STALEMATE

Why We Can't Win the War on Terror and What We Should Do Instead

Greg C. Reeson

GOVERNMENT INSTITUTES

An imprint of
THE SCARECROW PRESS, INC.
Lanham • Toronto • Plymouth, UK
2011

Published by Government Institutes
An imprint of The Scarecrow Press, Inc.
A wholly owned subsidary of The Rowman & Littlefield Publishing Group, Inc.
4501 Forbes Boulevard, Suite 200, Lanham, Maryland 20706
http://www.govinstpress.com

Estover Road, Plymouth PL6 7PY, United Kingdom

British Library Cataloguing in Publication Information Available

Library of Congress Cataloging-in-Publication Data
Reeson, Greg C., 1968-
  Stalemate : why we can't win the war on terror and what we should do instead / Greg C. Reeson.
    p. cm.
  Includes bibliographical references and index.
  ISBN 978-1-60590-771-0 (cloth : alk. paper) -- ISBN 978-1-60590-772-7 (electronic)
  1. Terrorism—Prevention. 2. Radicalism—Religious aspects. 3. United States—Foreign relations—21st century. 4. United States—Politics and government—21st century. 5. War (International law) 6. World politics—21st century. I. Title.
  HV6431.R438 2011
  363.325'15610973—dc23

                                                            2011022529

Contents

Acknowledgments

THIS BOOK WOULD NOT HAVE BEEN POSSIBLE without the direct and indirect support of many people, all of whom have my sincerest thanks for making this project a reality. In particular, I must recognize the influence of my closest friends, Ronnie, Andrew, Jack, and Jeff, who have challenged me intellectually for more than two decades with in-depth discussions of U.S. foreign policy and America's role in the international system. Next, I want to thank all the men and women, past and present, who have selflessly served their country in uniform as members of the armed forces of the United States. I am humbled by their devotion to duty and love of country and consider myself blessed to have been counted among their ranks. Special mention must also be made of the many heroes who have made the ultimate sacrifice for this great nation, especially my comrades-in-arms who gave their lives in Iraq: Major Matt Schram, Second Lieutenant Clifford Gadsden, Staff Sergeant Craig Davis, Specialist Luke Frist, and Private First Class Christopher Kilpatrick. Finally, and most importantly, I must thank my family: my parents, who have always been there with unconditional support and encouragement; my children, Jason, Amanda, Matthew, and Jacob, who give my life purpose and direction; and my amazing wife, Kelly, without whom nothing I attempt would be possible. She is the consummate military wife: strong, supportive, resilient, loving, and independent. She is the bedrock of our family, and to her, for all she does, I am eternally grateful.

Introduction

O N THE MORNING OF SEPTEMBER 11, 2001, nineteen Islamic extremists turned four hijacked American commercial passenger jets into improvised missiles in a shocking surprise attack on the United States that resulted in the murder of more than three thousand innocent people from dozens of countries across the international system. The horrific strikes carried out that fall day, in terms of scale and lethality, were the deadliest acts of terrorism ever committed against the American homeland, acts that together constituted a defining moment in the history of the United States and its citizens. Temporarily, at least, the American people were awakened to the lethal threat posed by a small minority of Muslims who practiced a fanatical ideology in which human life was not respected and nonbelievers were not tolerated. The 9/11 attacks also brought about the realization that the United States was embroiled in a global fight declared many years before by an enemy who defied traditional American beliefs about hostile forces and the proper conduct of armed conflicts. Less than a month after 9/11, the United States military was ordered into combat action to remove the Islamic fundamentalist Taliban regime from power in Afghanistan, eliminating the state-sponsored safe haven of Osama bin Laden's al Qaeda terrorist organization, and subsequently to depose the ruthless Ba'athist government of Saddam Hussein from its near quarter-century of dictatorial rule in Iraq. Now, a full decade after U.S. troops entered Afghanistan and more than eight years after the U.S.-led invasion of Iraq, it has become evident that while the men and women of America's armed forces, with the support of government workers in other federal agencies and some private-sector organization employees, are engaged in a violent struggle with extremists who practice a perverted form of their Islamic faith, the nation as a whole is not.

The American people have largely moved on since 9/11. Life in the United States has essentially returned to the way it was before the 2001 attacks, for the most part unaffected by the deadly combat the country's military forces are experiencing thousands of miles from America's shores in some of the most hostile and desolate places the world has to offer. Day after day, in cities and rural areas across the United States, it is business as usual with a small percentage of the population anxiously waiting at home for the safe return of their loved ones while the rest of the nation eagerly waits for the latest version of the iPhone or iPad to hit the consumer market, more aggravated than anything else about the increasing number of security inconveniences put in place after the 9/11 attacks. There are, of course, regular but brief reports on the conflicts in Iraq and Afghanistan during the evening news broadcasts and semiregular assessments by the president and the Department of Defense concerning the degree of progress America's military forces are making in overseas conflicts. By and large, though, the American public is more attuned to the latest movie releases, the continuing troubles in the economy, and the ongoing debate about controversial conservative and liberal domestic political agendas than it is to the global battle with Muslim extremists who regularly seek out opportunities to bring death and destruction to the cities and suburbs of the United States.

For the better part of the past two decades, I have closely followed the complex workings of the international security system, or more specifically U.S. foreign policy and the employment of American military forces as a component of U.S. national strategy designed to secure American interests abroad. During this time I have invested significant effort in studying the United States' ongoing fight against Islamic radicalism and the terrorists who use grossly warped interpretations of carefully selected portions of their faith as justification for committing acts of violence against American citizens and interests. As complacency to the Islamic extremist threat continues to set in across the nation, and as the reality of the 9/11 attacks steadily turns into a distant memory for most Americans, I have come to realize through multiple conversations with friends and family members and wide-ranging discussions in Internet chat rooms and on social networking websites that the average citizen is largely uninformed about the nature of the terrorist threat faced by the American people. Critical to the long-term management of that threat is an understanding of the enemy the United States faces, the goals he seeks to achieve in the international system, the reasons for the actions he takes, the danger he poses to Muslims and non-Muslims around the world, the tools available to the United States in this transnational conflict, and the likely course of events over the coming years as America continues its struggle against Islamic extremists who will not surrender, will not be defeated outright, and will not simply go away and leave us alone to live our lives as we see fit.

It is the average American for whom this book is written. U.S. foreign policy experts, international relations academics, diplomatic, military, and intelligence personnel, and those few ordinary citizens who have actively sought out detailed information on the United States' global battle with Islamic extremists will not find much here that is new or innovative. The goal of this effort is not to develop a new theory or craft a new grand strategy, although suggestions about the approach the United States and its allies should take in this transnational struggle are certainly offered. The goal, rather, is to educate typical Americans so that they may better understand the generational struggle the United States embarked upon when former president George W. Bush declared America was going to wage a "Global War on Terrorism" against Islamic extremist ideology and those radical Muslims who subscribed to its teachings. Arming the American public with a sound knowledge base will help foster intelligent, informed debate and sustained, active involvement by ordinary citizens in a conflict that is being fought on their behalf by a mere fraction of the population but that affects and will continue to affect every man, woman, and child in the United States in a profound and life-changing manner for many years to come. One thing should be perfectly clear: those Americans who believe the fight against Islamic radicalism is entering its final stages could not be more wrong. The absence of a successful major attack on the U.S. homeland since 9/11 should not be interpreted as indicative of a reduced Muslim extremist threat. Islamic terrorists continue to target the United States and the American people at home and abroad, citing religious principle as justification for their violent acts. Their efforts have not relented, and the measures undertaken by the United States to stop them must be aggressively and determinedly continued.

Because the objective is to provide basic but important information to those who are seeking to better understand the global conflict the United States has been engaged in, unwittingly at first, for the past several decades, the chapters that follow are purposely brief. There is more than ample subject-specific material available elsewhere for those who wish to expand their knowledge base with in-depth examinations of each of the topics covered. Official government publications, books, scholarly articles, and think-tank analyses and reports provide a constant, timely, and relevant stream of information that can be acquired at little or no expense, in most cases, to those individuals who wish to broaden their study of one of the defining international security challenges of the post–Cold War era. Pithiness is a critical aspect of this endeavor. By limiting the amount of material presented, I hope to give readers just enough information to establish a solid understanding of what the United States and its allies and partner nations are doing in this epic struggle and the elements and instruments of American national power being used to combat transnational Islamic extremists, without causing an information overload that leaves them confused about the nature of the conflict in which the United States is now and will continue to be engaged.

Chapter 1 begins by explaining how the international security environment changed suddenly in the 1990s from a decade characterized by a global balance of power, a bipolar security environment with the United States and the Soviet Union as the two dominant actors (a period known as the Cold War), to one in which the forces of globalization essentially turned state borders into meaningless lines on the world map, destroying traditional national barriers to outside intrusion by the forces of economics, technology, individual mobility, and cultural influence. Globalization brought different peoples with vastly different beliefs and value systems into close contact with one another, contact that often resulted in national responses ranging from mild resentment to outright hostility and, sometimes, open conflict. The gap between the world's haves and have-nots widened rapidly as a result of globalization, unleashing chaos in regions where people believed the West was growing rich through the exploitation of the natural resources of developing countries. Globalization's advances in communication and transportation technology facilitated the ability of individuals in every corner of the world to quickly and easily travel to new and distant locations, something the Islamic terrorists who attacked America on 9/11 took advantage of with deadly consequence. The United States responded to the 2001 terrorist strikes by launching a worldwide effort in which the goal was ideally, but unrealistically, to completely wipe out Islamic terrorism wherever it existed in the international system. In support of this goal, President Bush declared there would be no distinction made between the Muslim extremists committing their acts of violent terror and the state sponsors that directly or indirectly facilitated their barbaric deeds.

Chapter 2 briefly examines the questionably labeled "War on Terrorism," the U.S.-led global campaign to eradicate violent Islamic extremism that began after the Taliban regime in Afghanistan failed to meet American demands for the extradition of al Qaeda founder Osama bin Laden and his chief deputies, particularly second-in-command Ayman al-Zawahiri. The chapter explains the four general types of threats the United States can expect to face in the contemporary international security environment and argues that irregular or asymmetric warfare like that experienced by American military forces in Afghanistan and Iraq will remain the defining characteristic of the global threat environment for the foreseeable future. The chapter defines terrorism, explains the key characteristics used to classify certain acts of violence as terrorism, and discusses the primary reasons why various groups adopt terrorist tactics as a means for achieving their political and social objectives. The chapter also discusses how aggressive and proactive military and nonmilitary measures by the United States and its allies in Afghanistan resulted in the decentralization of al Qaeda into a networked grouping of like-minded and affiliated terrorist bodies collectively named al Qaeda and Associated Movements, or AQAM.

Chapter 2 continues by defining state sponsorship of terrorism, looking at the types of support states provide to various terrorist organizations, and discussing the measures the United States takes against those nations it classifies as state sponsors of terrorist violence. Each of the four states currently on the Department of State's list of state sponsors of terrorism (Iran, Syria, Cuba, and Sudan) is covered, as is the criteria that must be satisfied for a country to be removed from the State Department's list. An examination of the classification of the fight against Islamic radicalism as a "war" is undertaken before the chapter concludes that the increase in the number of extremist organizations targeting the United States and other nations since the 9/11 attacks, a direct result of the decentralization of al Qaeda, ushered in an era of "persistent conflict" that will see America and its allies and partner states engaged in a transnational battle with Islamic radicals lasting at least a generation and probably much longer, perhaps never reaching a conclusion. The likely duration of this conflict presents a significant challenge for U.S. policymakers charged with protecting American citizens from the Islamic terrorist threat. Quick and relatively bloodless battlefield victories in various hostile actions in the 1980s and 1990s conditioned Americans to expect the rapid defeat of those enemies foolish enough to challenge the armed forces of the United States in head-to-head battle. This era of persistent conflict will continue to test the patience and resolve of the United States to wage protracted armed struggles against fanatically committed opponents.

To effectively deal with the global Islamic extremist threat, the United States will need to continually refine its grand strategy so that the approach taken over the coming years is a comprehensive and coordinated one that utilizes all the elements of national power in a manner that over time efficiently and substantively reduces the risk of harm from terrorist activity to American citizens and U.S. national interests at home and abroad. Because the development of such a strategy requires a sound understanding of the international threat environment in which the strategy will be employed, chapter 3 reviews four frameworks that attempt to explain the reasons the Islamic terrorist threat exists in the contemporary international security system. The chapter explains what strategy is and provides an explanation of some of the barriers that can prevent those charged with strategy development from crafting sound strategic plans. National power is defined in this chapter, and the eight principles upon which strategy rests are described. The chapter details the three categories of national interest, vital, important, and peripheral, as well as the ends, ways, and means components that together make up a strategic plan. The elements and instruments of national power are introduced, as is the concept of risk, or the probability of failure for a given strategy. Chapter 3 also looks at why it is beneficial for the United States to have allies and partner nations assisting in the execution of U.S. national strategy and discusses the advantages and disadvantages of forming alliances or coalitions with other countries in pursuit of U.S. national interests in the international security environment. Finally, the chapter examines the North Atlantic Treaty Organization (NATO) and its struggle for a new and relevant identity in the wake of the collapse of the Soviet Union, the threat from which NATO, America's chief defense alliance, derived its purpose and direction in the decades between the end of World War II and the fall of the Berlin Wall.

Chapter 4 focuses exclusively on the diplomatic element of national power, the first element in the DIME acronym, which stands for the diplomatic, information, military, and economic elements of U.S. state power. The chapter provides a definition of diplomacy and an overview of American diplomatic efforts as an element of power employed as a means for achieving U.S. interests in the contemporary international system. The history and purpose of the United Nations, the primary forum for U.S. diplomatic efforts, are explained, as is the role the UN plays in facilitating or hindering U.S. diplomatic work with other countries within the confines of the UN Security Council and General Assembly. The global legitimacy that comes with UN approval is discussed, as is the prospect for reform of the United Nations' massive, inefficient, and ineffective bureaucratic structure, with particular emphasis on the dysfunctional rules governing the Security Council. Chapter 4 also looks at the special bond between the United States and Europe and the prospect of diplomatic negotiation with Islamic terrorist organizations like al Qaeda, the Taliban, Hamas, and Hezbollah. The chapter concludes with a review of the instruments or resources available to the United States for employment under the diplomatic element of national power.

Continuing with the DIME acronym, Chapter 5 examines the information element of power, including an introduction to the "war of ideas," alternately known as the "battle of narratives." In discussing the information element of power, the chapter looks at the message Islamic extremists are communicating to fellow Muslims and the need for a positive alternative message and counternarrative from the United States and its allies conveyed through moderate Muslim elements that do not have the West's credibility problem in Islamic societies. Ideology is defined before delving into the historical influence of Qutbism's advocacy of political violence on the contemporary radical Islamist viewpoint. The role of both traditional and nontraditional media, including the Internet, is examined, as is the critical importance of public opinion, both Western and Muslim. The chapter includes some of the actions the United States can take in the months and years ahead to help win the "hearts and minds" of moderate Muslim populations around the world, including increased levels of engagement with the global Muslim community through public diplomacy and the selective targeting of those specific elements within Muslim societies that promote Islamic radicalism and prevent mainstream Muslims from having their voices heard.

Chapter 6 deals with what is perhaps the most controversial of all the elements of U.S. national power: the military element. The chapter defines the military element of power and provides those factors that contribute to a nation's overall military capability. A review of the four generations of warfare leads to a discussion of some of the scenarios in which U.S. military power might be employed in the contemporary international security environment. The factors that shape the decision to use military power are examined, including the oft-referenced Weinberger and Powell doctrines, along with the advantages and disadvantages of using military power to deal with critical international security issues impacting U.S. national interests across the international system. The chapter looks at the difference between preemptive military strikes and preventive military strikes and concludes by discussing some of the ways military instruments might be used to combat Islamic radicalism in the years ahead. Those ways include the deterrence of states and nonstate actors behaving in ways contrary to U.S. interests, the training of host nation security forces in countries threatened by Islamic extremists, the conduct of security cooperation activities, the execution of current and future combat operations, the targeted use of special operations forces and unmanned aerial vehicles in discrete military operations, the enforcement of economic sanctions regimes, the provision of support to federal agencies charged with security of the homeland, the development of ballistic missile defense technology, and the overseas projection of America's unmatched military power to potential crisis points around the world.

Chapter 7 defines the economic element of power and discusses the reward-based and punitive economic tools used by the United States in its attempts to influence the behavior of other states and nonstate actors in a manner that advances U.S. national interests worldwide. These tools can include economic development aid, positive or negative trade relationships, and economic sanctions. Aid assistance and free and open trade can improve the global quality of life and undermine the extremist message that argues the plight of the developing world is a direct result of decades of exploitation by Western nations.

Negative trade relations and economic sanctions or financial restrictions are designed to inflict a measure of hardship on a targeted state (or, in the case of sanctions and financial restrictions, a nonstate actor like Hamas or al Qaeda) in the hope that severe economic difficulties will coerce the targeted actor to adjust its behavior in a way that is beneficial to the United States and its allies and partner nations. The chapter discusses the multiple problems associated with the imposition of sanctions regimes and concludes with an examination of the impact U.S. economic health has on the federal government's ability to exercise economic leverage in the international community and to invest in the resources necessary for a prolonged fight with Islamic radicals. Finally, the chapter discusses the need for increased military investment, along the lines of 6 to 8 percent of the nation's gross domestic product (GDP), and the likely effect of growing annual budget deficits and the ever-increasing national debt.

Chapter 8 moves beyond the DIME acronym for the primary elements of national power and examines two less prominent but no less important elements that often operate behind the scenes with results sometimes never known to the American public. This chapter, the last to deal with the elements of national power, begins with an introduction to the intelligence and law enforcement elements of power and discusses the vital role of timely, accurate, and actionable intelligence that can be shared across the federal government and with allied and partner nations participating in the transnational effort to combat the Islamic extremist threat. The chapter explains the need for a global human intelligence network and describes some of the problems inherent in a law enforcement–centric approach to the challenge of Muslim radicalism. Postapprehension procedures for processing individuals suspected of terrorist activity are addressed, including detention policy, the chain of custody for evidence, the provision of U.S. constitutional rights to terrorist detainees, the reason the Geneva Convention protections do not apply to Islamic terrorists, and the potential rules that could be used in the disposition of cases of suspected terrorist activity. The chapter covers the issue of U.S. border security, including the need for a delicate balance between preventing terrorist operatives from infiltrating the American homeland and the need for commerce and legal immigration hindered as little as possible by border security measures. In conclusion, the chapter briefly discusses some of the steps the federal government can take to better ensure smooth pre- and postattack efficiency and effectiveness.

Chapter 9 shifts focus away from the elements of national power and toward those places in the international system where the United States is most likely to be engaged against Islamic radicals over the next decade and beyond. The chapter begins with a review of the conflict in Afghanistan from the U.S. invasion in late 2001 to the present and discusses the reasons for the deteriorating situation in which the United States and its NATO allies now find themselves. Those reasons include a resurgent Taliban, a corrupt and ineffective Afghan government, and significant operational capability problems with the military forces of NATO's European member states. The critical relationship between Afghanistan and Pakistan is examined, with specific attention paid to the complex challenges posed by the Federally Administered Tribal Areas along the largely lawless Afghanistan-Pakistan border. The chapter continues with a look at the ongoing conflict in post–Saddam Hussein Iraq, which is increasingly becoming a purely Iraqi problem but will nonetheless continue to demand American political, economic, and military assistance for the foreseeable future. Reasons for the U.S.-led invasion of Iraq are reviewed, including the need to deal with an aggressive Saddam Hussein who demonstrated both the will and the ability to use weapons of mass destruction, harbored international terrorists, and consistently defied the demands of the international community as expressed through multiple United Nations Security Council resolutions. The progress made by U.S. military forces since the near civil war of 2006 and 2007 is described, as are the long-term interests the United States has in a stable and secure Iraqi state.

Chapter 9 also examines the significant security challenge failed and failing states pose for America and its allies in an increasingly complex international security environment. Failed and failing states are defined, and the process used by extremist groups to incrementally secure a foothold in areas characterized by weak or nonexistent governments and despondent populations is discussed. The desperate situation across much of Africa is described, along with the reasons why the African continent holds great potential for the establishment of relatively safe areas of operation for Islamic extremists, particularly in the Sahel and Horn of Africa regions. Poor standards of living and large Muslim populations make many African nations particularly susceptible to the influence of Islamic radicalism. Al Qaeda and affiliated group activities in the Islamic Maghreb and Somalia are looked at as part of the discussion of Muslim extremism in Africa, as are U.S. efforts like the Combined Joint Task Force–Horn of Africa, Operation Enduring Freedom–Trans Sahara, and the United States Africa Command.

Continuing with the discussion of potential U.S. focal points in the years ahead, chapter 9 examines the interests the United States pursues in the Middle East, the difficulties in securing peace between the Israelis and the Palestinians, the security problems posed by Hamas in the Palestinian territories and Hezbollah in southern Lebanon, the future of Iraq and its ongoing security and governance challenges, Iran's sponsorship of international terrorist acts and suspected pursuit of a nuclear weapons capability, the influence of Islamic extremist ideology in Saudi Arabia, and the developing political, social, and economic crises in Yemen, home to al Qaeda in the Arabian Peninsula (AQAP). The chapter briefly examines the less pressing but still important threat Islamic radicals pose to countries in Southeast Asia, particularly Indonesia and the Philippines, the possibility of North Korean nuclear and ballistic missile technology making its way into the hands of terrorists, and the rising threat of Islamic extremism in European nations allied with the United States.

Chapter 10, the final chapter of the book, questions whether the United States can ever "win" this global fight with Islamic extremists, ultimately concluding that victory, at least in the sense Americans traditionally think of when discussing victory and defeat in armed conflict, is not a realistic possibility. The chapter briefly reviews the threat to the United States and like nations and explains why the extremists ultimately have the advantage in this long-term and costly international struggle. The ways in which terrorist groups typically meet their demise are described, and special mention is made of the difficulties involved in neutralizing or destroying extremist organizations motivated by faith, a reality that causes particular concern for the United States as it continues to battle against a religiously inspired enemy constantly seeking to do it harm. This final chapter also discusses by element of national power the measures the United States is likely to embark upon, or in some cases continue to pursue, in the near term to reduce the threat posed by Islamic radicals to a level that minimizes the overall risk of injury or death from terrorist violence.

Under the diplomatic element of power, the need to continue to seek broad international support, despite the challenges to President Obama's "new era" of global engagement, is discussed, as is the need to maintain the United States' right to act unilaterally when it feels it must do so to protect its enduring national interests. In the information arena, the necessity for a credible alternative to the message put forth by Islamic extremists is stressed, along with the need for a targeted approach aimed at specific subsets within the broader Muslim community that may be able to influence the opinion and support of moderate Muslims across the international system. Militarily, the importance of seeing the conflicts in Iraq and Afghanistan through to conclusions that are satisfactory for U.S. national interests is reinforced, along with the urgent need for the United States to address the increasingly dangerous problem posed by failed and failing states. The importance of a strong forward military presence that allows the United States to deal with ongoing hostile actions and potential crisis areas in the world's most insecure regions is discussed, stressing that forward-deployed forces enable the United States to use its unparalleled military power to confront serious global security challenges before they reach America's shores. Given the myriad potential threats to U.S. national security, the importance of significant investment in the maintenance of a strong and balanced military force is emphasized because a powerful and capable military enables the United States to deter potential adversaries and, if deterrence fails, deal with both conventional and asymmetric challenges that will continue to surface across the international landscape.

In discussing the economic element of national power, the chapter argues the top priority for the United States must be significant improvement in the country's overall economic strength. Huge annual budget deficits and a ballooning national debt are crowding out spending on other national priorities like the sustainment of an overwhelming military capability that is equipped and trained to handle complex international security issues. Some important priorities will unavoidably be allocated fewer and fewer resources as interest payments on the debt and growing entitlement spending consume the limited funds available in the U.S. Treasury. Current economic trends make it unlikely that the United States will have the monetary resources necessary to invest a desirable level of 6 to 8 percent of the nation's gross domestic product in current and future national security and defense capabilities. Limited monetary resources also mean the United States will find it increasingly difficult to provide critical international development aid to countries in need, engage in fair and balanced trade with other nations, and mitigate the effects brought on by the imposition of UN or unilateral economic sanctions regimes. Finally, the vital roles played by the intelligence and law enforcement elements of national power in the transnational conflict with Islamic extremist groups are revisited. The United States will need to take aggressive action to ensure the cultivation of a capable global human intelligence network that can provide elected and civil service officials with timely, accurate, and actionable information that is disruptive to terrorist operations directed at the United States and its people. Recognizing there are terrorist suspects currently in U.S. custody and that more suspects will inevitably be captured and detained by U.S. military, intelligence, and law enforcement personnel, the chapter argues the development of clear and fair rules for the detention and ultimate disposition of these individuals will be critical to the overall effort to minimize the risk posed to American citizens and infrastructure. Switching to the issue of border security, the chapter reinforces the need to move the national debate away from the ideological extremes of amnesty or sealed borders and toward a balanced and sensible solution that prevents those who would do the United States harm from entering the country while not unnecessarily impeding the flow of legal immigration or the conduct of international commerce.

In conclusion, the book explains why the United States will have to maintain its dominant leadership role in international security affairs if there is going to be any semblance of global unity in the worldwide battle with Muslim extremists who choose not to coexist with those who do not subscribe to their radical belief system. The United States is an exceptional nation and, simply put, no other country in the world is capable of doing what the United States can do in the international environment to keep Islamic terrorists on the defensive and unable to launch massive attacks that result in large numbers of casualties in targeted nations. Superior economic and military capabilities impose on America the responsibility to lead other nations in the international system, a responsibility that puts the United States out in front as the leading target for the violence perpetrated by the extremists. Islamic radicalism and those who practice it radically changed the international security environment on September 11, 2001, and it will never again be like it was before that fateful day. Understanding where we have been and where we are going is critical to the national effort to manage the Muslim extremist threat in a way that ensures the maximum amount of safety and security for the people of the United States and the broader international community.

1

A New Era in International Relations

WHEN I FIRST ENROLLED AS A NEW UNDERGRADUATE STUDENT in the Russian area studies baccalaureate program at Louisiana State University in the late 1980s, I did so believing my chosen degree program would arm me with the knowledge I would need to secure a long and hopefully prosperous career as a Soviet analyst of some sort, probably for one of the branches of the United States military or one of the several federal agencies charged with analyzing, assessing, and countering the threat posed by the much-feared "evil empire" Soviet Union. To help fund my college expenses, I enlisted after high school in the armed forces as an airman with the Louisiana Air National Guard, just a few months after my eighteenth birthday. I started my military career as an air-to-air missile maintenance technician with the 159th Consolidated Aircraft Maintenance Squadron (CAM) before securing a position as a junior-level intelligence analyst with the 122nd Tactical Fighter Squadron (TFS) at the New Orleans Naval Air Station, a small base located in the suburb of Belle Chasse just across the Mississippi River from the Crescent City. At the time, the 122nd TFS was an F-15A fighter jet unit that expected one day to engage in aerial combat against Soviet military aircraft, fighting pitched battles that would play an important role in deciding the ultimate outcome of the great ideological struggle between the United States and the Soviet Union.

All of my work with the Air National Guard during those days was focused on the Soviet threat. I studied the various types of Soviet military aircraft and numerous Soviet offensive and defensive weapons systems, learning all I could about their known and suspected capabilities and weaknesses so that I could best prepare the fighter pilots in my unit for the threats they would one day be expected to defeat in battle. My daily readings and briefings consisted of classified and unclassified intelligence reports, Jane's Defense analyses, various think-tank studies and reports, and classified and open-source news stories about every topic imaginable concerning the Soviet military and Soviet foreign policy. I spent countless hours analyzing political, economic, and military events across the breadth of the Soviet empire, and my National Guard unit conducted regular war-game exercises and mission rehearsals that focused on the inevitable battle with Soviet military forces. There was little to no consideration of the possibility that soon the world would no longer be divided into two distinct ideological spheres, one American and one Soviet. It was East versus West, communism versus democracy, NATO versus the Warsaw Pact, freedom versus tyranny, and that was the way it was going to stay.

Outside of my military responsibilities, the Soviet Union played a similarly dominant role in my academic pursuits as a student at LSU. Formal and informal discussions with classmates and professors focused on key Soviet government figures and their day-to-day speeches and actions at home and abroad. We would meet at our favorite social establishments near campus and pass the time theorizing about the future of U.S.-Soviet relations and talking about the leadership styles and eccentricities of each of the Soviet general secretaries. We were especially fascinated by Russian jokes that made fun of the Soviet system, and we particularly enjoyed theorizing about how past Soviet leaders would handle current domestic and international issues. I signed up for a series of undergraduate courses that covered the structure and organization of the Soviet government, Communist Party politics, the central planning economic model, Russian literature and history, and Soviet foreign policy. I read, or at least tried to read with my limited knowledge of the language, Russian books and newspapers, subscribed to the English-language *Soviet Life* magazine, and requested informational materials from the Soviet Embassy in Washington to further my knowledge and understanding of America's great ideological and military rival.

My study of the Russian language provided me with an incredible opportunity to translate, albeit at a rudimentary level, for a high-school basketball team from Moscow conducting a goodwill sports tour in the United States. As the Russian visitors traveled to a series of Louisiana high schools for exhibition games against American teams, I and my fellow students bombarded our guests with questions about "real" life in the Soviet Union and tried to figure out which of their official escorts was the KGB agent sent to monitor their behavior and watch for potential defectors. We took snippets of conversations with the Russian players back to the classroom, sharing them with our primary language professor in order to broaden our discussion of the peculiarities of the Russian language. We traded cultural souvenirs of various sorts and learned as much as we possibly could about each other in the short time we had together. An intensive study of all things related to the Soviet Union consumed my everyday routine, both in and out of uniform. It was as if the U.S.-Soviet Cold War would continue without interruption, at least during my lifetime and, I suspected, through my children's lifetimes. There was never reason to believe the international system would be structured any other way.

For nearly half a century from the end of the Second World War until the collapse of the Soviet Empire, the international security environment was characterized by a relative balance of power between two very distinct ideological camps, one led by the United States and the other by the Soviet Union. Most of the other nations of the international system aligned themselves more or less with one of the two superpowers in an effort to enhance as much as possible their individual positions in the international arena. The Cold War was really more a clash of ideas and beliefs than it was a traditional shooting war, although proxy battles were sometimes fought in places like Korea, Vietnam, and Afghanistan. There were, to be sure, some very close calls and some terrifyingly tense moments, the most notable of which was undoubtedly the Cuban Missile Crisis in late 1962, in which the American and Soviet superpowers came dangerously close to becoming embroiled in an all-out, possibly nuclear, war. The U.S. and Soviet governments regularly pushed the proverbial envelope, always running the risk of escalating tense moments to actual combat by constantly locating their military forces in close proximity to each other on land and sea and in the air. But the world's two strongest powers always managed to pull back from the brink and prevent the ever-simmering tensions from erupting into a devastating full-blown conflict between nuclear-armed rivals.

Not once during those years did I imagine a world in which the Soviet Union did not exist. Such a concept was inconceivable, for me and for nearly everyone I associated with. I, along with many others in and out of government, accepted without hesitation that American and Soviet bipolarity would remain for many more decades the defining characteristic of the international security environment. Virtually no one suspected that in just a few short years the Berlin Wall, which nearly everyone assumed would stand forever as a symbol of the division between East and West, would be torn down as the Soviet government began to loosen its grip on long-held satellite nations and the Cold War adversary of the United States started its transformation into a relic of an era long past. The Union of Soviet Socialist Republics that had been formed just a few years after the 1917 revolutions that deposed Russia's last czar and the provisional government that followed his rule officially ceased to exist in December 1991, giving way to a conglomeration of fifteen separate countries suddenly forced to find their own way in a complex and dangerous world now dominated by a lone superpower. The Cold War that had threatened all the nations of the international system with the possibility of nuclear Armageddon ended relatively peacefully, without any direct force-on-force combat actions occurring between the two primary actors and very little blood being spilled in the Soviet empire's former republics.

From the Cold War to the Age of Globalization

As America's archenemy started to come apart at the seams, the world began to change in dramatic fashion. The bipolar structure that had existed for so many decades quickly disintegrated, and with it went the relative stability provided by the American-Soviet global balance of power. Political, economic, and military alliances across the international system had to be reconsidered and reconfigured as one of the world's two most powerful countries simply ceased to exist. The United States was left standing as the world's lone remaining superpower, and smaller, weaker states began to form a variety of alliances in an effort to counter America's dominance in the global security environment. A brief period of unipolarity for the United States quickly transformed into what renowned political scientist Samuel Huntington once described as a hybrid uni-multi-polar world in which the international community's only superpower was regularly challenged by multiple major powers, including France, Russia, China, India, and other lesser powers that had aligned themselves in order to limit the amount of influence the United States was able to exert across the international system.[1]

The global ideological and power balance of the Cold War was replaced by a new defining characteristic of the international system that ultimately would facilitate the horrific terrorist attacks on the United States on September 11, 2001. During the time between the collapse of the Soviet Union at the beginning of the 1990s and al Qaeda's 9/11 strikes on the American homeland, an era of globalization dominated nation-state interaction across the international community. Advances in transportation and communications technology facilitated the rapid transfer of people, goods, services, capital, technology, information, and ideas around the world. Cross-border trade increased significantly as new, previously restricted markets were opened to outside investment. Traditional barriers to commerce and cultural exchange were torn down, and individuals moved from country to country more freely and more easily than ever before. Nations and cultures came into increasingly close contact with one another as countries across the global landscape became more and more interconnected and states found it almost impossible to exercise any significant amount of control over who and what entered and exited borders that were at times nothing more than lines drawn on a map.

Advocates of globalization believed its sweeping changes to the global system would raise the overall international standard of living by facilitating the economic development of poor and less-developed countries through the promotion of free and open trade that would aid market growth and increase global investment. Opponents argued the major powers of the West would benefit economically at the expense of smaller, weaker, and less-developed nations as the former plundered the natural resources and wealth of the latter. Both advocates and opponents of globalization were essentially right in their predictions. Globalization has had both positive and negative effects on societies across the international system, and increased interaction among peoples and nations has impacted different states and cultures in significantly different ways. Global prosperity has generally increased, and the free flow of information, people, and ideas has exposed more individuals to the world around them while simultaneously promoting more trade and the opportunity for economic growth and development to struggling states in desperate need of foreign investment. The benefits of globalization, however, have not been universally shared, as its opponents feared, and the wealthiest and most fortunate of the international system have reaped the lion's share of the riches generated by the expansion of globalization. The gap between the so-called haves and have-nots of the international community has continued to widen as the overall level of global interconnectedness has increased.

As globalization failed to live up to many of its economic promises, and as inclusion in world markets became increasingly dependent upon following rules and regulations put in place by the powerful nations of the West, resentment and hostility among the populations of non-Western states steadily increased. Perceptions of the West, and particularly the United States, became increasingly negative, and resistance by non-Western peoples to cultural intrusion by Western and American customs, values, religion, and business practices became more and more pronounced. The have-nots were quickly able to see more clearly than ever before the disparity between the countries of the West and the countries of the rest of the world, and they did not like the picture being painted before their eyes. With the rapid spread of globalization, the peoples of Western nations began to realize that many states and cultures were not only unenthusiastic about American and Western influence, they were becoming openly confrontational and sometimes violent in their reactions. Western, and particularly American, values on the role of women, religious freedom, government institutions and practices, the fair and impartial rule of law, and economic enterprise came into conflict with national and cultural traditions in many places around the world. Globalization and all that came with it was frowned upon and sometimes rejected outright in countries and cultures not quite ready to embrace symbols of the West like McDonald's, MTV, and Abercrombie & Fitch.

The world of the 1990s was one in which globalization quickly extended American and Western ideas, values, and practices to places both receptive to and resentful of Western, and especially American, dominance of the international community. The citizens of the United States generally, although cognizant of the plights of other nations in the international system, did not pay much attention as a significant portion of the world around them began to seethe with anger at global imbalances of power, influence, and wealth. Of course, there were short-lived sideshows in the Persian Gulf, Somalia, and the Balkans that temporarily occupied the attention of the American public, but in the United States the times were generally considered to be pretty good. The Soviet Union had been defunct since the beginning of the decade and no longer loomed just over the horizon as a dangerous and potentially lethal threat. Trade markets were expanding, the economy was booming, and the United States was largely at peace. Much of the rest of the world, however, was growing increasingly volatile, complex, and dangerous, and the threats to U.S. national security were becoming less clearly defined than they had been in years past. Most Americans felt generally isolated from the world's growing troubles, protected by the United States' superior economic and military strength, friendly nations to the north and south, and two ocean barriers that kept dangerous actors at what was thought at the time to be a safe distance from America's shores.

U.S. foreign policy under presidents George H. W. Bush and Bill Clinton saw the United States become engaged more frequently and in more global hot spots than it had ever been since America joined the Allied powers to defeat German and Japanese aggression in the Second World War. The U.S. armed forces joined the militaries of other Western and non-Western nations in multiple deployments to every corner of the international system as the breakup of the Soviet Union unleashed varying levels of chaos and cultural conflict around the world. The United States, in its role as the lone superpower and de facto global leader, became the world's policeman, the cop on the international beat called upon by the global community of nation-states to support or take the lead in a series of seemingly endless but low-intensity conflict peacekeeping and nation-building operations. Economic and cultural globalization, along with a strong forward presence by the U.S. military, meant America and everything she believed in and stood for were broadcast loudly and intrusively to virtually every other nation in the world, whether the countries on the receiving end were amenable to the message being transmitted or not. During the 2000 campaign for president of the United States, then candidate George W. Bush promised American citizens that as commander-in-chief of the country's armed forces he would refocus the international efforts of the nation's military in order to limit engagement to only those places where it was clear the vital national security interests of the United States were at stake. Candidate Bush pledged during the campaign that America's military would no longer be the international community's "go to" rapid-response police force and that future nation-building efforts in the developing world would be relegated to a lower position on the list of U.S. priorities abroad. The primary focus areas for the American military establishment would be the modernization of the armed forces, the streamlining of day-to-day operations, and the enhancement of traditional war-fighting skills and capabilities in anticipation of the potential rise of another global superpower competitor. Other nations, especially America's allies in Europe, would be compelled under the Bush approach to start taking more responsibility for security problems in their own regions as it became clear to the countries of the international system that the United States would no longer be the default answer for the world's most troubled areas. Bush's chief goal was to limit the global presence of the U.S. military as much as he could without compromising America's national security interests, and he embarked upon his presidency in early 2001 determined to follow through on the promises made during his campaign. Then came 9/11, and everything changed.

A Different Kind of War

On September 11, 2001, I was serving on active duty as an Army logistics staff officer at Fort Lee, Virginia, a small training post just south of Richmond and only a two-hour drive on Interstate 95 from Washington, D.C. The day began no differently than any other had during my Army career to that point. Following an early morning physical fitness training session, I showered, put on my duty uniform, said goodbye to my wife and kids, and headed off to my job as an operations and training officer for one of the battalion headquarters charged with providing Advanced Individual Training (AIT) to new soldiers recently graduated from the Army's basic combat instruction course. In Army lingo, AIT is the period of instruction immediately after basic training in which a soldier learns how to do his or her job, or military occupational specialty (MOS), before joining a unit in either the active or reserve component. As the workday got underway, I was attending a change-of-command ceremony for a friend and fellow officer when my cell phone rang. After learning from my wife that a commercial jet had crashed into one of the World Trade Center towers in New York City, I dismissed the tragedy as a horrible and unfortunate accident, hung up the phone, and went back to the ceremony. A short time later, my cell phone rang again. Another plane had hit the other World Trade Center tower in New York. Everything changed in an instant as guests at the ceremony, also alerted by colleagues, friends, and family members to the tragic events unfolding to the north, began to wander off in search of a live news feed on the nearest radio or television. What had started as a routine day was turning out to be anything but business as usual. I remember telling my wife that this was no accident—the United States was under attack and there would surely be hell to pay as soon as we found out who had done this to us. As the devastating consequences of the 9/11 attacks started to become clear, it was obvious there was no way the United States was going to avoid fighting a war.

Listening to President Bush address the nation later that evening, I knew the lives of people in the United States and around the world were about to be altered dramatically and permanently. The international environment we had grown accustomed to since the collapse of the Soviet Union was changing, and just as in 1991, the change was going to be dramatic and lasting. The president vowed to find those who were responsible for the planning of the attacks and to make no distinction between the terrorists who had executed the horrific strikes on the American homeland and those who had aided and abetted them in their barbaric deeds. The line between terrorist and sponsor was eliminated with just a few words from the commander-in-chief. The president was trying to prepare the nation to fight a war that had been declared by a fanatical enemy many years before but that until the 9/11 attacks had been largely ignored by successive presidential administrations and Congresses of the United States government, even though some terrorism analysts within the U.S. intelligence community had been trying for years to draw attention to the growing Muslim extremist threat. While the 9/11 al Qaeda attacks were the most deadly acts of terrorism in American history, they were not the first time Islamic radicals had attempted to bring their war with the West to the United States.

Just a few minutes past noon on February 26, 1993, four Islamic radicals exploded a truck bomb in a public parking garage under the World Trade Center in New York, killing several people and seriously injuring more than a thousand others while causing more than $1 billion in damage to property.[2] Eventually, four Muslim extremists were convicted in U.S. federal court in connection with the bombing, and each was sentenced to more than two hundred years in prison. The 1993 bombing should have served as a grim warning of the deadly strikes to come just eight short years later. But Americans, like many of their Western allies, were not fully aware of what was going on in an increasingly unstable and hostile world around them. They were largely ignorant of the serious danger posed by fanatical Islamic terrorists with global aspirations, a raging hatred of the United States and the West, and the ability to reach out and target their enemies with lethal effect. The relatively quick identification and prosecution of individuals responsible for the 1993 bombing contributed to a false sense of security that would ultimately come back to haunt the United States and its people.

The National Commission on Terrorist Attacks Upon the United States, better known as the 9/11 Commission, was established in late 2002 to prepare a full account of the events leading up to the September 11 attacks and the execution of the attacks themselves. The commission identified in its 2004 report four features of the 1993 bombing of the World Trade Center that were relevant to the 9/11 attacks. First, the commission found the 1993 bombing was an indicator of a new terrorist threat to the United States that was fueled by a hatred that knew no bounds. It was a threat the United States did not fully understand in 1993 or in the eight years that had followed al Qaeda's first attack on the American homeland. Second, the commission found U.S. federal law enforcement agencies performed their duties so competently in the aftermath of the 1993 bombing that many in the United States, both in and out of government, concluded acts of terrorism could and should be treated primarily as criminal matters best left to the American legal system. Law enforcement, and not military action, became the preferred response to terrorist attacks against the United States and its interests abroad. Third, a consequence of the successful legal efforts following the bombing was that there was no sense of any immediate need to fully analyze the threat posed by radical Islamic terrorists. Very few in the United States believed Islamic extremism was anything more than a security "nuisance" that could be handled by law enforcement professionals on those rare occasions when terrorism-related incidents occurred. Last, the commission found the successful prosecutions of the persons responsible for the bombings contributed to an "underestimation" of the growing threat to American and allied interests worldwide.[3]

The United States failed to heed the warning given by Islamic terrorists led by Osama bin Laden and al Qaeda in 1993, and America paid a steep price for that failure on September 11, 2001. Reactions to the 9/11 attacks, which bin Laden and his followers referred to as the "planes operation," were wide ranging across the international system, from horror, anger, and sadness in the United States, Europe, and other countries to dancing in the streets in the Palestinian territories of the West Bank and Gaza Strip. There were, of course, the obligatory condemnations of the attacks issued by most of the world's heads of state, as well as the offering of condolences for the massive loss of innocent life. Conspiracy theories quickly emerged, suggesting the attacks were an inside job perpetrated, or at a minimum allowed to occur, by the government, more specifically the top levels of the Bush administration, so that the United States could wage war on the Islamic lands of Southwest Asia in order to secure the bulk of the world's oil supplies for America and its allies. The North Atlantic Treaty Organization, NATO, invoked for the first time in its history Article 5 of the NATO charter, declaring an armed attack against one or more member states in Europe or North America constituted an attack against all alliance member states.[4] Dr. Thomas P. M. Barnett, a former professor at the United States Naval War College and author of *The Pentagon's New Map* and other books, offered an interesting perspective on the attacks, describing the 9/11 strikes as "feedback" from a distressed world and an "amazing gift" that would force the United States to deal with the failings of the nations around it.[5]

Dr. Barnett was right in at least one sense. The United States finally came to realize after the 9/11 attacks that it could no longer ignore a world in which it prospered and other nations struggled for survival while being relentlessly bombarded with American influence and cultural excesses. The United States was now engaged in a global fight with Islamic radicals who expressed their discontent through the use of terror and violence, attacking indiscriminately and accepting that civilian casualties, Muslim and non-Muslim, were unavoidable and sometimes necessary and desirable in the pursuit of their extremist goals. This dangerous threat would have to be confronted in an aggressive and forceful way if the leadership of the United States was going to provide the country's citizens with the security they rightly demanded from their government. The confrontation with Islamic extremism could not be delayed another day. The illusion of invulnerability that had been fostered by overwhelming military and economic superiority and natural geographic defenses was forcefully shattered as the World Trade Center towers crumbled and the Pentagon burned. Americans could no longer dismiss Islamic radicalism and its use of terrorist violence as a distant problem unworthy of a response involving more than stepped-up law enforcement efforts or ineffective cruise missile strikes against empty desert training camps in the dead of night. The war declared years before by Muslim extremists had come to the American homeland with deadly ferocity, and the time to fight back was at hand.

The 9/11 attacks exposed the American people to an aspect of globalization they had previously been unaware of or had chosen simply to ignore. It was an aspect that was far more disturbing than the uneven distribution of globalization's economic benefits or the widening gap between the world's haves and have-nots. Globalization, through the reduction of communications and transportation barriers, facilitated the export of terrorism to America's shores with a degree of devastation never before seen firsthand by American citizens. The international system's growing interconnectedness had provided strategic reach to a radical movement with its headquarters based thousands of miles away from its target. Islamic terrorists, particularly Osama bin Laden and his al Qaeda organization, hated Western power and Western intrusion into Muslim-dominated regions. Globalization provided them with the means to strike out at those they considered aggressors and threats to their religion and way of life. Pulitzer Prize–winning author and *New York Times* foreign affairs columnist Thomas Friedman remarked once that globalization was "the integration of markets, finance, technology, and telecommunications in a way that is enabling each one of us to reach around the world farther, faster, deeper, and cheaper than ever before. And at the same time, is enabling the world to reach into each one of us farther, faster, deeper, and cheaper than ever before."[6]

Those words rang true with deadly cruelty on the morning of September 11, 2001, and the world would never again be the same. The 9/11 terrorist attacks fundamentally changed the Bush administration's approach to U.S. foreign policy. The United States had been targeted by terrorists before, but never had America's citizens experienced a coordinated assault on multiple locations inside the borders of the continental United States. As the magnitude of the attacks became clear, fear and grief gave way to mounting anger at those who had viciously taken the lives of so many innocents and to a unified national determination to take on once and for all Islamic terrorism and those who practiced and supported it. Al Qaeda's 9/11 attacks on the United States were the sort of events that have been described in international affairs as "fault lines," traumatic experiences that significantly alter the international environment and require a major adjustment by the nations of the international community.[7] The course correction by the United States and the Bush administration came quickly and with an aggressive determination to confront Islamic terrorism wherever it existed, regardless of cost and difficulty.

The September 11 attacks changed the way Americans thought of the world around them and the way in which the United States under President Bush and future presidents would engage that world. A new era of international relations was ushered in, and globalization took a back seat to an unprecedented international effort to eradicate the threat from transnational Islamic extremism. The perpetrators of the attacks on the United States and the Afghan nation that harbored them would be the first targets in America's revenge-seeking crosshairs. They would not, however, be the last. The world was put on notice. Heads of state across the international system had a decision to

2

The Global War on Terrorism

I N AN OCTOBER 7, 2001, ADDRESS TO THE AMERICAN PEOPLE, President Bush announced that military action against the al Qaeda terrorist network and the Taliban government had begun with attacks on training facilities and government installations throughout Afghanistan. Prior to the launching of hostilities, President Bush made several demands of the Taliban that the regime of Mullah Mohammed Omar, the radical clerical leader of the religious movement and government, failed to meet within Bush's time line. Those demands included the closing of all terrorist training camps in Afghanistan, the handing over of senior al Qaeda leaders, particularly Osama bin Laden and Ayman al-Zawahiri, and the safe return of all foreign nationals detained by the Taliban, regardless of country of origin.[1] Declaring the United States and a coalition of willing partners would wage a global campaign against terrorism, President Bush emphasized the fight in Afghanistan was just the beginning of what would ultimately be a much broader endeavor to stop terrorist violence wherever it existed in the international security environment. The "War on Terrorism," as it was called then, would be fought in multiple geographic locations and across many different fronts, from the disruption of terrorist financial networks and funding pipelines, communications mediums, and logistical support systems, to the targeting of key individuals and sovereign nation-states engaging in or facilitating violent terrorist acts, either passively or actively. Any place where terrorists and their sponsors operated in the international system would be considered fair game for targeted action and would be subject to the full might of the United States, with all its diplomatic, technologic, military, economic, intelligence, and law enforcement resources, could bring to bear. There would be no safe haven for the sort of Islamic radicals who viciously struck the American homeland on 9/11, killing thousands of innocent and unsuspecting people going about their daily lives, most not even knowing about, let alone understanding, the fierce hatred being directed at them.

Identifying and Understanding the Terrorist Threat

The successful prosecution of any war or armed action requires a sound understanding of the threat posed to the nation waging the conflict, the individuals who pose the threat, and the goals and interests the threatening party is interested in securing in the international security environment. Threats to the United States, or any nation for that matter, can generally be divided into four broad categories: traditional, irregular, catastrophic, and disruptive. Traditional threats are those threats posed by other nation-states using conventional military forces in ways generally accepted in armed conflict. Irregular threats, in contrast, stem from irregular or nontraditional forces, such as individuals, groups, or nation-states using unconventional methods like insurgency or terrorism as a way of offsetting any real or perceived advantages a stronger opponent like the United States might possess. Catastrophic threats arise from the possession or use of weapons of mass destruction (nuclear, chemical, biological, radiological) or methods that produce weapons of mass destruction-like effects. Finally, disruptive threats come from technical advances that have the potential to negate the technologic advantage the United States and some of its key allies have over other nations, both friendly and hostile.[2]

The potential for traditional state-on-state conflict, the type of war that usually comes to mind when individuals think of armed struggles, is generally believed to be waning, at least among the major powers of the international system.[3] The likelihood of massive armies facing off on a battlefield with armored vehicles, large formations of troops and equipment, and overhead air attack assets has become less likely since the collapse of the Soviet Union and the subsequent degradation of the once mighty and much-feared Red army. The realities of contemporary international relations, however, dictate that major nation-states will always be involved in some level of competition with one another, constantly seeking power and advantage over other states within the international system. Constant competition among countries results from what is known in international affairs circles as the security dilemma: steps taken by one nation to increase its security or power generally decrease the security or power of other nations, resulting in a need to respond in order to negate the advantage enjoyed by the state taking the initial action. This is how arms races happen. For example, if Iran is successful in developing a nuclear weapon, other states in the Middle East will likely feel compelled to pursue nuclear weapons technology in order to level the playing field so that no one state in the region becomes too dominant or enjoys too great an advantage over other states in the region. Despite the decreasing likelihood of traditional major power conflict, the United States and its allies must maintain the capability to counter traditional conventional threats that America and other Western nations could face from strong competitor countries like an increasingly powerful China looking to expand its global influence and a resurgent and assertive Russia once again pushing its way into European affairs.

Both China and Russia have invested heavily in recent years in military modernization and conventional force growth, devoting significant percentages of their national budgets to defense-related expenditures designed to increase operational capability and general efficiency and effectiveness in conventional warfare. China appears to be focusing most of its energy on air, missile, antiship, and air defense capabilities.[4] The People's Republic is also working on the production of unmanned aerial vehicles, with some designs capable of firing missiles like American and Israeli UAVs and at least one design that is jet powered.[5] These and other efforts like the planned building of an aircraft carrier will ultimately give the Chinese government the ability to move beyond territorial defense of its homeland to worldwide projection of its military power to support international outreach efforts designed to increase China's regional influence and secure needed natural resources for the Chinese people.[6] Particularly worrisome for the United States, the only other significant military power in the Asia-Pacific region, is China's faster-than-expected progression in stealth aviation technology. An early 2011 test flight of a stealth fighter prototype caused great concern among U.S. and Western military and intelligence personnel watching China's growing military capabilities.[7]

Russia has concentrated its military modernization efforts on restoring the advanced military means that disappeared with the collapse of the Soviet Union in 1991. It has been projected Russia will spend more than $60 billion, or almost 20 percent of its annual budget, on national security and defense programs over the course of 2011.[8] Russia is also working to modernize its naval base at Tartus on the Mediterranean Sea while maintaining its longtime naval presence at Sevastopol, Ukraine, on the Black Sea for the next quarter century.[9] Over the coming decade, the Russian government estimates it will spend more than $600 billion on modernization and rearmament programs for Russia's armed forces, with a primary focus on strategic nuclear assets, air defense capabilities, communications, intelligence, naval capabilities, and development of fifth-generation fighter aircraft.[10] These efforts will allow the Russian military to achieve a level of global reach indispensible to a nation looking to reassert its power across the international security system.

The United States has the most capable, best-fed, best-led, best-trained, and best-equipped military force the world has ever seen. Several key U.S. allies have respectable conventional military forces, but even these lack anything close to the level of capability possessed by the American armed services. The result of this disparity is an extreme dependence on U.S. military might for general stability and security across the international system. No nation in the world can compete with the United States in a traditional military sense, at least for now, and terrorist groups or terrorism-sponsoring states are unlikely to try to do so in the near term. The disparity between the military power of the United States and its competitors and enemies is just too great for direct, head-to-head conventional confrontation with American forces to be anything but suicidal. The potential for conventional conflict between the armed forces of state actors does still exist over the long term, though, and the current gap between the United States and its nearest conventional military competitors could rapidly shrink without continued U.S. investment in traditional force-on-force war-fighting capabilities. It would be far better for the United States to be prepared to wage traditional warfare against potential state rivals like China and Russia and not have occasion to do so than it would be for a conventional conflict to erupt unexpectedly and have the American armed forces unprepared for such an event because of a failure to invest sufficiently in conventional war-fighting equipment and training.

Catastrophic-level threats hold the greatest potential danger for the United States in terms of both damage to national infrastructure and loss of human life. In an increasingly unstable and insecure world, the likelihood of a catastrophic event involving a weapon of mass destruction occurring within the United States or some other Western nation continues to grow each year. While many of the countries in the international system have some level of chemical or biological weapons capability, only a handful of states are currently known to possess or are suspected of possessing nuclear weapons that can be accurately delivered to a targeted site. The so-called nuclear club includes the People's Republic of China, France, Russia, the United Kingdom, the United States, India, Israel, and Pakistan. Russia is estimated to have the greatest number of nuclear weapons, with 12,000, followed by the United States with 9,600, France with 300, China with 240, the United Kingdom with 225, Israel with 80, Pakistan with between 70 and 90, and India with between 60 and 80.[11]

Of course, some of these estimates are purely speculative, as in the case of Israel, which neither confirms nor denies its possession of nuclear weapons even though the United States and the rest of the international community has suspected an Israeli nuclear weapons capability for several decades. At least one recent estimate says Pakistan's arsenal is larger than generally thought, at more than one hundred nuclear weapons and growing, as Islamabad continues to build its nuclear capacity as a safeguard against possible aggression from neighboring India.[12] All of the states in the nuclear club save Pakistan, which is in the midst of an intense and violent counterinsurgency campaign against Islamic radicals attacking it from within its borders and from safe havens in neighboring Afghanistan, can be considered at least relatively stable and secure. Of the eight nuclear club member nations, three, Pakistan, India, and Israel, have not agreed to the Treaty on the Non-Proliferation of Nuclear Weapons. Outside of the nuclear club, two other states pose a serious nuclear security challenge for the international community that will have to be dealt with in the near term if the risk of a catastrophic event is going to be effectively minimized.

The Islamic Republic of Iran has been ruled since the 1979 Islamic revolution by a fundamentalist clerical regime headed by a supreme religious leader. The theocratic government in Tehran is believed by most Western nations, led by the United States and a few key European allies, to have been pursuing a clandestine nuclear weapons program for at least the past decade and probably longer. The capability to produce nuclear weapons, when combined with Iran's continuing advancements in medium- and long-range ballistic missile systems, could provide Iran with deliverable nuclear bombs capable of reaching targets in Western Europe or possibly even the United States in the very near future. The Democratic People's Republic of North Korea is a Stalinist-type statist dictatorship largely protected in the international system by neighboring China. The North Korean government claimed in early 2003 that it possessed nuclear weapons and in the following years conducted multiple tests of nuclear devices. At least one estimate says North Korea has between one and ten nuclear weapons, but Western nations have still been unable to verify, or at least publicly acknowledge, that North Korea has a nuclear weapon capable of being delivered in an attack against a specific target.[13] The ability to deliver a nuclear weapon to a predesignated target is a key consideration when evaluating a given nation's nuclear capability. It is no small feat to master the technology required to marry up a nuclear weapon with a delivery system capable of accurately striking a target. It is unclear whether North Korea has achieved such an advanced level of technologic know-how. With respect to both Iran and North Korea, it is the volatile and dangerous nature of the regimes in power that exacerbates the concern over their nuclear activities. The presence of nuclear weapons in either or both of these states would be much less worrisome if democratic governments accountable to their people were in place in Tehran and Pyongyang.

One other nation merits mention in any discussion of nuclear weapons or the pursuit of a nuclear weapons capability. Syria has long been considered a nuclear proliferation risk by the international community, despite ratification of the Nuclear Non-Proliferation Treaty in the late 1960s and the signing by Damascus of a nuclear safeguards agreement with the International Atomic Energy Agency in the early 1990s. In late 2007, Israeli warplanes struck a target at the Al Kibar nuclear site inside Syria that many suspected was a partially constructed nuclear reactor purchased from North Korea, fueling concerns that the Syrian government was secretly developing a nuclear weapons capability. Other reports of additional secret nuclear sites have done nothing to allay Western concerns about Syria's nuclear intentions, although those concerns have not yet risen to the level of worry attached to the Iranian and North Korean nuclear programs. If Syria is indeed pursuing nuclear weapons, another destabilizing force would be introduced into an already volatile and dangerous region, forcing the United States and its allies to divert at least some of their already stretched counterproliferation attention to Damascus.

There is no shortage of nations in the international system seeking a nuclear capability, although not all are necessarily interested in possessing nuclear weapons. Some countries, including a handful of Muslim countries in the Middle East, are legitimately considering only peaceful civilian nuclear energy programs. The calculus of those countries could change quickly, though, if Iran's nuclear program progresses to the point where it allows Tehran to join the nuclear club and fundamentally alter the balance of Middle Eastern power, or if a North Korean nuclear capability proliferated by a dangerous and unpredictable regime introduced nuclear weapons into states that currently do not possess such technology. The greater the number of states with a nuclear capability of any kind, the greater the likelihood of a deliverable nuclear weapon or the knowledge necessary to produce a deliverable nuclear weapon making its way into the hands of violent terrorists who could then use a weapon of mass destruction to strike the homelands of the United States and other Western countries or their interests across the international system.

Of the four threat categories, disruptive threats are the type least likely to be utilized effectively in the near term by Islamic terrorists targeting the United States, although some state sponsors of terrorism may in the not-too-distant-future provide increased disruptive capability to their sponsored terrorist organizations. That is not to say radical Islamists are not interested in a disruptive threat capability. Indeed, they are. The disruptive capability of these extremist individuals and groups, however, has not yet risen to the threat level posed by competitive state actors like China and Russia. Cyber, directed-energy, space-based, and other such threats will in the near term likely continue to come from established state competitors whose ready access to advancements in technology is steadily eroding the advantage currently enjoyed by the United States and its Western allies.

For the foreseeable future at least, irregular threats from radical Islamists employing nontraditional or asymmetric methods of warfare will pose the greatest immediate danger to the United States and like-minded nations in the international system. Fanatical Islamist extremists like the nineteen hijackers who struck the American homeland on 9/11 will continue to use terrorist violence, insurgency, and other unconventional methods in order to minimize their exposure to superior U.S. military might and over time erode the patience and political will of the American public and U.S. government officials. Muslim extremists can be expected to continue a long-term, deliberate, and patient approach in their confrontation with the "nonbelievers" in general, and with the United States in particular. The ultimate goal for the extremists is to make the cost of continued U.S. involvement in Muslim lands too high to maintain the support of the American people, ultimately forcing a reduction in U.S. and Western influence in the Middle East and parts of Africa and Asia. It is this asymmetric, irregular threat the U.S.-led "Global War on Terrorism" was launched to counter.

Terrorism in one form or another is not a new or even semirecent phenomenon. The Islamic extremist threat to the United States is simply the latest manifestation of the use of terrorist violence in pursuit of political goals. At least four periods of terrorist brutality have occurred in the global system in the past century and a half: the anarchist period that began in the late 1800s, the anticolonial period that came into being in the 1920s, the left-wing period of the twentieth century, and the current religious period that has its beginnings in the Iranian Revolution and Soviet invasion of Afghanistan, both of which occurred in 1979.[14] The "wave of terror" concept was developed by Dr. David Rapoport, who theorized a wave of terror consists of a cycle of terrorist activity characterized by expansion and contraction phases in a given time period that can last for about four decades.[15] If Rapoport's time line is even close to being accurate, the current wave of Islamic terrorism threatening the United States and other nations in the international system should be entering its final phase within the current decade or shortly thereafter. There are no substantive indications, however, to suggest this will be the case. Ongoing U.S. and allied military action in Afghanistan and Iraq, less overt operations in other Muslim nations, and the continuing presence of American and Western influence in traditionally Islamic lands will likely have the effect of making the Islamist wave last considerably longer than Rapoport's theoretical life expectancy for waves of terror.

The Islamic extremist security challenge is not going to suddenly disappear or slowly fade away, a reality the American public must be prepared to accept if the United States is going to effectively manage terrorist violence in the years ahead. Even though Islamic terrorism had been growing increasingly common in the international system since 1979, Americans generally thought of suicide bombings, hostage takings, hijackings, and other types of terrorist attacks targeting innocent civilians in the name of religious ideology as events that took place in other countries far from the safety of the American homeland. The threat from Islamic radicals existed for decades prior to the September 11 attacks on the United States, but it took the destruction of the World Trade Center towers in New York and the ramming of a civilian airliner into the military's Pentagon headquarters to awaken, even if only momentarily, the American people and their government to an extremist ideological movement that had been increasingly setting its sights on the U.S. homeland and vulnerable U.S. interests abroad. The full force of violent Islamic radicalism finally reached into the lives of average Americans on 9/11, and it did so with a terrifying and devastating effect that shook the nation to its core and fundamentally altered the way the United States conducted its foreign policy activities in the international system.

Terrorist Violence and Justifications for Its Use

Defining terrorism or what constitutes a terrorist act is essential to understanding the global Islamic extremist threat. Multiple definitions of terrorism are available from a wide variety of sources, but all essentially say the same thing. For example, a paper submitted to the 2008 Copenhagen Consensus described terrorism as the premeditated use (or threat of use) of violent acts by individual persons or nonstate groups against noncombatants in pursuit of some political or social objective through the intimidation of an audience beyond that of the immediate victim.[16] In another example, the United States government characterizes terrorism as the premeditated and politically motivated use of violence by subnational groups or individuals who target noncombatants with the objective of influencing a particular audience.[17] Finally, renowned strategist Colin Gray has written that terrorism is the sustained use (or threat of use) of violent acts by a small group for some political purpose like instilling fear, drawing attention to a complaint, or provoking a drastic and heavy-handed response.[18] Each of these definitions is essentially consistent with criteria identified by counterterrorism expert and former national intelligence officer for the Near East and South Asia Paul Pillar, author of *Terrorism and U.S. Foreign Policy*, who argued that for an event to be considered an act of terrorism, it had to be premeditated, politically motivated, aimed at noncombatant targets, and committed by either subnational groups or clandestine agents.[19] Putting minor differences in wording aside, most definitions of terrorism have one basic theme: violence against civilians or noncombatants for the purpose of achieving a political goal, although Gray's definition does not single out civilians or noncombatants as targets.

The reasons for adopting terrorism as a tactic designed to achieve political gain vary widely among extremist groups. Some of the more common reasons include ethnic nationalism, separatism, perceived or real social injustices, and fundamentalist religious beliefs. The Islamic terrorists who attacked America and prompted the "Global War on Terrorism" subscribe to a twisted ideology that perverts elements of the Islamic faith to justify the murder of innocent people, including women and children, as a means for correcting what they claim to be political, social, and economic injustices and cultural intrusions at the hands of Western nations and those secular regimes in Muslim countries allied with the United States and the West. These extremists are dangerous, and their ability to bring death and destruction to the United States must not be underestimated. They have already demonstrated the capacity to inflict considerable physical and economic harm on the American homeland and on U.S. and allied interests worldwide. Given the opportunity they will do so again. The effect of their violent acts is not limited to death or injury to humans or damage to equipment and infrastructure. Acts of terrorism also disrupt the global freedom of movement enjoyed by the United States and its citizens and hinder American diplomatic relations with other countries across the broader international system.

The use of terrorist violence provides radical enemies of the United States with an effective, relatively cheap and easy-to-use weapon that negates many of America's traditional national strengths and has the potential to inflict large numbers of casualties on American citizens at home and abroad. The motivation to use terrorism can be rationalized with multiple justifications: *as leverage for bargaining*, in which practitioners of violent terrorist acts are seeking some degree of influence that will help them attain a sought-after objective; *for political or diplomatic disruption*, where an attempt is made to send a political message to a specific target audience; *to influence the behavior of a fearful population* in order to increase support for the terrorists or lessen support for a nation's government; *to provoke a government* into reacting harshly and indiscriminately; *to "show the flag"* by attempting to demonstrate a particular terrorist organization is still a powerful force that has to be dealt with; to exact a measure of *revenge* against those who have done harm to the terrorists; as an act of *simple hatred* directed at those who do not agree with the terrorists' motives or objectives; and *to carry out a divine mandate*, touted by groups such as al Qaeda, Hezbollah, Hamas, and other Islamic terrorist organizations that claim to be defending their religious beliefs.[20]

A 2007 Rand research brief offered four hypotheses that sought to explain the reasons extremist organizations engage in violent terrorist activities. While Rand focused specifically on the motivations of bin Laden's al Qaeda network, the hypotheses outlined in the brief can generally be applied to any individual Islamic terrorists or terrorist groups threatening the United States and its allies in the contemporary international security environment. Rand's *coercion* hypothesis argues that terrorists seek to inflict some measure of pain in order to force policies sympathetic to the terrorists' cause. A good example can be found in the terrorist bombing of the Madrid commuter train system three days before Spain's general election in 2004, ostensibly to force an end to Spain's support for the U.S.-led war in Iraq. The *damage* hypothesis theorizes that terrorist attacks weaken the economy of a targeted country and make it harder for that country to stay engaged in Muslim-dominated lands. Next, the *rally* hypothesis says terrorist attacks within the United States and other Western nations are designed to attract new recruits and new sources of financial and material support by demonstrating the capability of the organization to strike Americans and other Westerners on their home soil. Finally, the *franchise* hypothesis holds that contemporary Islamic terrorists are focused more on local or regional issues than they are on global issues and cannot be considered part of the original al Qaeda organization that existed prior to the United States' "Global War on Terrorism."[21]

This last Rand hypothesis argues that al Qaeda as a transnational terrorist organization has decentralized itself into small regional and local cells that receive little, if any, substantive support from the individuals who make up the core al Qaeda leadership. These local and regional terrorist groups often affiliate themselves with or pledge their allegiance to the original al Qaeda organization in order to focus more attention on their particular cause and to gain some measure of credibility as bona fide Islamic terrorist groups worthy of support from the broader Muslim community. The decentralization of al Qaeda's once-global terrorist movement is discussed in more detail in the next section of this chapter. For all the reasons presented here, Islamic terrorists have targeted and will continue to target the United States and American interests abroad whenever given the opportunity to do so. American officials finally came to understand in the aftermath of the 9/11 attacks that they could no longer ignore or simply wish away the growing lethal threat posed by a fanatical enemy determined to strike the United States, its citizens, and its interests and those of its allies, in every corner of the international system.

Identifying the Enemy and His Evolving Structure

In the days and weeks following the 9/11 attacks, the United States began to focus its attention on Osama bin Laden and the al Qaeda terrorist network based in Taliban-controlled Afghanistan. Bin Laden was already well known to American defense and intelligence officials, having declared war on the United States once in 1996, in his *Declaration of Jihad on the Americans Occupying the Country of the Two Sacred Places*, and again in 1998, in his *Declaration of the World Islamic Front for Jihad against the Jews and the Crusaders*. His goals, and by default the goals of his al Qaeda terrorist network, articulated in various formats (bin Laden liked to issue *fatwas*, or Islamic religious rulings, but lacked the credentials of a true Islamic scholar) and pursued through the violent actions of his extremist operatives, included the expulsion of American and Western influence from Muslim countries, the removal of secular governments in Muslim states, the elimination of Israel, and the restoration of the Muslim empire to its farthest historical boundaries. In executing its plan to achieve these goals, al Qaeda conducts a global campaign of terrorist violence that utilizes attacks on the United States, its allies, the West in general, and secular Muslim governments in the Middle East, Africa, and Asia while simultaneously promoting the expansion of radical Islamist ideology with an aggressive and effective information campaign designed to influence global public opinion and win support in both Muslim and non-Muslim societies across the international system.

Since the United States embarked upon its "Global War on Terrorism," bin Laden's al Qaeda network has suffered prohibitive losses in both personnel and capability as well as the loss of its Taliban-sponsored terrorist safe haven in Afghanistan. Once a powerful Islamic extremist organization with legitimately global reach, al Qaeda has seen a large percentage of its senior and mid-level leadership captured or killed and has had its operational effectiveness degraded to such an extent that the al Qaeda that struck the United States on 9/11 essentially no longer exists. The core al Qaeda of bin Laden and al-Zawahiri, sometimes referred to as al Qaeda proper or al Qaeda prime, has been subjected to such a massive onslaught of U.S. national power since late 2001 that it is no longer capable of conducting effective strategic planning or controlling major terrorist activities in any meaningful fashion. Even in this weakened state, though, al Qaeda prime still poses a serious but not necessarily existential threat to the United States and its allies and partners. As key al Qaeda leaders have been killed, captured, or otherwise taken out of the fight by being forced into hiding to avoid death or detention, others have stepped up to take their place in the leadership hierarchy. Such losses necessarily result in some degradation of experienced extremist talent, but there has been no shortage of radical Islamists eager to take on more responsibility and make their mark on the global jihadist movement. Al Qaeda is not the powerful force it was just a few years ago, but the terrorist network continues to fight for survival and relevance while carrying the banner of Islamic extremism as a model for other radical groups to emulate.

Remnants of al Qaeda still threaten international coalition forces operating in Afghanistan and Pakistani forces trying to bring some semblance of order to the tribal areas located along the Afghanistan-Pakistan border. Al Qaeda's propaganda campaign, conducted primarily through the release of a steady stream of audio and video messages, has not relented in its effort to rally Muslim support, recruit new fighters, undermine Western opinion, and nurture the perception that bin Laden's terrorist movement is still a significant and dangerous force capable of striking U.S. and other national interests across the international system. Bin Laden's followers remain committed to a prolonged and bloody conflict with the United States and any other nation that does not subscribe to their radical Islamist ideology. While the potential for serious harm inflicted by the original al Qaeda organization on the United States and its allies has been significantly lessened, it has not been eliminated or reduced to the point where American officials need not worry about the death and destruction that would accompany an al Qaeda prime or al Qaeda prime–sponsored attack on the United States or on U.S. interests overseas.

Al Qaeda proper has long been regarded as the most dangerous Islamic terrorist organization in the world, the vanguard of Muslim radicalism. It is a terrorist force that must still be reckoned with, but not on the same level as in the past. While some of the core leadership has been neutralized, it is fair to assume that al Qaeda leaders, along with their inner circle of trusted and dedicated operatives, will do whatever they can to remain relevant to the global Islamic extremist movement and to ensure their long-term viability as leaders of a worldwide Islamist struggle against the United States, its allies, and other like-minded nations. It is critical that the United States continue to target key al Qaeda leaders for death or capture whenever and wherever they can be found, without letting such efforts overshadow the broader strategic challenge of transnational Islamic radicalism. Killing or capturing one man or a small group of men is a difficult task best prioritized as a target of opportunity. The death or detention of the most widely recognized al Qaeda personalities, including bin Laden, would not end or even diminish significantly the overall threat from Islamic extremism. It would likely inflict a powerful psychological blow on Muslim radicals everywhere, but such an effect would be temporary and would cause limited overall damage to radical Islamist ideology. Morale among Islamist foot soldiers would probably suffer in the short term, but the strategic effect on terrorist operations would be negligible.

Al Qaeda prime, though largely marginalized and severely weakened, remains relevant even if only in the form of an ideological inspiration for other Islamic radicals seeking to achieve their goals through the use of violence directed against anyone that stands in their way. As al Qaeda proper has decreased in significance and lost operational capability in the years since 9/11, a new and greater threat to the United States and its allies has emerged. The most serious danger now comes from al Qaeda and Associated Movements, or AQAM, a vast association of Islamic terrorist groups that consists of the original al Qaeda organization and a multitude of affiliated and associated extremist organizations that operate at both the local and regional levels around the world.[22]

Almost immediately after the United States invaded Afghanistan in late 2001, al Qaeda prime was forced to decentralize its operations to have any chance of surviving the American military's campaign to eliminate it as a viable transnational Islamist terrorist group. This decentralization led to the establishment of multiple local and regional terrorist organizations loosely affiliated with the original al Qaeda, sometimes in name only. These post-9/11 Islamist groups represent a threat to the United States and its allies that is much less structured than before, with al Qaeda prime evolving into a more diffuse global movement where dispersed terrorist cells focus their efforts primarily on local and regional objectives while sharing the broader extremist ideology of bin Laden and al-Zawahiri. AQAM can be divided into three basic levels: the core al Qaeda that perpetrated the 9/11 attacks on the United States; al Qaeda affiliates and like-minded groups, including official al Qaeda franchises and regional groups that maintain some degree of independence despite their links to al Qaeda prime; and al Qaeda-inspired but nonaffiliated terrorist groups and individuals who draw inspiration from bin Laden and al Qaeda prime.[23]

Non-al Qaeda prime AQAM groups plan their own terrorist operations, provide their own funding, recruit their own fighters, and employ their own homegrown tactics while looking to al Qaeda prime for inspiration, ideological guidance, and legitimacy. A successful operation or series of operations for any one of these groups enhances the Islamist reputation of all Muslim terrorist groups, regardless of their level of involvement. It is this conglomeration of local and regional extremist cells combined with al Qaeda prime in a global terrorist association unified by a shared ideology that poses the greatest danger to the United States and its allies. Al Qaeda franchises, affiliates, and like-minded terrorist organizations are critical to al Qaeda prime's ability to maintain its status as the leading ideological force of the global Islamic extremist movement. Al Qaeda franchises are terrorist groups officially recognized by al Qaeda leaders as branches or extensions of al Qaeda prime. Only three regional Islamic terrorist groups have achieved a level of success sufficient for obtaining official franchise status: al Qaeda in Mesopotamia (Iraq), al Qaeda in the Islamic Maghreb (Western Africa), and al Qaeda in the Arabian Peninsula (Yemen). Becoming an al Qaeda franchise is a long and complex process, often taking many years, in which an aspirant group's credibility is established to a degree sufficient for al Qaeda prime to accept it into the base organization. Designating official franchises allows al Qaeda proper to extend its influence while gaining validation of its global Islamist vision.[24] The "like-minded" grouping of terrorist organizations in the second tier of AQAM includes other regional Islamic entities that have links to al Qaeda prime and aspire to achieve the same level of success and notoriety of the al Qaeda base and its official franchises. The most notable terrorist group in this category is the radical al Shabaab Islamist movement in Somalia, which has begun to expand its operational reach into neighboring African countries while making its case to al Qaeda prime for recognition as an official franchise.

AQAM is a resilient and adaptive enemy that is largely focused on local and regional causes but that never loses sight of the broader global battle with the "nonbelievers" that ties the various individual Islamic terrorist groups together. A shared ideology and a common desire to target those who do not subscribe to radical Islamist beliefs increase the likelihood of an attack on the United States or its allies by these groups as their ability to execute violent acts of terrorism grows. The organizations that make up AQAM do not recognize international laws, do not engage in what is generally considered to be acceptable behavior for resolving differences or conducting armed conflict, and are not interested in a peaceful coexistence with those who do not subscribe to their extremist beliefs. They are willing to engage in barbaric acts of violence, they usually lack definitive areas of operation that can be easily targeted, and they are often extremely difficult to identify until after an attack has been attempted or successfully carried out. They are wildly unpredictable and they are exceptionally dangerous, to our allies in the Middle East and Europe in the near term, and to the United States itself in the long term. It is essential that the United States focus its attention on this broader Islamist network and not solely on the original al Qaeda, no matter how much national satisfaction might be had in seeing al Qaeda leaders brought to justice through death or capture for their acts of terror against the United States and its citizens.

The "Far" and "Near Enemy" Strategic Approaches

Al Qaeda prime favors a strategic approach that focuses its efforts on the "far enemy," those countries like the United States and European nations outside areas traditionally dominated by Muslim populations. Al Qaeda's franchises and associated movements, in contrast, generally focus their efforts on the "near enemy," those secular governments in Muslim lands that are allied with the United States and the West and are opposed to the political agenda of Islamic extremists. That is not to say al Qaeda's franchises and affiliates do not take advantage of opportunities to strike at the "far enemy" when those opportunities arise. Multiple terrorist plots foiled by Western and non-Western governments since the 9/11 attacks on the United States show an increasing level of intent and capability by al Qaeda in the Arabian Peninsula and other extremist groups to extend their reach beyond their traditional operating areas. There are several advantages to pursuing a strategy focused on the "far enemy," including a unifying and rallying effect among Muslims in Islamic societies across the international system, the provision of greater sanctuary for extremists in states supportive of the Islamist agenda, and the easy portrayal of violent terrorist acts as part of a religious war between Islam and the West. Disadvantages associated with a strategy focused on the "near enemy" include the creation of divisions among Muslims, the localization of support, the risk of significant pressure from state security organizations, limits to sanctuary, uncertainty among Muslims about conflicts between local political issues and broader Islamic religious matters, and a lack of substantive impact on Western support for secular governments in Muslim-populated states.[25] Bin Laden believed a powerful, mass-casualty-producing terrorist strike like the 9/11 attacks on the "far enemy," the United States, would result in a disproportionate Western response in Muslim countries.[26] Such a response, bin Laden believed, would prompt Muslims around the world to rise up in the defense of Islam and drive non-Muslim powers from Muslim territories. Bin Laden was right in one respect. The 9/11 attacks were met with a massive and, some would argue, disproportionate response from the United States and its allies, in Afghanistan and then subsequently in Iraq. The spontaneous uprising of the Muslim masses envisioned by bin Laden and his deputies never materialized, though, and does not seem likely to in the foreseeable future.

The "near enemy" strategic approach favored by al Qaeda's associated movements cannot continue indefinitely given the broader ideology of conflict with the West shared by al Qaeda prime and its franchises and affiliates. "Near enemy" targets are logistically easier to attack, especially for local and regional groups that may suffer from a limited supply of resources available for carrying out their terrorist strikes. Eventually, though, the real source of power and security for "near enemy" targets, the United States and its Western allies, will have to be dealt with if Muslim extremists are going to accomplish the goals set forth by Osama bin Laden in his declarations of war against the United States and the West. One al Qaeda–affiliated radical Islamic terrorist group traditionally focused on the "near enemy," the Pakistani Taliban, claimed responsibility for and subsequently was linked to an attempted car bombing in New York City's Times Square, carried out by Pakistani-born American citizen Faisal Shahzad in early 2010. A potentially mass-casualty-producing attack was averted only when the would-be bomber's device failed to function properly and alert citizens quickly notified local law enforcement personnel of the smoking sport utility vehicle used to carry Shahzad's bomb. In another incident, Yemen's al Qaeda in the Arabian Peninsula shipped explosive materials hidden in laser printer toner cartridges aboard commercial airliners destined for Chicago, Illinois. Law enforcement and intelligence officials suspected the bombs were meant to detonate somewhere over the continental United States, destroying the planes and killing all those on board.

Georgetown University security studies professor Bruce Hoffman, who also serves as a senior fellow at the United States Military Academy's Combating Terrorism Center, has theorized that al Qaeda developed and implemented a new strategy at least as long ago as early 2009. While Hoffman's focus was on al Qaeda prime, it is likely the second- and possibly third-tier elements of AQAM would adopt some of the base organization's tactics given the level of association of the groups that make up al Qaeda's global extremist network. Calling the new strategic approach "death by a thousand cuts," Hoffman divided the strategy into five parts. First, U.S. intelligence collection assets are being bombarded with multiple threat warnings, some real and some bogus, that overwhelm and exhaust America's limited and already stretched intelligence resources. Second, al Qaeda is increasingly conducting a form of economic warfare with the goal of forcing the United States to implement expensive and resource-intensive countermeasures designed to protect American citizens from a wide variety of possible terrorist threats. Third, al Qaeda is attempting to divide the international coalition arrayed against it by conducting terrorist attacks against coalition member states that are politically vulnerable with their populations (for example, the Madrid, Spain, attack in 2004, the London, England, attack in 2005, and attacks against NATO forces that lack strong public support for their participation in the war in Afghanistan). Fourth, al Qaeda is aggressively seeking to exploit failed states and ungoverned or undergoverned spaces like Somalia, Yemen, and the Federally Administered Tribal Areas in Pakistan that offer terrorist operatives relatively safe places to operate. Finally, al Qaeda is attempting to enlist new operatives who can infiltrate the United States and other Western nations with relative ease so that it is less difficult to carry out violent acts of terrorism. One recent example of this aspect of al Qaeda's new strategy can be found in the case of Umar Farouk Abdulmutallab, the Nigerian Christmas Day bomber who attempted to set off explosives hidden in his underwear while traveling to the United States aboard a commercial passenger jet. Abdulmutallab did not fit the expected Muslim terrorist profile because he was not Arab and he was not from the Middle East.[27]

The economic aspect of al Qaeda's war with the West is important to understand and can be further broken down into several components: the general use of terrorist violence to inflict damage on the economies of targeted countries; forcing targeted countries into bankruptcy with expensive and protracted resource-intensive conflicts like those in Afghanistan and Iraq; targeting the world's supply of oil so that energy costs for Western nations increase dramatically; and carrying out violent acts of terror with greater frequency rather than focusing on spectacular, mass-casualty-producing terror strikes.[28] A greater frequency of attacks causes a targeted country to repeatedly react with security countermeasures that increase the costs required for a nation to defend itself. Economics has played a much greater role in Islamic extremist strategies since 9/11. Al Qaeda and its franchises and affiliates know they cannot defeat the United States and the West militarily, but they can inflict a level of economic harm sufficient to weaken the will of Western populations to remain engaged in foreign expeditions that target Islamic radicals. Aggressive offensive actions taken by the United States and its allies since 2001 have forced the groups that make up AQAM to shift their strategies and become more creative or else risk failure in pursuit of their strategic goals.

The Threat from "Lone Wolf" Terrorists

Radicalized individuals who draw inspiration from al Qaeda prime have become increasingly active in targeting American citizens and U.S. interests over the past decade. These "lone wolf" terrorist actors, who are generally categorized as a subset of AQAM's third tier, are not formally affiliated with any particular terrorist organization. Because they are not part of an official command structure in a known extremist group, lone wolf radicals are difficult to identify and track, making it easier for them to commit their acts of terrorist violence while simultaneously making it extremely difficult for those charged with protecting American citizens from Islamic radicalism to stop these individual actors before it is too late. Lone wolf Islamic extremists who have attempted or successfully conducted attacks on American soil include Hesham Mohamed Hadayet, who opened fire at the El Al ticket counter at Los Angeles

International Airport in 2002; Mohammed Reza Taheri-Azar, who drove his vehicle into a crowd of students at the University of North Carolina at Chapel Hill in 2006; Naveed Abzal Haq, who shot several people at the Seattle Jewish Federation in 2006; Abdulhakim Mujahaid Muhammad, who opened fire at a U.S. military recruiting station in Little Rock, Arkansas, in 2009, killing one American soldier and wounding another; and U.S. Army Major Nidal Malik Hasan, who went on a shooting rampage at a soldier readiness processing center at Fort Hood, Texas, in 2009, killing thirteen people and wounding dozens more. Another lone wolf Islamic extremist who was serving in the ranks of the United States military overseas when he committed his act of terrorist violence was U.S. Army Sergeant Hasan Akbar, who attacked his fellow service members with grenades at a military camp in Kuwait in 2003 as his unit prepared to move north into Iraq as part of Operation Iraqi Freedom.

State Sponsors of Terrorism

When former president Bush announced the United States would make no distinction between the terrorists who attacked America and those who harbored and assisted them, he made it clear to the American public and to the international community that rogue groups acting outside the nation-state structure of the international system would not be the only targets in the U.S.-led "Global War on Terrorism." The countries of the world were put on notice—the United States would hold them accountable for their actions if they chose to directly or indirectly support Islamic radicals targeting America or its allies. Bush's declaration was an important recognition that the support of a state sponsor significantly enhances the ability of a terrorist group to conduct acts of violence in pursuit of its political agenda. State sponsors of terrorism act as "force multipliers," to use a common military term, providing critical resources that groups without such support simply cannot get on their own. State sponsors of terrorism are able to deliver into the hands of dangerous terrorist groups the financial resources, weapons, equipment, safe havens, protection, and training facilities they require if they are to be effective terrorist entities capable of striking targets on a regional or global basis.

There are three categories of state sponsorship of terrorist activity. Active state sponsorship occurs when a nation makes a deliberate decision to provide some measure of support to a particular terrorist group or to several terrorist groups. Passive state sponsorship happens when a nation knowingly tolerates terrorist activity either because it is unwilling or unable to take action to stop such activity. And finally, state-sanctioned support for terrorism occurs when a given terrorist group is not an official arm of a state's government but is provided with some level of state assistance that does not compromise the group's ability to operate independently.[29] State sponsorship of terrorism can also be divided into five different levels according to the severity of the state's actions. Those levels, in order of declining severity, are as follows: active sponsors who provide direct financial and material support to terrorists and who typically fail to cooperate with the international community on terrorism-related matters; nation-states that make deals with terrorist groups for amnesty and regional independence; countries that allow terrorists to raise money and operate freely within their territory; states that do not apprehend or extradite terrorists identified within their borders; and states that have not taken the steps necessary to fulfill their terrorism-related responsibilities to the international community.[30]

Under United States law, the Export Administration Act of 1979 established a list of state sponsors of terrorism and granted the secretary of state the legal authority to place countries on that list.[31] As of this writing, four nations are currently classified by the United States as state sponsors of terrorism: Iran, Syria, Cuba, and Sudan. Two countries recently removed from the list are Iraq, taken off in 2004 following the U.S.-led invasion that toppled Saddam Hussein's Ba'athist regime, and North Korea, removed in 2008 following Pyongyang's cooperation with the international community on inspections of its nuclear program. The list of state sponsors of terrorism is often used as a diplomatic lever that allows the United States to apply a degree of pressure with the goal of coercing a targeted state into changing its behavior. In some cases, the objectionable behavior the United States seeks to correct has nothing at all to do with support for terrorist violence. A good example can be found in the case of North Korea, which some in the United States have argued should be returned to the state sponsors of terrorism list despite a lack of concrete evidence that Pyongyang definitively supports terrorist activity. A return to the list, advocates say, would put pressure on North Korea for its human rights violations, its repression of North Korean citizens, and its continued irresponsible behavior with regard to its nuclear and ballistic missile programs.

The Islamic Republic of Iran is considered by the United States to be the most active state sponsor of terrorism in the international system. An unclassified U.S. government report on Iran's military power described Iranian support for terrorism with the following statement: "We assess with high confidence that over the last three decades, Iran has methodically cultivated a network of sponsored terrorist surrogates capable of conducting effective, plausibly deniable attacks against Israel and the United States."[32] Added to the U.S. State Department's terrorism sponsorship list in 1984, just five years after the Islamic revolution that swept a clerical dictatorship into power, Tehran provides significant material and ideological support to a variety of terrorist groups as a means for pursuing its goals throughout the Middle East. Hezbollah, Hamas, multiple militant groups in Iraq, several Palestinian terrorist organizations, and the Taliban in Afghanistan all benefit from Iranian state sponsorship of terrorist activity.[33] Iranian support to these groups includes the provision of money, weapons, training, logistical assistance, equipment, and ideological guidance. Particularly worrisome for the United States is the help Iran provides to Shia militias targeting American interests in Iraq. Iranian assistance to these militias opposed to the U.S. presence and to the Iraqi government includes explosively formed penetrators (EFPs), improvised explosive devices (IEDs), antiaircraft weapons, mortars, rockets, rocket-propelled grenades (RPGs), small arms, and various types of explosives.[34] Iran is also suspected of being actively involved as a state actor in the planning and execution of terrorist attacks in the Middle East as well as serving as a safe haven for several senior figures of al Qaeda prime.

Syria was designated a state sponsor of terrorism in 1979 and has been on the State Department's list longer than any other country. The Syrian government provides state support to multiple terrorist organizations, including Lebanese Hezbollah, Hamas, and various Palestinian organizations that use terrorist violence against Israeli civilian and government targets. Syria also allows several terrorist groups to operate organizational offices within its borders, maintains strong ties with regional powerhouse, terrorism sponsor, and would-be nuclear power Iran, and facilitates the flow of weapons and radical Muslim fighters into Iraq to attack American and host-nation security forces.

Cuba, the only nation in the Western Hemisphere to appear on the state sponsors of terrorism list, received its designation nearly three decades ago in 1982. The Cuban government has ties to fellow state sponsors of terrorism Iran and Syria and is suspected of providing safe haven to members of various regional terrorist groups, even though Havana announced in 1992 that it no longer actively supported foreign insurgents or terrorist organizations.

Finally, the African nation of Sudan, added to the list in 1993, is believed to be providing safe haven to fugitive members of multiple Islamic terrorist groups, including Hamas and the Palestinian Islamic Jihad.[35] In an early 2011 referendum, southern Sudan voted overwhelmingly to secede from the country's north. In response to the referendum's results, the Obama administration declared its intention to remove Sudan from the state sponsors of terrorism list and recognize Southern Sudan as a sovereign nation in mid-2011.

When a country is placed on the State Department's list of state sponsors of terrorism, that nation is subjected to a series of U.S. government-imposed sanctions that includes a ban on arms-related exports and sales, controls over the export of dual-use items (those materials that can be used for both civilian and military purposes), prohibitions on economic assistance, and the imposition of multiple financial and other restrictions against the targeted state.[36] For a country to be removed from the terrorism sponsorship list, the president of the United States is required to certify to Congress that the government of that country has not supported international terrorism for at least the preceding six months or has experienced a shift in leadership and government policies (as in the case of post–Saddam Hussein Iraq) that has resulted in an abandonment of support for terrorism, and that a state has promised to refrain from support for terrorist violence in the future.[37] Being named a state sponsor of terrorism and the subsequent imposition of sanctions by the United States does not appear to have had a substantive effect on the behavior of the countries on the list of terrorism-sponsoring nations. None of the list's current residents has demonstrably changed its policies or behavior since being designated a state sponsor of terrorism, and it is unlikely any will do so as a result of U.S. blacklisting.

Of course, there is a certain amount of international embarrassment associated with a state sponsor of terrorism designation, and diplomatic pressure can be applied to both the targeted state and to America's allies and partners to possibly force a change in state terrorism-supporting practices. But there will no doubt always be some nations, like the ones currently on the State Department's list, that will not be influenced by U.S. labeling or by any potential or real effects associated with economic sanctions unless there is a broad and united international front arrayed against them, or unless the threat of military action appears to be imminent. For terrorist groups and individuals that do not have the benefit of a state sponsor and thus cannot be placed on the state sponsors of terrorism list, the United States has other classifications available under the Immigration and Nationality Act and Executive Order 13224. Under the former, non–state-sponsored terrorist groups can be designated as foreign terrorist organizations (FTOs) while under the latter, individuals can be categorized as specially designated global terrorists (SDGTs).[38] Each of these designations carries with it specific economic and freedom-of-movement restrictions.

In today's complex, dangerous, and uncertain international system, Islamic terrorists with or without the benefit of state-level active or passive support represent the greatest threat to the United States, its people, and American interests worldwide. The threat from these extremists, initially spearheaded by Osama bin Laden's transnational al Qaeda terrorist network, has morphed into the al Qaeda and Associated Movements grouping of like-minded Islamic extremist organizations, a decentralized set of local and regional radical Muslim cells that use terrorist violence as a means for achieving short-term, local, and regional objectives while remaining focused on the long-term global struggle against the United States and other Western nations. When given the opportunity to commit their acts of violence, these terrorists have demonstrated the will and the ability to join forces against America and its allies and partners on battlefields both near to and far from their homes. U.S. and coalition forces in Afghanistan and Iraq have regularly encountered foreign Islamic fighters from Pakistan, Turkey, Syria, Saudi Arabia, Yemen, and a host of other countries, including some in the West. Active Islamic terrorist cells have been identified on nearly every continent, and spectacular, mass-casualty-producing attacks have been carried out in countries across the Middle East, Europe, Asia, North America, and other places where Islamic radicals live and operate, often with help from state sponsors or local populations. In 2008, there were roughly twelve thousand terrorist attacks worldwide resulting in more than fifty thousand injuries and deaths.[39] In 2009, the number of such attacks dropped slightly to eleven thousand in more than eighty countries, with a death toll of nearly sixteen thousand.[40] The Islamic extremist threat exists throughout the international security environment, and what may seem like an isolated local or regional threat is unlikely to remain so in today's increasingly globalized, interconnected, and interdependent world.

An Era of Persistent Conflict

Since the United States first embarked on its global quest to rid the world of Islamic radicalism and its use of terrorist violence in pursuit of political and social goals, one question has repeatedly been asked by both supporters and opponents of the transnational effort: Can the U.S.-led fight against Islamic radicalism legitimately be classified as a war? Former president Bush's administration quickly identified its response to the 9/11 attacks as a "war," the purpose of which was to neutralize the threat posed to the United States by terrorists and the nation-states that supported them. The "war" label was reinforced in the president's 2006 *National Strategy for Combating Terrorism*, which stated, "America is at war with a transnational terrorist movement fueled by a radical ideology of hatred, oppression, and murder,"[41] and again in the 2007 *National Strategy for Homeland Security*, which said, "The terrorist attacks on September 11, 2001, were acts of war against the United States and the principles of freedom, opportunity, and openness that define the American way of life."[42] Critics immediately countered that it was impossible to wage war on terrorism because terrorist violence was a tactic and not an identifiable enemy that could be decisively defeated in combat on the battlefield. Since the launching of the "Global War on Terrorism," there has been a significant amount of debate in the United States and around the world regarding this issue.

A good starting point for this discussion is the definition of the word *war*. Merriam-Webster defines war as "a state of open and usually declared armed hostile conflict between states or nations" or "a state of hostility, conflict, or antagonism."[43] Most Americans, when thinking about whether or not a particular conflict is or is not a war, consider the inclusion of national governments, uniformed soldiers, organized armies, defined rules of engagement, identifiable territories, and a clear end-state or objective as critical factors necessary for designating an armed action as a war, regardless of whether Congress formally declares war in a particular crisis situation. This creates a bit of difficulty when Islamic terrorists are identified as the enemy the United States is seeking to defeat. The Muslim extremists threatening the contemporary international security environment do not wear easily identifiable uniforms, nor do they abide by conventional and accepted rules of warfare. They are often not very structured in their organization, and they generally do not hold specific pieces of territory, or at least they do not do so for long. They may or may not have state sponsors providing critically needed and capability-enhancing support, and they are unlikely to be beaten in the traditional Western sense of wartime victory and defeat. Historical notions of war, therefore, do not support the proposition that the United States is engaged in a "Global War on Terrorism" and instead provide backing to those who argue terrorist violence is largely a criminal matter best left to law enforcement and other nonkinetic methods and not a military matter to be dealt with by America's armed forces.

Supporters of the war classification tend to argue terrorism is at least a form of warfare, even if it is not a formal war. Organized and trained Islamic fighters, they say, conduct offensive military and paramilitary operations involving the use of violence against their targets, just like the armies of nation-states. Treating terrorism as a criminal matter, the argument goes, limits the range of responses available to only those that are reactive and defensive in nature. Reactionary responses and defensive postures do not allow the United States to stop terrorist attacks before they can cause death and destruction on American soil. Supporters of the war classification maintain that since terrorism is a form of warfare, it can be answered only with war. Writing in *The Lessons of Terror*, military historian Caleb Carr put it this way: "One can refuse to call such people an army, if one wishes; yet they are organized as an army, and certainly they conduct themselves as an army, giving and taking secret orders to attack their enemies with a variety of tactics that serve one overarching strategy: terror."[44]

Shortly after President Obama was sworn in as the forty-fourth commander-in-chief of America's armed forces, the United States moved away
from the Bush administration's "War on Terrorism" jargon in favor of
"overseas contingency operations" (OCOs) and the "campaign against al
Qaeda and transnational terrorist organizations" (CAAQATTO). Whether
one chooses to call the global fight against Islamic extremists a war or a
contingency operation, it has become increasingly clear over the past several
years that the armed struggle against Islamist terrorism is going to last a very
long time and will possibly never be ended. There are several reasons for this.
First, because of its status as the world's lone superpower, the United States is
constantly in the crosshairs of multiple Islamic terrorist groups who actively
seek out opportunities to demonstrate a strong commitment to their cause
by striking out at the most powerful symbol of the West. A large and active
overseas presence puts U.S. military personnel, embassy workers, nonprofit
and humanitarian organization employees, businesspeople, and tourists in
constant danger of being attacked by Islamic radicals who have no qualms
about targeting innocents as a means for achieving their goals. Second, the
United States is facing an enemy who is fanatically committed to his faith and
who sees U.S. support for Israel and secular governments in the Middle East
as justification for his hatred of America and its policies. When religion is the
motivating factor behind a given cause, it is extremely difficult to dissuade its
followers from taking action in support of that cause. Third, there are many
more Islamic terrorist groups than the United States could possibly confront
at any one time, or even in a relatively short period of time. The diversity and
number of terrorist organizations threatening the United States and its allies
and partner nations in the international system dictate a measured response
prioritized by the capabilities and potential for global reach possessed by each
individual terrorist group. Such an approach requires an investment of significant resources and a considerable amount of time, probably a minimum
of several decades.

In short, there is no quick solution to the threat posed by Islamic radicalism. An effective strategic response to extremist violence requires patience,
multiple and varying coalitions and alliances, and efforts to deal with those
entrenched aspects of globalization like freedom of movement and communication that work to the terrorists' advantage and make it harder to defend
free and open societies like those of the United States and the West. This is
problematic for the United States as it attempts to wage a long-term battle
against radicals dedicated to the continuation of their struggle against the
West, and particularly, the United States. Americans in general are opposed to
prolonged conflicts because they entail huge costs in lives and national treasure and because the citizens of the United States have been conditioned by

quick military victories since the end of the Vietnam War to believe crushing defeats of America's enemies in short order were indicative of the immense power of their country. Swift triumphs in Grenada, Panama, the Persian Gulf, and the Balkans fed the belief that the United States could win its wars quickly and with little overall cost to the nation's limited and most valuable resources.

Americans, especially those who do not fully comprehend the Islamic extremist threat, need to understand this is a prolonged battle against an enemy that ultimately cannot be defeated but that can be managed to such an extent that his impact on the lives of U.S. citizens becomes almost negligible. Islamic terrorism itself will never be completely eradicated, but it can be curtailed through the implementation of a deliberate and consistent strategy sustained at least for the foreseeable future and probably indefinitely. The years to come promise to be an era of "persistent conflict," to borrow a phrase first used by Army Chief of Staff General George W. Casey in 2007 and subsequently enshrined in U.S. Army doctrine. "Persistent conflict" refers to the protracted confrontation among state, nonstate, and individual actors increasingly willing to use violence to achieve their political and ideological ends.[45] Referring to the contemporary and future international security environments, General Casey identified several trends he believed would shape the strategic environment, including the continuing advance of globalization, increased technological diffusion, radical shifts in worldwide demographics, increasing competition for scarce natural resources, climate changes and natural disasters, the proliferation of weapons of mass destruction, and the destabilizing effect of failed and failing states.[46] There is little doubt each of these trends will have a significant impact on the stability of the overall international security environment over the coming years. Each of these, however, must take a back seat to an increasingly hostile and violent Islamic extremist movement actively seeking to carry its Islamist vision to the far corners of the earth, willing to kill anyone who does not succumb to its radical dream.

3

U.S. Grand Strategy and the Role of Allies

IF THE UNITED STATES IS GOING TO EFFECTIVELY MANAGE the lethal threat posed by Islamic radicals operating in a volatile and uncertain world, American policymakers will need to continue to adapt and execute a comprehensive grand strategy that employs all the elements of national power in a manner that coordinates efforts across the U.S. government and with allied and partner nation stakeholders throughout the international system. Critical to getting the strategy right is an understanding of the difference between the proximate cause of the conflict and the long-term cause of the conflict. The proximate cause, simply put, is the immediate spark that caused the conflict to begin. In the United States' battle with Muslim extremists, the proximate cause of the "War on Terrorism" was the coordinated al Qaeda terrorist strike on the U.S. homeland on September 11, 2001. The long-term cause, in contrast, is the often-overlooked, underlying tension that will continue to generate conflict until the reasons for the friction are resolved, even if the proximate cause of the conflict is dealt with by the opposing parties. In the global effort to combat Islamic radicalism, the root cause of the conflict can be historical grievances, the effects of globalization, the actions taken by repressive Muslim governments supported by the United States and the West, Islamic extremist ideology, U.S. and Western policies and influence in traditionally Muslim areas, or a combination of any of these.[1]

The multitude of Islamic extremist groups operating within the international system have varying reasons for lashing out at the West, making it extremely difficult for the United States and its allies to pinpoint and address the long-term cause or causes of this global conflict. An understanding of the root problem, as complex and elusive as it often proves to be, is critical if those charged with developing an American grand strategy are going to effectively focus their efforts on enduring strategic solutions to the United States' security challenges and not on knee-jerk reactions to whatever immediate crises may pop up at a given point in time. One of the world's foremost counterterrorism and counterinsurgency experts, former Australian infantry officer Dr. David Kilcullen, developed four frameworks that attempt to explain the long-term source of the current international threat environment and the role played in that environment by the Islamic extremists targeting the United States and its Western and Muslim allies. Kilcullen gained his counterterrorism and counterinsurgency experience in Asia, Africa, and the Middle East and served as an adviser to General David Petraeus, author of the strategy that brought Iraq back from the brink of civil war, and to former Bush national security adviser and former secretary of state Condoleezza Rice.

In his *backlash against globalization* framework, Kilcullen argues the forces of globalization have resulted in a Western-dominated world culture and an interdependent and interconnected global economy that features a world of haves and have-nots. In this globalized international system, anger and resentment against cultural intrusion and material deprivation have resulted in multiple "wars of globalization." Under this framework, individual conflicts across the global landscape may differ slightly in character and nature, but all are connected by one common theme: a violent response to the forces of globalization that have been spreading through the international system in recent decades. The second framework, the *globalized insurgency*, theorizes the world is witnessing a large-scale, transnational globalized Islamic insurgency that requires a counterinsurgency approach rather than a counterterrorism approach. The difference between the two is important to understand. Counterinsurgency doctrine concentrates on securing populations and protecting innocent civilians from terrorist attacks while building host nation governance capacity and training host nation military and police forces to provide for their country's security. The targeting of individuals and groups committing violent acts is part of counterinsurgent doctrine, but the kinetic effort takes a back seat to population security and governance capacity activities. Counterterrorism doctrine, in contrast, focuses its efforts on targeting for detention or death individuals and groups committing terrorist violence, with all other efforts relegated to a secondary role.

The third framework, the *civil war*, argues there is an internal struggle raging between moderates and extremists within the global Muslim community and that the West and other nations affected by spillover violence from Islamic countries are simply targets of opportunity in a larger battle for leadership of the Islamic faith. According to this model, the real threat is to the existing status quo within Muslim countries as secular Muslim regimes are directly threatened by individuals and groups seeking to establish Islamic states in the Middle East and other areas dominated by Muslim populations. Finally, the *asymmetric warfare* framework proposes that the use of terrorist violence by Islamic extremists is a deliberate and necessary reaction to overwhelming U.S. military superiority. Faced with the dominant capabilities possessed by U.S. armed forces operating in every corner of the international system, America's enemies have no choice but to resort to nontraditional, asymmetric forms of warfare or risk complete destruction.[2] No one of these frameworks is dominant over the others. Each plays some role in the transnational battle between Islamic radicals and the West, making it extremely difficult for the United States and its allies to identify and remedy the specific core issues that are provoking Muslim radicals to take violent action.

In the years since the 9/11 attacks on the American homeland, the United States has followed a grand strategy largely focused on the military element of national power, with less attention paid to other equally important elements of power. This is understandable, to a degree, because the initial response to 9/11 was appropriately a reaction to an armed strike that killed thousands of innocent and unsuspecting people from many nations. This armed forces–centric approach, however, has frequently left the other elements of national power wanting for limited but desperately needed budget and personnel resources. The grand strategy employed by the United States needs to be continually refined so that a well-balanced effort, with less attention given to highly visible and aggressive military action, is put forth with more focus on the other tools available in the arsenal of American national power. This does not necessarily mean a radical reduction in current U.S. military efforts around the world. In fact, the ongoing security situations in both Afghanistan and Iraq and secondary efforts in Yemen, Somalia, Djibouti, and other global crisis spots probably preclude that possibility, at least for the next half decade or more. Over the long term, though, more attention will need to be given to the other elements of national power in a balanced and comprehensive approach tailored not only to the individual Islamic terrorist organizations pursuing their goals through acts of violence, but also to the environments in which they live, train, and operate.

U.S. strategy must be both realistic and flexible enough to be supported by the American public and by different presidential administrations and Congresses, regardless of political party affiliation or ideological outlook. This is no easy task. The degree of partisanship in Washington makes politicians of both major parties extremely hesitant to embrace anything offered by the opposition, regardless of a measure's sensibility or overall worth to the security of the nation. The nature of the strategy pursued will also affect the willingness of allied and partner states that will vary in their levels of participation and their commitment of critical resources as conditions change and as opportunities and threats present themselves or fade away. The involvement of other nations in this endeavor is critical. In crafting a grand strategy for a long-term conflict with Islamic radicals who threaten scores of nations in every region of the international system, every effort should be made to enlist the support of allied, partner, and like-minded countries that can provide resources and capabilities beyond those possessed by the United States. Assistance from other nation-states will be essential because no one country, including the superpower United States, has all the resources necessary for a generational struggle with religious fanatics dispersed in local and regional cells on multiple continents across the international system. A shared effort among nations can provide far greater global security than if individual states attempt to act independently, concerned only with securing their own national interests.

Understanding Strategy and Its Components

Before discussing the components of strategy, it is necessary to understand what is meant by the word *strategy* itself. Strategy can be defined as a course of action that integrates ends, ways, and means to meet policy objectives.[3] Grand strategy is the set of objectives that brings together a country's policies and provides a consistent view over a long period of time.[4] Simply put, a strategy is a plan that provides guidance and direction for the application of the various elements of American national power in pursuit of specific U.S. national interests. It is a structured approach to the employment of the nation's resources as a means of achieving a desired goal or objective. Putting together a sound strategic plan is no easy task, and multiple barriers to good strategy development make even the seemingly easy difficult to plan and execute. At least five such barriers have been identified by noted defense policy analyst Dr. Andrew Krepinevich. The first is a tendency to think of strategy as a list of desirable outcomes or results. Results are end states, not a plan of action to get to an end state. Equating strategy with outcomes is likely to result in a product that lacks depth and fails to consider either potential obstacles that could prevent success or potential courses of action to overcome those obstacles. Second, there is often a failure to understand the enemy being targeted with a particular strategy. That failure limits the ability of strategy developers to identify those areas that might be exploitable during the implementation of the strategy. Third, among senior national security decision-making officials there are varying levels of strategic competence. The insight necessary to craft good strategy is, Krepinevich has argued, relatively rare. Fourth, strategy is affected by the resources available to the nation for use in the strategy's execution. The United States does not have an infinite supply of national resources, which means the number of courses of action available to strategists is necessarily limited. Finally, the nature of bureaucracies themselves, with their organizational agendas and resistance to change, prevents the formulation of fundamentally sound strategic plans.[5] British-American strategist and professor of international relations Colin Gray once noted, "Strategy is an extraordinarily difficult enterprise primarily because it is a bridging function between unlike elements."[6] Attempting to integrate and synchronize diplomatic, information, military, economic, intelligence, and law enforcement efforts in pursuit of a national objective is a complex undertaking. The multiple government agencies and organizations that play a role in strategy formulation each have their own unique agendas and approaches that create conflict and make unity of effort toward a common goal, even that of national security, hard to achieve.

The United States seeks to use its national power to increase America's strength and to secure U.S. interests in the international system. National power refers to the ability of the United States to exert its influence on other countries. It can be divided into two types: hard power, which is the capacity to compel other states to take a desired action or abstain from an undesirable action, and soft power, or indirect influence that coerces other states to follow a particular path. Hard power typically includes the threat or actual use of military force (although military force can also be used as soft power, such as when special forces soldiers train troops from other nations), economic sanctions, and other direct and punitive methods designed to change the behavior of other nation-states. Soft power generally involves less stringent methods like diplomacy and positive reinforcement of acceptable or desirable behavior. The idea behind soft power is that persuasion may be the best way, in some situations, to convince a given country to act in a way that is desirable and beneficial to the United States and its allies. It is important to note that strategy is not the same as policy. Policy is a political activity. It sets the national goals, objectives, or end states that strategy seeks to achieve through the employment of the different elements of national power. Policy can be based on an ideal end state, whereas strategy cannot. Strategic plans have to be grounded in a reality based on the international system as it actually is at a given moment in time. Crafting sound strategy is a much harder endeavor than making national policy.

Because it is complex and difficult to do, strategy development relies on eight basic principles designed to help make strategic plans relevant and effective at the least possible cost to the nation. First, strategy must be proactive and anticipatory, meaning it must be vision based or forward looking. Second, it must have a clear end state or desired goal or objective to be achieved as a result of the strategy's implementation. Third, it must have a good balance between the objectives sought and the methods and resources used to pursue those objectives. In other words, it must be realistic. Fourth, it must always be driven by policy. Policy sets the objectives that strategy tries to achieve. Fifth, it must be hierarchical, meaning it must flow from the top levels of government down to the organizations responsible for its execution. Sixth, it must be comprehensive. Seventh, it must be developed after a sound and thorough analysis of the strategic situation and the international environment. And finally, eighth, it must address the risk or possibility that the strategy will not achieve its objective.[7] Any given strategy must also pass three critical tests: suitability, feasibility, and acceptability.[8] For a strategy to be suitable, it must accomplish the desired end state or policy objective. For it to be feasible, it must be able to accomplish the end state or objective with the resources available for the strategy's execution. And, finally, for it to be acceptable, the importance of the end state or objective must justify any risk or cost involved in the implementation of the strategy.

U.S. grand strategy is ultimately driven by the country's enduring national interests. Interests can be thought of as conditions in the international system that the United States finds desirable. National interests provide the objectives or desired end states that tell those responsible for strategy development and execution why a particular national policy is important. They can be separated into three basic categories: vital, important, and peripheral. Vital interests are those interests that could affect national survival and for which there can be no compromise by the nation's leaders. They are nonnegotiable, no matter what costs might be incurred as a result of their pursuit, and they tend to remain steady over time. A nation will do whatever it takes in terms of commitment in both blood and treasure to defend its vital national interests. U.S. vital national interests are generally considered to be the physical security of the American homeland, the promotion of the values and ideals of the United States, a stable international order, and U.S. economic prosperity.[9] The *2010 National Security Strategy* listed the nation's enduring vital national interests as the security of the United States, its citizens, and U.S. allies and partners; a strong, innovative, and growing U.S. economy in an open international economic system that promotes opportunity and prosperity; respect for universal values at home and around the world; and an international order advanced by U.S. leadership that promotes peace, security, and opportunity through stronger cooperation to meet global challenges.[10] Important interests can be defined as those national interests not immediately threatening to the national survival, as vital interests are, but that have the potential to affect the overall well-being of the nation if not addressed over long periods of time. Last, peripheral interests are those national interests unlikely to have an appreciable effect on national survival if they are not achieved. They are relatively important, but failure to achieve them does not pose an existential threat to the country. A state may or may not defend important and peripheral national interests, depending on the costs involved and the relative significance of the interest at a given point in time.

When thinking about the components of strategy, it is helpful to consider the model taught in strategic arts courses at the U.S. Army War College. Developed by a retired colonel named Art Lykke, the model uses an image of a three-legged stool in which each leg is labeled with a critical component of strategy: ends, ways, or means. The three legs support the seat, which represents the strategy. The stool in the model shows the interconnectedness of the individual components of strategy with the overall strategy itself. If any of the legs of the stool are missing, the strategy is likely to fail. Ends or objectives explain what the strategy is trying to accomplish. They describe a future condition and give the strategy developer purpose and direction in support of a particular national interest. When crafting a strategy, it is the ends or objectives that are most important because the remaining components of strategy flow from the desired end state. Ways, the next component of strategy, explain the manner in which the ends or objectives will be achieved. A good way to think about ways is to view them as courses of action to be taken in pursuit of defined ends or objectives. Means, the third leg of the stool in the model, are the actual resources employed in the execution of a given strategy. While the ends tell what the desired result or objective is, and the ways tell the courses of action to be taken in pursuit of the ends, the means define the specific instruments or tools to be used by those executing the strategy. The resources employed can be tangible or intangible, with tangible instruments being those that can be quantified in some way, like military forces, equipment, or money. Intangible instruments are those things like public support or national will that cannot be quantified but nonetheless have an effect on the overall viability of a particular strategy.[11]

In crafting a strategy for this era of persistent conflict, it is important that U.S. officials and the American public maintain a long-term outlook for what has already proved to be an enduring challenge that will continue without a substantive decrease in intensity for many years to come. Strategic patience is a must. The temptation to seek out short-term solutions that may produce immediate results must be avoided if the long-term threat from Islamic radicalism is going to be efficiently and effectively managed. Reducing the danger posed by Muslim extremists to a reasonable level will take many decades at a minimum and will require not only persistence and sustained effort, but periodic adjustments to the national strategy that allow the United States to respond effectively to changing conditions in the international security environment. The strategy pursued over the long term must be a wide-reaching one that employs all the elements of national power, attacks the problem of Islamic radicalism on multiple fronts, and enjoys unity of effort from all agencies and departments within the federal government and, ideally, allied and partner nations. The focus must be twofold: to eliminate the immediate threat to the U.S. homeland and U.S. interests worldwide and to begin to address the long-term problem of the conditions and attitudes that feed extremist ideology and spur radical groups and individuals to use violence against the United States.

One additional strategic consideration must be noted. The threat from radical Islamists, as mentioned earlier, is not manifested in one particular individual, like Osama bin Laden, or in one specific group, like al Qaeda. The threat is transnational in nature and exists in the form of multiple terrorist organizations that subscribe to a radical Islamist ideology and that sometimes share a common purpose but often pursue individual, local, or regional agendas. A one-size-fits-all strategy is destined to fail, as is a strategy that focuses on one or two Islamic extremist groups or individuals that put a recognizable face on the threat. The efforts undertaken by the United States will have to be adapted to specific terrorist groups in numerous locations and under widely varying domestic and international conditions. Attempting to treat all Islamic extremists in the same manner will result in an unsuccessful effort to manage the threat posed by disparate groups of Muslim radicals spread across the entirety of the international landscape. Instead, everything about a particular terrorist enemy must be taken into account—its culture, its ideology, the nature and character of its leadership, its strengths and weaknesses, its history, its level of popular support, its degree of global reach, and more. Each group or cell of individuals must be addressed separately and not lumped together as one enemy. Finally, the multiple factors affecting strategy formulation will have to be reconsidered each time national strategy has to be adjusted as a result of changing circumstances or changing target groups. Those factors include the resources available to the nation, the time it will take to implement strategic options, the risks involved in the pursuit of strategic options, the estimated costs involved, and domestic and international constraints that determine the relative permissiveness of the environment in which strategic options will be executed.

All strategies begin with defined end states derived from the nation's interests. The United States' *National Military Strategic Plan for the War on Terrorism* identified two ends, or objectives, for the global fight against Islamic radicalism: the defeat of violent extremism as a threat to the American way of life and the creation of a global environment inhospitable to extremists and those who support them.[12] To these should be added a third and seemingly obvious objective, already mentioned in this chapter—the protection of the American homeland from another 9/11-type terrorist attack. There are multiple ways, or courses of action, that can be undertaken in pursuit of these objectives. Broadly speaking, they can be classified as the diplomatic, information, military, economic, intelligence, and law enforcement elements of national power. It is from these elements of power that the resources or instruments necessary to execute a strategy are drawn. The individual elements of national power are made up of both natural and social determinants, the natural determinants consisting of the population, geography, and natural resources of the country and the social determinants consisting of the ways in which the population is organized and how the people alter the environment surrounding them.[13]

Each of the elements of national power is made up of instruments or resources that are employed in the pursuit of a given strategy. Instruments of national power are subordinate components of the elements of national power. For example, naval blockades, forward projections of military assets in a show of force, and military exercises unilaterally or in partnership with other nations are all instruments of the military element of national power. Instruments are simply the various tools or resources utilized in the execution of a particular strategy. All instruments of national power, if they are to be effective, must have three basic characteristics: capability, meaning the nation employing the instrument must actually be able to use the instrument; credibility, meaning the target of the instrument has to believe the employing country will use the instrument; and efficacy, meaning the country employing the instrument must be able to use it in a way that will accomplish the desired end state.[14] The chapters that follow will outline the various elements of national power and some of the instruments or tools within each element that could potentially be used in the execution of a strategy designed to combat the transnational Islamic extremist threat.

All strategies involve some degree of risk or uncertainty. No government can ever be completely sure whether the strategy it pursues will succeed either fully or only in part, and if in part, to what degree success will be achieved. When talking about grand strategy, the probability of failure or partial failure is known as strategic risk. Constant assessments and reassessments of risk are essential during both the formulation and execution of strategy to ensure the success of the course of action embarked upon by the nation. Assessments and reassessments of risk allow those responsible for the development and execution of strategy to quickly identify problems or potential danger areas, as well as the second- and third-order effects or potential consequences of a strategy, and to make periodic adjustments that will increase the likelihood of success for the strategy being implemented. If the strategic risk of a given strategy is considered to be too great, changes can be made to the objectives or end states, to the ways or courses of action, to the instruments or tools being used, or to a combination of any or all of the components of the strategy in order to reduce the degree of risk present in the strategy. In some cases, the level of risk will be deemed too great, and a proposed strategy will have to be abandoned altogether, forcing those responsible for strategy formulation to come up with an entirely new strategic plan.

Allies and Partner Nations

The dangers of Islamic radicalism do not threaten the United States alone. In fact, the greatest peril is likely in the Middle East, Asia, and Europe, where America's allies are in much closer proximity to the threat than is the American homeland. Even many of America's interests abroad are at less risk than the cities and government institutions of our allies and partners in the international system. It is far easier for the extremists to strike the "near enemy" than it is to strike the "far enemy," especially when desperately needed resources are under constant U.S. and allied economic and military pressure. The best way to confront this transnational threat is with a broad international response that uses collective action whenever and wherever possible to prevent and respond to terrorist attacks. Because the threat is a global one, and because no one nation-state has the capacity to fight Islamic radicalism entirely on its own, at least not in an effective way that substantively reduces the risk of injury or death for innocent people, the U.S. strategy for the battle against Muslim terrorists should seek to include at every opportunity possible the cooperation and participation of other nations also threatened by the extremists. By combining the resources of the United States, the means of strategy development, with those of other countries, the capabilities of all nations fighting Islamic radicalism are enhanced, and there is a greater likelihood of success for U.S. grand strategy over the long term. Intelligence collection, arms interdiction, disruption of finances, counterproliferation efforts, sanctions enforcement, criminal apprehensions and prosecutions, and full-fledged combat operations are all made significantly less difficult when like-minded states work together to reduce or eliminate a common transnational threat.

The best way for the United States to secure international cooperation for the fight against Islamic terrorists is through the formation of alliances and coalitions tailored to specific operations or efforts. An alliance can be defined as a relationship between two or more countries that results in a formal agreement concerning broad, long-term objectives. A coalition, on the other hand, is more of an ad hoc arrangement generally put together for a single action of limited duration.[15] Consider this example: the United States belongs to the NATO defense alliance, a grouping of twenty-eight nations with common long-term defense interests that bind them together in a collective security organization. The NATO alliance was formed in 1949 with the signing of the North Atlantic Treaty, a formal collective defense agreement. In contrast, the United States formed a coalition of more than two dozen countries to confront the Iraqi army after its 1990 invasion of neighboring Kuwait. At the conclusion of Operations Desert Shield and Desert Storm, which blocked Iraqi troops from a potential invasion of Saudi Arabia and then removed those troops from occupied Kuwait, respectively, the U.S.-led coalition assembled in response to the aggression of Saddam Hussein was disbanded, and the temporary security arrangement assembled for the Persian Gulf War ceased to exist. Both alliances and coalitions are agreements between nation-states to work together toward a common goal, the chief differences between the two being their degree of formality and the length of time they are expected to be sustained.

Not every nation the United States would like to be aligned with will be interested in participating in either an alliance or a coalition. The United States and other countries in the international system will weigh the benefits and consequences of partnership against those of nonpartnership on a case-by-case basis as international crisis situations present themselves and as national interests dictate. In attempting to persuade other states to join in the fight against Islamic radicalism, there are several themes the United States should emphasize. The most obvious is the large-scale nature of the threat facing America and other nations across the breadth of the global system. The Muslim extremists threatening international stability and security are transnational in nature. No country is immune from their violent acts, and no country should believe it can indefinitely ignore the extremist threat. Second, the United States should express its desire to reduce the terrorist threat without a prolonged presence in other nations. Potential partner countries should understand the United States does not have any imperial interest in the territory of other states and is concerned only with furthering the security of the American people and the broader international community. America's benign intent must be clearly articulated to and understood by other nations. Third, the United States should make it clear to potential partner states that any degree of assistance, no matter how trivial it might seem, will be accepted and appreciated. Every task undertaken by another country is one less task the United States has to perform on its own with limited and valuable American resources. Finally, the United States should offer assistance to other nations through various mechanisms like financial aid, military trainers and advisers, intelligence sharing, law enforcement, and logistics. These forms of assistance can help recipient countries increase their own capacity to combat Islamic extremism without foreign military help. Bolstering the self-reliance of other nations will ultimately reduce the likelihood that an intervention by the United States will be needed at some point in the future.

All alliances and coalitions have advantages and disadvantages. When nations join together for collective action against a common threat they enjoy greater strength and capability than they possess by themselves, greater public support for their actions than if they act independently, and greater legitimacy in the eyes of the international community as governments are seen offering one another support for the betterment of the broader international system. International legitimacy is generally easy to obtain when agreement is reached in a globally accepted intergovernmental forum like the North Atlantic Treaty Organization or the United Nations. Alliances and coalitions also benefit from burden sharing as requirements for combat troops, support personnel, supplies, transportation assets, technical expertise, use of territory, and funding are spread out among participating members rather than being borne by one state acting unilaterally. That is not to say all nation-states contribute to alliances or coalitions equally. They do not, nor should they. Individual countries will have different capabilities and different areas of expertise that can be provided in support of other nations in a given collective action. What is important is not necessarily the level of contribution but the presence of the contributing nation in a capacity that adds value to the alliance or coalition. Finally, a potential benefit of alliances and coalitions is the potential to work as a deterrent force against bad actors who may be more hesitant to confront a grouping of nations unified against them than they would be to confront one state acting unilaterally.

A significant problem with alliances and coalitions is that they can be difficult to put together. They generally take a considerable amount of time to assemble as the particular concerns of each potential member state have to be dealt with before any agreement on the way forward can be achieved. The nature of the desired end state or objective may also pose a problem when trying to enlist the help of potential alliance or coalition members. Collective defense agreements and humanitarian or post-hostility alliances and coalitions in troubled countries are generally more agreeable to potential member states than those requiring offensive military operations that could result in large numbers of casualties and a loss of political support at home. Additionally, some states may have serious reservations about surrendering some or all of their authority over decision making to another nation or grouping of nations. The issue of which country gets command of an alliance or coalition or the leading role in such an endeavor can be an extremely sensitive one.

Even when an alliance or coalition can be formed, the difficulties inherent in the complex relationships between nations can continue to cause problems. Since all states tend to look out for their own national interests first, reaching agreement within an existing alliance or coalition can be extremely problematic. National interests and values are not always in harmony, and the political wills of member states will often differ greatly depending on the issue or issues involved. Common interests may be given differing levels of priority by member nations, and members will often disagree about which approach to a particular problem is the correct one to pursue. Differences in capability can result in some participating members bearing significantly more of the burden than other members, and some countries may be added or dropped as time passes and the conditions that brought about the alliance or coalition change. During the Persian Gulf War in 1991, there was great concern among the members of the coalition arrayed against Saddam Hussein and the Iraqi military that Arab states would abandon the coalition if Israel responded with force to Iraqi missile attacks on Israeli cities. Israel refrained from retaliatory action and the coalition remained intact. In the years since the United States launched its second war against Iraq, several nations have left the original coalition of nearly four dozen countries while others have increased their levels of contribution. Similarly, the broad coalition of nations involved in the U.S.-led effort in Afghanistan has had member states depart the country, announce future withdrawals, and make regular changes to their levels of contribution.

Despite the many and sometimes complicated challenges involved in forming and maintaining alliances and coalitions, the advantages of collective action usually outweigh the disadvantages associated with bringing other countries on board in the pursuit of U.S. national interests. Broad international cooperation, whenever possible, is the preferred method for the United States to deal with global security challenges like the threat posed by Islamic radicals who are not interested in accommodation with those who do not subscribe to their extremist ideology. What is ultimately most important for the United States to remember when it comes to allying with other states is that each crisis situation or global security problem is unique. The United States has no permanent allies, it has been said. It has only permanent interests. Those enduring national interests, and not the desirability of having other nations join the effort to ease the burden on America and its people, should ultimately drive the decision about whether the United States deals with its security issues through the formation of partnerships, alliances, or coalitions, or whether it chooses to deal with international challenges on its own. In this era of persistent conflict, the United States will need to strengthen and expand existing relationships with countries like Great Britain, Australia, Canada, and other like-minded nations, pursue new opportunities with countries in strategic locations like Eastern Europe and the Caucasus, and transform or abandon those partnerships like the North Atlantic Treaty Organization that have become outdated or irrelevant in the contemporary international security environment.

The United States' NATO Challenge

The North Atlantic Treaty Organization, NATO, was formed in the aftermath of World War II to provide a security guarantee for Western Europe, underwritten by the military might of the United States, against a potential attack by the Soviet Union. The end of the Cold War found NATO in search of new purpose and direction in an international security environment lacking a clearly defined enemy or easily identifiable threat. Within hours of the 2001 terrorist attacks against New York and Washington, NATO for the first time in its history invoked Article 5 of its charter, the collective defense article, which states an armed attack against one or more NATO member states in Europe or North America is an attack against all NATO member states and directs each member state to assist the nation or nations attacked in a manner determined to be appropriate by the nation providing assistance.[16] In a matter of just a few months, NATO countries had armed forces in Afghanistan fighting alongside the United States against the Taliban and al Qaeda fighters. The Afghanistan mission, however, turned out to be far more dangerous and complex than NATO anticipated. In the years since the alliance entered Afghanistan, NATO has struggled to the point where its credibility has been severely undermined, and its relevance has been appropriately questioned as critical weaknesses in both policy and capability have been brought to the surface.

There are multiple challenges threatening NATO's viability as a collective defense alliance.[17] First, NATO has a credibility problem as a result of its efforts in Afghanistan. The realities being experienced by NATO member states in the former al Qaeda safe haven do not match the expectations that preceded the commitment of NATO military forces to the U.S.-led effort. Anticipating a role in reconstruction and government institution building, NATO forces instead encountered deadly combat operations that severely tested the viability of the alliance as an organization. In response to the unexpected conditions experienced in Afghanistan, major alliance member states like Germany and Italy generally took the relatively easy route in the fight against the Taliban and al Qaeda, largely limiting their forces to noncombat operations like development and humanitarian work while their American, British, Dutch, Danish, and Canadian partners did the bulk of the fighting and dying in bitter asymmetric combat on formidable terrain. Popular among American soldiers assigned to the International Security Assistance Force (ISAF) mission in Afghanistan was a joke that said ISAF stood for "I Saw Americans Fight." Restrictions on the rules of engagement used by NATO's European forces, fueled by waning support among European publics for the war in Afghanistan and a fundamental difference in opinion about the nature of the threat from Islamic radicals, have limited the ability of alliance commanders to effectively combat a steadily deteriorating security situation in which the Taliban is increasingly thriving and the NATO alliance is increasingly failing. Terrorist plots and attacks across Europe have clearly demonstrated why the fight against Islamic extremism should be a priority for NATO's European member states. It seems, though, that America's allies in Europe are not getting the message.

NATO's second problem is a qualitative one. A substantial capability gap between the armed forces of the United States and the armed forces of its European NATO allies threatens the alliance's ability to accomplish current and future missions. NATO's European members have largely been spared the costs of maintaining modern and capable military forces because their security has been guaranteed by the United States for nearly three quarters of a century. The great Soviet threat of the twentieth century was countered by the presence of large numbers of American troops and firepower in Europe from the end of World War II until the Soviet Union's collapse in late 1991, allowing NATO's European members to focus on domestic social matters without having to worry about providing security for their citizens. Even after the Soviet menace was gone, the nations of Europe were able to continue their inward focus knowing that any serious security issues that might arise would still be handled by their superpower ally, the United States. Now, faced with a growing Muslim extremist problem in several major European nations, NATO's member states in Europe are playing catch-up in an effort to improve their armed forces and homeland security capabilities. The challenge is a daunting one. Significant levels of spending on domestic social programs have depleted European treasuries, leaving few funds available for critically needed security programs that would close the capability gap with the United States.

NATO's third challenge deals with the alliance's willingness to confront threats to international peace and stability. Originally founded to confront the possibility of a Soviet land invasion of the European continent, NATO has proved itself unwilling to stand up to a resurgent and increasingly aggressive Russia that provides critical energy supplies to European nations while simultaneously increasing its involvement in complex European security affairs. Even if Georgia, a former Soviet Republic and aspiring member of NATO, had been part of the alliance when Russian military forces invaded a portion of the country in 2008, ostensibly to protect ethnic Russians in the Georgian province of South Ossetia, it is doubtful NATO would have fulfilled its obligations under Article 5 of its charter and come to the aid of the government in Tbilisi. There is little doubt Russia noticed NATO's inaction on the Georgia issue and was emboldened by what it saw.

The fourth problem plaguing NATO is one of doubt over the alliance's relevance as a global defense organization. NATO as an alliance has been a virtual nonplayer in what is undoubtedly one of the greatest threats to international peace and security since the collapse of the Soviet Union: Iran's suspected pursuit of a nuclear weapons capability. Some NATO members have been strongly supportive of U.S. efforts to limit Tehran's ability to produce nuclear weapons, but there has been no unified action of any substance on the part of the entire alliance. The national interests of individual states understandably differ. But when those national interests prevent NATO from addressing critical international security issues like Iran's suspected pursuit of nuclear weapons, it is appropriate to question the alliance's relevance when it comes to global security challenges. If NATO cannot find its post-Soviet, post–Cold War purpose in combating the threat from Islamic radicals who indiscriminately target innocent civilians in Europe and elsewhere, in enhancing its security capabilities to ensure it has the most modern and effective forces possible, in confronting a resurgent and increasingly belligerent Russia that is extending its influence once again into European affairs, or in taking a hard line against the clerical regime in Iran over a nuclear program that could expand the presence of nuclear weapons in the most volatile region in the world, it is of little future benefit for the United States to remain part of the alliance.

There have been indications that some within NATO recognize the danger to the alliance's continued relevance in today's complex and volatile international security environment. At a NATO foreign minister's meeting held in April 2010 in Estonia, Secretary-General Anders Fogh Rasmussen warned the alliance that NATO's goals and purpose must be shaped in a way that would strengthen the relationship between the United States and NATO's European members.[18] NATO member states must realize that without the United States, NATO has no real meaning as a collective defense alliance. Without the backing of U.S. military power, NATO is nothing but a hollow shell of a treaty organization incapable of defending Europe against outside aggression or preventing or defeating aggression in other regions of the world. The nations of Europe are woefully incapable of providing for their own defense after having their security guaranteed by the United States for nearly seven decades. This reality was likely instrumental in NATO's adoption of a new strategic concept in 2010, the alliance's first such concept in more than ten years. The concept, titled *Active Engagement, Modern Defence*, characterized the alliance as a provider of global security and committed NATO to an expeditionary capability that will be essential if the alliance is to be a relevant force for peace and stability across the global system.[19] The document's focus on worldwide security challenges reflects a clear recognition that NATO faces threats very different from those that existed at the alliance's founding. The new concept also recognizes that the likelihood of "out-of-area" missions is as great as, if not greater than, the likelihood of missions in Europe. The realities of the current global security environment cannot be dismissed or wished away. NATO's Cold War Soviet enemy has been replaced by unconventional challenges that should prompt the alliance's European member states to reconsider defense expenditures that are at present woefully inadequate.

Riding the United States military's coattails for more than a generation, total defense spending among NATO's European members has steadily declined over the years, falling to just $272 billion in 2009.[20] Total defense expenditures across Europe, with few exceptions, fall well below the NATO target of 2 percent of member states' gross domestic products, a situation that is not expected to get better in the near future.[21] In fact, the United Kingdom plans to cut its defense budget by nearly 10 percent over the next four years by reducing the number of troops in uniform, delaying an upgrade of Britain's submarine-based nuclear force, decommissioning an aircraft carrier, and cutting its inventory of tanks and fighter aircraft, while France plans to reduce its defense budget by 3 percent, or more than a billion dollars, and cut more than fifty thousand defense-related jobs over the next four years.[22] The road ahead will be a long and difficult one. Additional planned spending cuts across Europe, if carried out, will degrade NATO's overall defense capability, forcing the alliance's European members to rely even more heavily on their superpower ally, the United States, for security assistance. Additionally, on most relevant security issues, there is considerable disagreement among NATO member states about the types of missions the alliance should be engaged in and the places in which the alliance should commit its military forces. Some believe NATO has demonstrated its limits in Afghanistan and such "out-of-area" missions are unlikely in future years.[23] Differences of opinion within NATO are significant, and finding areas of mutual concern and priority will be difficult. NATO's new strategic concept is a good start, at least on paper. It recognizes the political and military challenges that exist in the contemporary international security environment and, if translated into concrete action by NATO's member states despite the distaste European publics have for expeditionary operations, will pave the way for a stronger alliance that will not only make Europe and the United States more safe but will enhance the level of security across the entire international system.

When it is possible to work with other nations on global security issues, whether those nations have been traditionally allied with the United States or not, U.S. government officials should make every effort to do so. The right to undertake unilateral action, though, in the defense of American citizens and U.S. national interests must always be maintained if willing international partners prove hard to come by in confronting global security threats. American power is not unlimited, and assistance from friends and partners will be critical to the long-term fight against Islamic radicalism. The cost of that assistance, however, must be reasonable and must not pose a threat to other priorities the United States has to address. Those nations willing to cooperate with the United States should have an amount of influence proportional to the contributions they make to the overall fight against the extremists. Ultimately, it has to be U.S. interests that are the driving force when the United States chooses to include or exclude other nations from the actions it feels compelled to take to safeguard its citizens and their homeland. America has no permanent friends or enemies, and it should not forsake its national interests in an attempt to attract other states to join the fight just so it can say the effort is one with an international face. What is ultimately most important is for the United States to make sure the rest of the world understands it will not act unilaterally just because it has the ability to do so but will sometimes be forced to take action without the consent or assistance of the international community because there will be some situations in which it believes it has no choice but to do so.

4

The Diplomatic Element of National Power

D IPLOMACY CAN BE DEFINED AS THE CONTINUAL ASSESSMENT of other countries' power potential, perceived vital interests, and relationships with other nation-states as a means for maximizing one's own country's freedom of action in the international system.[1] A less complicated definition is that diplomacy is simply the use of a state's influence to create and maintain alliances or isolate opponents.[2] It is the principle means by which the United States engages other nations and nonstate actors in the global system, and it is critical to securing strong international cooperation in the pursuit of vital and important U.S. national interests. Diplomacy seeks to achieve the national interests of the United States through dialogue and negotiation, both friendly and threatening, rather than through the use of hard power instruments like military force or economic sanctions. The U.S. Department of State is the federal government agency with direct responsibility for the planning and implementation of American foreign policy, and the agency's head, the secretary of state, serves as the primary adviser to the president on the nation's foreign policy matters. Diplomatic relations between states generally involve the articulation of a nation's policies and goals to other states in the international system and the reaching of agreement, where possible, on areas of mutual concern or interest. All states use diplomacy to advance their own national interests, usually, but not always, at the expense of the interests of other nations.

The United States is the principal actor in the global system when it comes to matters of international security. In its capacity as the strongest economic and military power in the world, and as a beacon of hope for much of the rest of the international system, the United States carries significant weight in the conduct of international diplomatic relations and is often expected to guide and direct diplomatic efforts in both regional and international forums. Diplomacy is a critical element of U.S. national power and a foundational pillar of President Obama's approach to foreign policy because diplomatic efforts can help secure international cooperation on a wide range of issues important to the United States and its allies and partner nations. A significant number of U.S. counterterrorism efforts are accomplished through the day-to-day diplomatic work of nearly sixty thousand State Department employees interacting with their peers in the governments of more than 180 nations worldwide, often behind the scenes and away from the spotlight of national and international media organizations.[3] Whether in the form of full-scale embassy operations, minimally manned diplomatic outposts, or the presence of just a few American advisers, every interaction between representatives of the United States and officials and citizens of other countries contributes to or detracts from the overall effectiveness of U.S. diplomatic efforts.

In the fight against transnational Islamic radicalism, diplomatic efforts can, through bilateral and multilateral negotiations, secure agreements with allies and nonallied nations on the extradition of suspected terrorists, legal proceedings, cooperative investigative work, intelligence sharing, detention operations, and a host of other critical issues. When pursuing such agreements through diplomacy, it is important to respect the values, judgment, and interests of other nations to the greatest extent possible without sacrificing the values and interests of the United States in the process. There will, of course, be times when the national values and interests of other countries are in conflict with those of the United States. In those instances, it will take careful and attentive diplomatic effort to focus on areas where mutual interests and concerns can lead to greater international cooperation that ultimately benefits the United States to the greatest degree possible. Diplomacy is messy, difficult, and often unappreciated work, and the United States will have to engage in much give-and-take in the international system in order to effectively utilize the diplomatic element of national power in pursuit of vital and important U.S. national interests.

Diplomacy and the United Nations

A significant portion of the United States' diplomatic work with other countries is done within the confines of the General Assembly and the Security Council at the United Nations headquarters in New York. The UN was formed more than six decades ago in the chaotic aftermath of World War II in the hope that an international organization structured to encourage and facilitate dialogue and compromise among the nations of the world could help prevent future conflicts while working to ensure basic human rights and individual freedoms. Article 1 of the UN charter outlines the organization's purpose:

> 1) To maintain international peace and security, and to that end: to take effective collective measures for the prevention and removal of threats to the peace, and for the suppression of acts of aggression or other breaches of the peace, and to bring about by peaceful means, and in conformity with the principles of justice and international law, adjustment or settlement of international disputes or situations which might lead to a breach of the peace; 2) To develop friendly relations among nations based on respect for the principle of equal rights and self-determination of peoples, and to take other appropriate measures to strengthen universal peace; 3) To achieve international cooperation in solving international problems of an economic, social, cultural, or humanitarian character, and in promoting and encouraging respect for human rights and for fundamental freedoms for all without distinction as to race, sex, language, or religion; and 4) To be a center for harmonizing the actions of nations in the attainment of these common ends.[4]

Undertaking diplomatic efforts within the United Nations system is important to the United States because actions approved by the UN tend to enjoy greater domestic and international legitimacy than actions taken by countries without the blessing of the UN. International legitimacy matters both to the American people, who will be more likely to support punitive measures employed by the United States if other nations are in agreement, and to many of the United States' allies and nonallied but like-minded countries who generally prefer international consensus to unilateral action. Americans like to feel their nation's cause is just and that other countries are on board with whatever the United States is trying to accomplish. At the same time, other countries like their views to be heard, considered, and potentially accepted before providing any level of support or assistance to a given endeavor. There are legitimate concerns among some in the United States that international legitimacy could come at the price of unacceptable constraints on U.S. national power. The potential benefits of international legitimacy, however, are worth some degree of limitation on what the United States is able to do in the international security environment provided, and this is a critical caveat, U.S. national interests are still achieved at a cost that is considered acceptable by the American people.

The United States conducts diplomatic relations through organizations like the United Nations in order to promote international peace and security

to the greatest extent possible; to protect innocent peoples in harsh and repressive societies; to advance individual freedom, human rights, democratic
institutions, and economic development around the world; to address vital
humanitarian needs across the international system; and to improve the overall global quality of life.[5] Despite the efforts of the United States in pursuit of
these worthwhile goals, the reality is that the United Nations has been more
often than not an abject failure when it comes to the most serious security
issues facing the international community. Simply put, the UN has fallen
woefully short of achieving the goals articulated at its founding. Genuine collective international security has not existed in the past, does not exist now,
and will not exist in the foreseeable future because of anything the bureaucratic and inefficient United Nations might be able to accomplish. Unless the
UN honestly confronts the internal problems plaguing it as an organization,
it will remain an unreliable venue for dealing with serious threats to global
security and prosperity.

The United Nations is a bureaucratic monstrosity that consistently fails to
secure meaningful agreements between the major international powers on
matters of global peace and stability. Each of the five permanent members
of the Security Council (the Russian Federation, the Republic of China, the
Republic of France, the United Kingdom, and the United States) seeks first
and foremost to increase its own power and influence in the international
community while limiting the amount of power and influence other states
are able to wield. The major nation-states of the international system often
work against one another so that no one country becomes too dominant at
the expense of others. Russia and China consistently obstruct the efforts of the
United States in the UN Security Council, and the United States and United
Kingdom often ally with each other in opposition to positions taken by Moscow and Beijing. France in years not so long past actively worked to thwart
the interests of the United States, but Paris has become a friendlier and more
reliable U.S. ally in recent years. The result of competing national interests is
often partial action of limited effectiveness or no action at all on the many
important global security issues that come before the council.

Perhaps the most glaring examples of the Security Council's impotence
can be found in the ongoing efforts of the international community to deal
with the nuclear programs of Iran and North Korea. For years, the United
Nations has attempted to deal diplomatically with both Iran and North
Korea to gain a good understanding of the scope and depth of their nuclear
efforts. Iran has rejected every proposal suggested thus far and continues to
advance its nuclear program despite UN objections and multiple rounds of
UN-imposed economic sanctions. While Tehran maintains its nuclear program is strictly for civilian energy purposes, the United States and its West-

ern allies suspect Iran is working to develop a nuclear weapons capability that would alter the balance of power in the Middle East and threaten Israel, America's strongest ally in the region. In response to the ineffectiveness of the UN on the Iran issue, the United States and the European Union have both taken measures to unilaterally impose additional sanctions designed to supplement the largely meaningless measures passed by the UN Security Council. North Korea has already conducted tests on multiple nuclear devices and is actively working on missile technology that could facilitate the development of an accurate delivery system for nuclear weapons. UN efforts to slow down or stop the weapons programs pursued by North Korea have been mostly ineffective, and there is no indication Pyongyang will acquiesce to international demands in the foreseeable future, at least not fully. Occasionally, the North Korean government will make slight concessions in exchange for international assistance of some sort, like food aid for its starving people or economic help for desperately needed government-provided services. But real concessions that could pave the way for long-term international cooperation with the North Korean regime have been and will continue to be difficult, if not impossible, to come by.

Efforts by the United States and its Western allies to impose stringent economic sanctions against Iran have been largely stymied by Russia and China, countries with extensive business ties to the Iranian government. Russia has a significant financial stake in Iran's nuclear program, and China imports a large percentage of its oil from the Islamic Republic. Neither country has thus far demonstrated a willingness to agree to the kinds of tough measures against Iran that could potentially damage their economic interests. Moscow and Beijing also obstruct efforts to sanction North Korea, which is seen by both nations as a buffer to U.S. influence in Asia. China engages in significant levels of trade with North Korea, and Beijing is keenly aware that a failed North Korean state, which could result from meaningful economic sanctions, would likely result in a unified Korean peninsula allied with the United States and a significant and resource-draining refugee problem for China. Unable to secure harsh sanctions against Iran or North Korea, the United States and its allies have been forced to settle for a series of relatively weak UN Security Council resolutions stripped of their toughest provisions in order to get Russia and China on board. International consensus has consistently trumped meaningful action within the Security Council. And, to no one's surprise, Iran and North Korea have continued to work on their nuclear programs virtually unobstructed as the international community has continued to struggle in its search for an acceptable solution. As long as Moscow and Beijing continue to prevent meaningful international action in the Security Council, neither Iran nor North Korea will be forced to change its strategic calculus.

Outside the Security Council, in the General Assembly of the United Nations, the United States is getting a poor return in terms of international support on its foreign aid investment in other nations. A report by the conservative think tank Heritage Foundation found U.S. foreign assistance has not led to a demonstrable level of support from non–Security Council states in the General Assembly. Heritage analysts examined the six sessions of the General Assembly that took place immediately prior to their report and found more than 90 percent of U.S. foreign aid recipients voted against the United States a majority of the time on nonconsensus votes and over 74 percent voted against the United States a majority of the time on nonconsensus important votes.[6] While economic investment in other countries should not be contingent entirely upon support for the U.S. position at the United Nations, it is not unreasonable to expect a greater degree of cooperation from countries receiving U.S. economic aid than the United States is currently getting in the General Assembly. Most of these nations rely heavily on American financial resources, and some degree of leverage can and should be exercised to gain support for the United States' diplomatic efforts.

The impotence of the Security Council and the poor return on investment in the General Assembly beg the question: is the United Nations worth the time, effort, and money expended by the United States in pursuit of international legitimacy or global consensus? The answer is far from being clear-cut. There are legitimate reasons to doubt the ability of the United Nations to deal with both current and future global security challenges across the international system. However, it is important to the American public that the United States government make every attempt possible to secure the support of other nations and to have any potential action the United States might be considering viewed as legitimate by as many members of the international community as possible. While international legitimacy may be important to the American public and many American policymakers, the United States cannot allow the UN and countries like Russia and China to dictate the direction its foreign policy will ultimately take. No nation with a choice in the matter allows another nation to determine its future or its behavior. International legitimacy or consensus is good to have if it can be achieved for meaningful action that actually helps make the world a more stable and secure place in which the citizens of all nations can live in relative peace. Ultimately, though, the vital and important national interests of the United States, above all other factors, must drive U.S. foreign policy, even if that means taking action on occasion without the consent of the international community.

Since it is unlikely the United States will withdraw entirely from the United Nations, it is critical that American policymakers work hard to reform the UN as much as possible so that the most benefit for the United States may be drawn from diplomatic efforts in the General Assembly and in the Security Council. The United States' potential leverage at the UN should not be underestimated. In 2009, American taxpayers were charged with 22 percent of the regular UN budget and more than 25 percent of the peacekeeping budget, far more than any other member nation.[7] Total U.S. contributions amount to more than $5 billion each year, an amount that should, but does not, provide the United States with a great deal of influence over the structure and function of the UN.[8] The core problem for the United States lies in how annual member state dues are assessed. Funding for much of the UN comes from member state contributions that are calculated according to the ability of a nation to pay.[9] Since the United States is able to pay more than, say, Poland, the American contribution to the UN budget is significantly higher than the contribution of the Poles. Most decisions, however, are not based on a nation's financial contribution. Instead, they are made on the basis of "one country, one vote," which means the United States, which funds 22 percent of the regular UN budget, gets the same level of direct influence as Poland, which funds significantly less of the regular budget. Overall, the 128 lowest-paying countries account for barely more than 1 percent of the entire United Nations budget.[10]

Reform efforts have to be focused and sustained. Bureaucracies like the United Nations do not change willingly or easily. The United States must make a concerted effort to ensure financial accountability, influence proportional to the U.S. contribution, greater burden sharing in global security operations, and a reform-minded restructuring of the Security Council to make it more representative of the contemporary international environment. For example, when looking at the composition of the Security Council, it is hard to understand why France should continue to hold a permanent seat. Paris was granted permanent member status after being thoroughly devastated in World War II, but rising power India is a more critical player in the current international security system and thus more deserving of the seat currently held by France. Of course, it is doubtful the French would agree. President Obama, like some of his predecessors, recognized the composition of the Security Council did not reflect the realities of power in the international system when he voiced support for a permanent seat on the council for India, just as President Nixon supported a permanent seat for Japan and President Clinton supported a permanent seat for Germany.

Making changes to the composition of the council is not a new idea. In 2005, three primary models of reform were introduced by different groupings of UN member states. The first was put forth by the Group of Four, which consisted of the countries of Brazil, Germany, India, and Japan. This reform model proposed expanding the Security Council to twenty-five members by adding six permanent seats and four temporary seats. The second reform model, proposed by Italy, Pakistan, Spain, Argentina, Canada, Mexico, and other nations under the name "Uniting for Consensus," also recommended expanding the Security Council to twenty-five members but by adding only temporary seats. The third proposal came from the African Union (AU), which recommended expanding the council to twenty-six members by adding six permanent and five temporary seats with more representation on the council for the countries of Africa. A fourth proposal that has received less attention than the three described above was introduced jointly by the Group of Four and Uniting for Consensus. This proposal recommended adding more temporary seats to the Security Council and giving those seats terms longer than the current two-year mandates for temporary members.[11] The Security Council currently has ten nonpermanent seats.

Each of these reform proposals centers on expansion of the Security Council. Simply increasing the size of the council, though, may not be the wisest course of action and could very well lead to even greater ineffectiveness on international security issues, as hard as that might be to imagine. If the United States is going to support a Security Council with a greater number of temporary or permanent members, the best approach may be one that is criteria based. Criteria for membership could include an established history of political stability; a globally or regionally deployable military force and civilian capabilities the prospective nation is willing to employ in support of the United Nations; a minimum level of financial contribution to both the regular and peacekeeping budgets; a demonstrated willingness to participate in global sanctions enforcement, international interventions, and, when necessary, the use of force; a willingness and ability to work toward regional and global solutions through collective action; and a record of abiding by and enforcing global security rules.[12] Such an approach would shift the focus of efforts to expand the council from geography to desirable state characteristics that could be utilized in support of international security operations.

Substantive changes to the composition of the Security Council would enhance the body's legitimacy with the broader international community, but not even one of the proposed reform models is likely to gain any traction at the UN for two simple reasons. First, real reform of the council would require some very important international players to relinquish some of the power and influence they currently enjoy within the UN system. Second, the requirement for changing the UN's charter, approval by two-thirds of the General Assembly and all five permanent members, is difficult if not impossible to meet. With real reform of the council likely a bridge too far, the United Nations will remain only marginally effective when it comes to the serious security issues facing the countries of the international system.

Since reform ideas are being tossed around, though, another proposal even more equitable than the ones discussed thus far would be a UN Security Council in which there were no permanent seats at all. The composition of the council could be based upon a majority vote by the General Assembly in which each UN member state voted for the five most powerful and influential nations on an annual basis. This would force regular reassessments of the power brokers in the international system and a constant shifting of seats within the Security Council. Current permanent members Russia, China, and the United States still fit the bill, but Great Britain and France are not the international players they once were and would likely be removed from the council under this proposal. Another major reform that should be considered for the council is the elimination of the veto power currently enjoyed by the council's permanent members. The ability of a permanent member to veto any Security Council resolution creates gridlock and often leads to inaction, even when the council is faced with serious international security issues like Iran's suspected pursuit of a nuclear weapons capability. Much more could be accomplished by instituting a rule set that allows decisions on global security matters to be made by a majority vote of the council. Of course, none of the current permanent council members, including the United States, is likely to go along with such a proposal because to do so would mean a more balanced playing field in the Security Council at the expense of individual states' national power. The road ahead for the Security Council looks bleak. Real reform is highly unlikely, and the council will continue to fail in its primary responsibility for the maintenance of global peace and international security.[13]

The United Nations is on the verge of becoming wholly irrelevant when it comes to serious international security issues. Some would no doubt argue it has already reached the point of irrelevance. The Security Council has virtually no credibility left in the international system, especially when it comes to confidence in the council's ability to deal with problem nations like Iran and North Korea, and accusations of bias, corruption, fraud, and waste undermine global confidence in the UN's ability to play a meaningful role in contemporary international security affairs. Essentially, nothing other than about $5 billion a year in U.S. taxpayer-funded revenue is lost by the United States if it continues to work through the United Nations while maintaining a hard push for serious reform of the organization. Ultimately, though, those charged with leading the United States through difficult international security challenges must recognize that what does or does not happen at the United Nations, in the Security Council or in the General Assembly, will not be the final word when it comes to deciding what actions the United States will or will not take to secure its national interests and defend its people at home and abroad. America's political leaders must be open to potential alternative courses of action, including other existing and not-yet-created international forums, when the United Nations proves unwilling or unable to take the steps necessary to address critical international stability and security issues.

The European Connection

The United States has a long history of shared values with the countries of Europe, a history that has fostered an extremely close-knit and generally cooperative relationship on matters of international security. Strong ties to Europe are critical to U.S. diplomatic efforts, both at the United Nations and outside of the UN framework. U.S. security interests in Europe are fourfold: the United States, which has underwritten European security since the end of World War II, is tied to the well-being of Europe through shared membership in the North Atlantic Treaty Organization; European nations are important trade partners of the United States; Europe serves as a strong counterweight to the expanding power and influence of a resurgent and increasingly bellicose Russian state; and the proximity of Europe to other key regions of the world provides the United States with a force projection capability that is essential to securing U.S. national interests across the international system.[14] Since Europe emerged from the devastation of World War II, its nation-states have been some of America's most steadfast allies in good times and bad. Great Britain, the Netherlands, and Poland, especially, have been consistently supportive of U.S.-led efforts in Iraq and Afghanistan, and France and Germany have moved closer to the United States in recent years as governments more friendly to Washington have come to power in Paris and Berlin. When American blood has been shed in armed conflict around the world, European blood has typically been shed with it.

It has largely been the nations of Europe that have stood with the United States in confronting the nuclear programs of Iran and North Korea, with the European Union adopting its own economic sanctions after failing to achieve the tough measures sought in partnership with the United States at the UN. Recent years, however, have seen the European-American relationship strained by the wars in Afghanistan and Iraq, the former due to the national caveats that restrict the utility of some European forces in confronting the Taliban and al Qaeda, and the latter due to a lack of substantive support from some European states for the removal of Saddam Hussein from power, the issues of NATO expansion, and the deployment of U.S. ballistic missile defense systems in European countries. The United States is also concerned about the European Union's continued development of its Common Security and Defence Policy that threatens the viability of NATO through the duplication of critical roles and structures. There are not enough resources available for the countries of Europe to man, fund, and equip a European defense capability separate from the NATO alliance. Most of NATO's European members do not currently meet the alliance's target of 2 percent of gross domestic product investment in military capabilities. Shifting already limited funds away from NATO will only serve to weaken the alliance even further. If the United States is going to remain part of the NATO alliance, it must push its European allies to focus on NATO's primacy in the role of European defense. An additional source of tension between the United States and the countries of Europe is the status of Turkey, a member of NATO since the early 1950s. The European Union's reluctance to accept Turkey as a full member has resulted in a Turkish drift toward Iran and other Islamic countries instead of a solidification of Turkey's position as a reliable Western ally. Turkey's location is strategic in that it serves as a critical bridge between the countries of Europe and the countries of the Middle East, making it imperative that Western nations embrace Turkish participation in European political, economic, and military affairs. A failure to do so opens the door for Iran to extend its influence into one of the most strategic areas in the international system.

Despite significant differences on some key international security issues, the United States and Europe will remain closely allied in the years to come if for no other reason than mutual defense against common threats across the international system. Europe has been working on creating a single strong European "state" since long before the formation of the European Union under the Maastricht Treaty in late 1993. A unified Europe could potentially rival the economic and military might of the United States, but nationalist sentiments have thus far prevented the emergence of a cohesive European superpower. In the absence of a single, cohesive European authority, the dangers of Islamic radicalism, nuclear proliferation, piracy, failed and failing states, and increasingly aggressive rhetoric and action by a Russian government once again exercising its influence in Europe will require significant cooperation between the United States and its European allies in order to ensure the protection of American and European citizens, resources, and assets worldwide.

Diplomacy with Terrorists

U.S. diplomatic efforts are appropriately directed primarily at nation-states and not at nonstate actors, although engagement with nonstate actors does occur when specific situations warrant such discussions. It is sovereign countries, whether allied with the United States, nonallied but tolerant of U.S. policies or supportive of U.S. interests, or antagonistic toward the United States that are still the primary actors in international relations, as they have been since the Treaty of Westphalia in 1648. The role of nonstate actors in the international security environment has increased dramatically since the end of the Cold War and the demise of the Soviet Union, but it is still at the nation-state level where the most substantive and effective diplomacy takes place.

The Islamic terrorists threatening the United States and other countries adhere to a radical ideology that does not allow for good faith diplomacy or negotiation with those who do not subscribe to the worldview of its adherents. There is little to no common ground upon which to build, and there is almost never any willingness on the part of the radicals to reach an accommodation that would allow peoples of differing faiths to live together in peace and security. It is for this reason that hard-core individual Islamic terrorists and terrorist groups should not be part of any negotiation or diplomatic effort except as a measure of absolute last resort. Calls for appeasement should be rejected when possible because concessions to terrorists will likely lead to more acts of terrorism against those offering the concessions. Radical groups like al Qaeda, Hamas, and Hezbollah are only willing to negotiate when they believe they have the upper hand on their adversary, even if it means only an incremental step toward their long-term goals. The Islamic extremists targeting the United States are willing to murder innocent people in the name of religion. The only way to deal with such people is through those measures designed to destroy them or, if they cannot be destroyed, to disrupt their operations and minimize their influence in the international arena as much as possible.

The United States should not hesitate to call terrorist groups what they are by designating them as foreign terrorist organizations (FTOs) under the Immigration and Nationality Act (INA) or under the Antiterrorism and Effective Death Penalty Act (AEDPA) of 1996. Under both the INA and the AEDPA, a group can be labeled a foreign terrorist organization if it is foreign based, engages in or has the capability and intent to engage in terrorist activity or terrorism, and threatens the security of American citizens or U.S. national security.[15] The United States may not be able to avoid diplomatic relations with terrorist groups entirely, particularly when those groups gain political power through a legitimate political process as Hamas did in the Palestinian territories, Hezbollah did in Lebanon, and the Taliban did in Afghanistan. When the terrorist group in question has both armed and political wings, it may be possible to isolate one wing from the other with diplomatic efforts focused on the political elements of a movement and not on the armed elements. Another technique for facilitating negotiation with terrorist groups focuses on creating divisions within the groups through a dual-track approach that isolates common foot soldiers from their leadership. The United States has pursued such an effort with the Taliban in Afghanistan through programs called "reintegration" and "reconciliation." Reintegration involves attempts to lure low- and mid-level terrorist fighters away from their sponsoring organizations with incentives like employment or money. Reconciliation is an effort to negotiate deals with terrorist leaders that offer them some level of influence in a state's affairs in exchange for a cessation of hostilities. The United States should, as a matter of national policy, avoid diplomatic relations with hard-core Islamic terrorists whenever possible. Deradicalization is the process of getting a radical to abandon an extremist worldview and conclude it is not acceptable to use violence to bring about social change.[16] It is an iffy prospect at best because the truly devoted Islamists, those who are engaging in terrorist violence because they believe it is required for them to be true to their faith, are not likely to be swayed from their twisted worldview. When diplomatic relations with such individuals are absolutely unavoidable, great care must be taken to ensure if at all possible those with American blood directly on their hands are held accountable for their actions.

The Instruments of Diplomacy

There are several tools or instruments available to the United States under the diplomatic element of national power. Some of these instruments are designed to reward, some are designed to coerce, and some are designed to punish the target of the diplomatic instrument being employed. The main instrument of diplomacy is simple negotiation, formal or informal, with the governments of other nation-states. Sometimes the negotiations are overt and transparent, particularly when the talks are between allies, and sometimes the negotiations are covert or through intermediaries, such as when the United States conducts behind-the-scenes talks with countries with whom it has no diplomatic relations, like Iran. An absence of formal diplomatic ties can also be compensated for with a diplomatic outpost like the one the United States maintains with its island neighbor, Cuba. A diplomatic outpost is useful for exchanging important information and conducting informal governmental negotiations without establishing a formal state-to-state relationship. It allows countries on not-so-friendly terms to maintain a channel for continuing dialogue.

Diplomatic efforts are critical to the United States' global fight with transnational Islamic radicals who see violence as the best means for obtaining their political, economic, and social objectives in the international system. Diplomatic negotiations conducted at any level of government can help the United States bolster its image abroad, strengthen and reform its alliances,

form new international bonds when old ones fail or when international crises warrant, develop law enforcement partnerships, expand the sharing of
intelligence information, facilitate the conduct of military exercises and operations, provide humanitarian aid to people and nations in need, negotiate
treaties and trade agreements, and foster intergovernmental cooperation and
coordination. Coercive or punitive instruments designed to punish a targeted
state for a particular behavior the imposing nation finds objectionable include
suspending or severing diplomatic relations, withdrawing ambassadors, ex-
pelling representatives from other countries, publicly supporting reformers in
repressive states, pressuring other nations to take or abstain from a particular
action, and adding or removing states from specific bad actor lists like the
State Department's list of state sponsors of terrorism.

Each diplomatic situation the United States finds itself in will be unique,
and the measures employed will depend upon a host of factors, including the
players involved, the amount of time available to resolve the situation, the
particular issue or issues at stake, and the degree of importance attached to
those issues. No matter which diplomatic instruments are used in the pursuit
of U.S. national interests, ultimately all diplomatic efforts should be designed
to mold the international environment in a manner that is most beneficial to
the United States and, when possible, its allies and partner nations. Consideration of the interests of other states is important because the manner in which
the United States exercises its power will have an effect on the willingness of
other nations to follow America's lead in confronting international security
issues. Diplomatic efforts must also reflect the values and beliefs Americans
hold dear if those efforts are going to receive the support of the American
public. Actions deemed inconsistent with traditional American values and
beliefs and lacking public support are unlikely to be politically sustainable
over the long term. Neither the interests of other states nor the support of the
American public will completely dictate the diplomatic actions of the United
States, but both are important to the ultimate outcome of those actions.

When it comes to the use of diplomacy, whether in international forums
like the United Nations or through direct dialogue with individual states or
groups of states, one thing is certain: American leadership is essential and
desired by most of the international community. Even some countries that
decry U.S. actions publicly look to the United States privately when important
international issues need to be resolved. The United States is the only nation
in the world capable of leading the countries of the international system and
there are very few issues of international concern that can be resolved without
U.S. participation in the resolution process. When serious global issues arise,
the rest of the world looks to the United States for guidance and direction.
Not all nations will agree with every U.S. action that is undertaken, but all

nations will certainly be watching to see what the United States does or does not do in response to international security issues. The American public knows this and realizes, generally, that the United States has no choice but to be proactively engaged in international security affairs. Isolation from the rest of the world is not a realistic or desirable option. In a globalized international system, a superpower like the United States cannot avoid impacting other states, no matter what actions it does or does not take, and it cannot avoid being impacted by other states, no matter how hard it might try to do so. Americans, like the citizens of other nations, want diplomacy to be the primary mechanism for their government's conduct of international relations. But diplomacy by itself is insufficient. It cannot function in isolation from the other elements of national power and often is dependent on other elements of national power for its credibility and effectiveness.

5

The Information Element
of National Power

THE GLOBAL BATTLE AGAINST ISLAMIC EXTREMISM is at its core a battle for the hearts and minds of ordinary moderate Muslims throughout the international system. The radicals that threaten the United States and its allies today depend upon the support of the global Muslim community, the *ummah*, in order to grow and sustain their extremist movement as a viable political and ideological force. This contest for the support of mainstream Muslims, often referred to as the "war of ideas" or the "battle of narratives," can be thought of as a competition of drastically different visions for the future of Muslim and non-Muslim societies everywhere. On one side are the radical Islamists who seek to exploit their religious faith and vulnerable young Muslims for their own personal political gain. On the other side are both Islamic and non-Islamic countries, including the United States and its allies, who are seeking to protect their national interests and, in some cases, promote liberty and democracy around the world.

Wars of ideas or battles of narratives can be divided into four general categories: intellectual debates; ideological wars; conflicts over religious doctrine; and advertising campaigns.[1] The war of ideas in the current transnational struggle against Islamic extremism is a battle of the second type, that of ideological warfare, while a simultaneous conflict of the third type, a dispute over religious tenets between moderates and radicals within Islam, is being fought out among the citizens of Muslim societies across the international community. The battle of narratives is being waged on the ground within Muslim societies through local information campaigns and the management of public perception, and over the airwaves through both traditional media like television and radio broadcasts and nontraditional media like Internet websites, chat rooms, and bulletin boards that appeal to the global Muslim populace. The competition for support from ordinary Muslims is a battle even more important than the physical combat occurring in Iraq, Afghanistan, Pakistan, the Philippines, Djibouti, Somalia, Yemen, and other countries. It is a battle that is without question the single most critical of the overall campaign against the hateful and intolerant ideology of Islamic radicalism and those who commit violent terrorist acts in the name of that ideology. It is a battle that targets both Muslim and non-Muslim publics, and it is a battle the United States and its allies are clearly losing to their extremist opponents. After nearly a decade of war in two Muslim countries and a series of proxy conflicts in other contested global hot spots, the United States and like-minded nations have essentially surrendered the information battlefield to the radicals who continue to threaten international peace and stability.

The Islamic Extremist Message

Radical Islamists have proved to be extremely adept at getting their message out and promoting their extremist ideology to Muslim and non-Muslim audiences worldwide. Ideology can be defined as an organized set of ideas or beliefs, in particular about human life or culture.[2] It is important because it serves as a reason or justification for specific actions taken by a particular group or by individuals.[3] It explains why the methods employed by individuals and organizations are considered to be legitimate and acceptable. Muslim extremists subscribe to the ideology of Islamism, or the idea that the legitimacy of a political order should be derived from the principles of the Islamic faith.[4] Islamism calls for strict adherence to the religion of Islam as a means for countering non-Islamic influence that is described to target audiences as corrupt, immoral, and a threat to traditional Muslim values and beliefs. The form Islamism takes can range from the mild, in which followers work to merge Islamic principles within a given political system, to moderate and extreme strains, in which followers temporarily accept non-Islamic political systems until Islamic principles can prevail or reject them outright as illegitimate and in defiance of Allah's will.

Islamist ideology breaks the world up into two distinct groups: the House of Islam, or *dar al-Islam*, and the House of War, or *dar al-harb*. The House of Islam is made up of those countries that have subjected themselves to pure Islamic rule based on Sharia law. The rest of the world, the House of War, is considered to be in conflict or at war with Allah's will, making it incumbent on the House of Islam to fight the nations of the House of War until everyone is subjected to Sharia-based Islamic governance.[5] Many Islamic terrorist groups, including al Qaeda prime, base their ideological precepts on Qutbism, a radical school of Islamist thought grounded in the writings and teachings of Sayyid Qutb, one of the most prominent Islamic thinkers of the modern era until his execution by Egyptian authorities in the mid-1960s. Qutb was a member of the Muslim Brotherhood, a radical Sunni Islamist group formed in the 1920s by Hasan al-Banna as an Islamic revivalist movement. A significant number of Sunni Muslim extremist groups operating in the contemporary international security environment, including al Qaeda, came out of the Muslim Brotherhood, which is still active in Egypt today. Qutbism uses Islamic teachings to justify violent action in the name of Islam. It has had a profound influence on current Muslim extremist groups and is a driving force behind the idea of offensive jihad. One of Qutb's works from the early 1960s, in particular, is cited as a contemporary justification for the use of terrorist violence. In *Milestones*, Qutb wrote that governments and individuals not following "true" Islam (or Islam as the radicals interpret it) are in a state of ignorance and must be changed, through the use of force if necessary.[6]

While Qutbism serves as a modern inspiration for violent Islamic extremists, the works of Sayyid Qutb are actually derived from earlier writings by a fourteenth-century Syrian Islamist named Shaykh Taqi al-Din ibn Taymiyya (1263–1328), who authored the "Mardin fatwa," a religious decree that provided Muslims with an Islamic justification for politically motivated violence.[7] A conference of more than a dozen Islamic scholars sponsored by two Muslim nongovernmental organizations, the Global Center for Guidance and Canopus Consulting, convened in Turkey in March 2010 to review the works of ibn Taymiyya, including the Mardin fatwa. Two important conclusions were reached at the conference. The first was that Muslims do not have the right to decide of their own accord to declare or wage jihad. The second was that the Mardin fatwa and other Islamic texts used to justify political violence in the name of Islam have been misinterpreted and misused by the extremists.[8] These findings will not, of course, change the philosophical outlook of Islamic radicals like those belonging to al Qaeda and other Muslim extremist groups, and they will not have any sort of appreciable effect on the violent principles these groups preach and practice. They do, however, provide a useful Islam-based starting point for the United States and its allies and partner nations to work on building support among moderate Muslim populations around the world that may be susceptible to radical Islamist influence.

The Islamic extremists that threaten the United States and its allies today exploit the perceived victimization and humiliation of Muslims by the West, and particularly the superpower and allegedly imperialist United States. A constant theme of the extremists' message is that the United States and its allies are waging war on Islam and it is the solemn duty of all Muslims to come to the defense of their faith.[9] Perceptions about the intentions of the United States in Muslim lands are critical to the Islamist message. A heavy reliance by the predominantly Christian United States on the use of military force in Muslim countries over the years has reinforced the extremist claim that America is waging a war of faiths, has hindered U.S. efforts in the Middle East and other Muslim-heavy regions, and has provided motivation for disaffected Muslim youths to heed the call of the radicals and join the fight in defense of their Islamic beliefs. Muslims have long been skeptical of U.S. motives in Islamic countries, and charismatic extremist leaders with strongly persuasive speaking skills have been wildly successful in securing support from Muslim populations by portraying the United States as an imperial power with territorial ambitions in the lands of Islam.

In 2009, Zogby International and the University of Maryland conducted an Arab public opinion poll in the Middle East countries of Egypt, Jordan, Lebanon, Morocco, Saudi Arabia, and the United Arab Emirates. Respondents to the survey named Hassan Nasrallah, head of the Lebanese terrorist group Hezbollah, as the most admired leader in the Arab world. More than 80 percent of those surveyed had an unfavorable view of the United States, and most of the individual respondents considered the United States and Israel to be the biggest threats to the Middle East.[10] A 2010 follow-up to the poll found President Obama's efforts to reach out to the Muslim world had not made an impact on Muslim perceptions of the United States or its political leadership. When asked about their view of Obama, more than 60 percent responded negatively while 20 percent responded positively. In 2009, those numbers were 23 percent negative and 45 percent positive.[11] In a volatile and dangerous region where terrorism and dictatorial regimes abound, where brutality and the repression of whole societies are the norm, where the people seldom get to influence their futures or the directions their countries take, it is nothing short of stunning that the populations of Middle Eastern nations consider the United States to be a greater danger to their societies than a radical clerical regime in Iran that seems determined to acquire nuclear weapons or than violent extremists who use brutal tactics like suicide bombings and beheadings against those who do not subscribe to their specific belief system, even if they are fellow Muslims.

Islamic extremist organizations and their leaders seize upon the general fear and loathing many Arabs have for the United States and the West and upon the general disaffectedness of Arab populations unhappy with dictatorial governments that often fail to meet their basic societal and individual needs. Muslim radicals skillfully use audio and video media products and, perhaps most importantly, expertly exploit the capabilities offered by the Internet to spread their message of hate for the United States, the broader West, Israel, and the secular governments of the Middle East. Bin Laden and al-Zawahiri developed a competent and effective media arm for al Qaeda prime, Al Sahab, which regularly broadcasts the group's message through the production of audio and video messages aired by radio and television networks and posted on the Internet. Increasingly, al Qaeda is taking advantage of English-language websites to facilitate the dissemination of its radical message to Muslim audiences outside the Middle East. The number of such websites active on the Internet has risen from around thirty in 2002 to more than two hundred now. Conversely, the number of Arabic-language websites devoted to al Qaeda's message has plummeted from around a thousand in 2002 to only about fifty today.[12] This trend is indicative of an attempt by al Qaeda to expand its extremist audience base to English-speaking Muslims outside of traditionally Muslim areas. Social networking sites like Facebook, too, offer radical Islamists an easy-to-use means for reaching out to target audiences. Extremely popular and with millions of subscribers, Facebook is being used by Islamic extremists to find recruits, conduct operational planning, disseminate propaganda, exchange ideas, conduct reconnaissance and targeting activities, and direct prospective jihadists to other radical websites and forums.[13] Another example of jihadists' use of the Internet can be found in the online English-language magazine created by the media arm of al Qaeda's affiliate in Yemen, al Qaeda in the Arabian Peninsula, or AQAP. The al Malahem–produced magazine, called *Inspire*, provides its readers with bomb-making instructions and methods for contacting members of the al Qaeda network.[14] *Inspire* targets Muslims in the English-speaking world with advanced graphics and interviews with infamous jihadists who preach the virtues of martyrdom and conflict with the United States and the West.[15]

The international reach of the Internet facilitates the rapid dissemination of the extremist message and allows for real-time communication through websites, chat rooms, and bulletin boards dedicated to the spread of Islamic radicalism. The Internet can also be used to gather intelligence on potential targets, conduct surveillance, post militant training materials, seek strategic or tactical advice from other extremists, recruit new fighters, disseminate propaganda, create publicity, deliver threats, connect with like-minded individuals, raise funds for terrorist operations, and reduce the need for a fixed base of operations, thereby lowering the overall risk to Islamic terrorists. The information contained on extremist websites could, in the hands of the right individuals or groups, be used with deadly consequences. A 2010 posting that circulated on English-language websites provided readers with a book called *The Explosives Course*, a how-to guide that provides instructions on bomb making, explosives laboratory building, and the availability of chemicals used in bomb production. Published by al Qaeda's Global Islamic Media Front, *The Explosives Course* is considered one of the most comprehensive and sophisticated jihadist manuals ever produced.[16]

Websites used by Muslim extremists have come a long way in a very short period of time in terms of functionality and user friendliness. These sites can be divided into five basic groups. The first consists of those websites affiliated with al Qaeda prime and can be further subdivided into sites run by al Qaeda traditionalists (followers of bin Laden and al-Zawahiri) and sites run by neo-Zarqawiists (followers of the tactics favored by deceased al Qaeda in Iraq leader Abu Mus'ab al-Zarqawi). The second group is made up of those extremist sites that support the multitude of Sunni insurgent groups formed in the chaos of post-Saddam, Shiite-dominated Iraq. The third group is dominated by Salafist-Wahhabi–influenced sites used by individuals and groups dedicated to promoting the Salafist version of Islam. Salafism is the belief that the Muslim faith must be returned to its purist roots (as interpreted by the Salafis). The fourth group consists of websites focused on support for the multitude of Palestinian groups involved in the Israeli-Palestinian conflict. The fifth and final group is a conglomeration of miscellaneous websites not linked to a specific terrorist organization or cause. The sites in this group direct their efforts toward generating broad-based Islamist discussions.[17] In terms of perception management, which is essential to winning the war of ideas and gaining the support of ordinary Muslims across the international landscape, the Internet offers Islamic radicals an extremely valuable medium that has been expertly taken advantage of at every opportunity.

Islamic extremists have a firm understanding of the value of traditional and nontraditional forms of media and the effect that media products can have on target audiences. Al Qaeda prime, its officially designated franchises, and the various movements affiliated with al Qaeda through AQAM all recognize that information operations are critical to their success or failure in the global war of ideas and in the ultimate achievement of their religious and political goals. Because they understand the power and influence of the media, these extremist groups regularly publish a variety of media products with great effect, through both traditional and nontraditional communications outlets. Just a few years ago, in July of 2007, nearly 80 percent of the Islamist media products that contained an identifiable geographic focus were concentrated on the war in Iraq, while only 10 percent were focused on the war in Afghanistan.[18] During this period, the American "surge" of military forces to Iraq was at its peak, and operations in Afghanistan were considered by the broader international community to be a mere sideshow to the U.S.-led effort that removed Saddam Hussein from power. Now, with the American military present in Iraq in significantly smaller numbers than in years past and scheduled to withdraw completely by the end of 2011, the former Saddam Hussein stronghold has been relegated to the back burner as a steadily increasing level of violence and rising U.S. and NATO troop numbers in Afghanistan have shifted the focus of jihadists across the international system to the original Islamist battleground that saw the extremists defeat in combat the mighty Soviet superpower.

What Can the United States Do?

There are two general schools of thought that deal with how the United States and its allies should fight the war of ideas against the radical vision put forth by Islamic extremists. The first approach advocates using public diplomacy in an effort to engage the global Muslim community through positive outreach and supporting that engagement effort with concrete, visible programs designed to reinforce the engagement message. The second approach favors treating the war of ideas as if it were a "real" war and recommends taking kinetic action designed to destroy the extremist ideology and its leading proponents.[19] Public diplomacy can be defined as the promotion of a country's national interests through engagement, persuasion, and influence with foreign populations. Public diplomacy traditionally focuses its efforts on long-term relationship building and a few core activities like broadcasting and exchange programs. Public affairs, on the other hand, is typically focused on short-term programs designed to engage the media and influence the twenty-four-hour news cycle while reaching out to both domestic and foreign target audiences.[20]

Public diplomacy efforts to engage the global Muslim community should have as a central feature an emphasis on highlighting Muslim victims of Islamic extremism. Followers of the Islamic faith have a huge stake in the war of ideas because it is Muslims who are most often the victims of Islamic extremist violence. An analysis conducted by the Combating Terrorism Center at the United States Military Academy at West Point found that only 15 percent of the fatalities from al Qaeda attacks between 2004 and 2008 were Westerners.[21] The killing of large numbers of Muslims inflicts harm on the Islamic extremist movement by reducing the level of support for the extremists' cause among mainstream Muslims, a phenomenon known as the "Shayma effect," named for a young Egyptian girl killed by a terrorist bomb in Egypt.[22] The United States and its allies and partner nations should promote the idea that whatever perceived fears exist about Western influence on Islamic culture, an even greater threat is posed by extremists who indiscriminately kill and maim innocents, regardless of the faith they practice, in pursuit of their political objectives.

Another critical aspect of the public diplomacy approach should be the targeting of moderate Muslim states, groups, and individuals with the ability to promote an alternative vision for the future than the one being offered by the extremists. In targeting moderate Muslim states, the focus should be on those countries with relatively strong governments and moderate to weak Islamist movements. Possibilities for engagement, at least initially, include Morocco, Jordan, and potentially Egypt, depending on the final composition of whatever post-Mubarak government solidifies its hold on power. In these countries, Islamic radicalism is generally under control and anti-Americanism is less rampant than in other Muslim states. One example of a moderate individual, and there are many more in Muslim societies, who could potentially be leveraged against the extremist message can be found in Egyptian cleric and television preacher Dr. Umar Abd al-Kafy. In a July 2010 interview with Dubai's al-Arabiya television channel, Dr. al-Kafy rejected Osama bin Laden's religious decree calling on Muslims to kill Americans in Islamic countries and offered heavy criticism of al Qaeda's strategy and the theological basis of its ideology.[23] Moderates like Dr. al-Kafy exist in all Muslim societies, often lacking only a platform from which to make their voices heard.

It is important, also, that the emphasis be on promoting moderation and not on the adoption of democratic principles. Democracy cannot be imposed. Instead, it must be chosen by the people. Pushing too hard for democracy in Muslim states could lead to a rise to power by elements not friendly to U.S. interests, like Hezbollah in Lebanon, Hamas in the Palestinian territories, and Shiite radicals loyal to Moqtada al-Sadr in Iraq. This does not mean the United States should avoid quietly promoting democratic reforms in Muslim countries. Democracy promotion is an enduring U.S. national interest that should be conducted behind the scenes as much as possible and with as little fanfare as can be managed. In targeting moderate groups and individuals, the focus should be on those organizations and persons with significant influence in Muslim communities, like aid and charity groups, and specific role models, including religious and educational figures. Listening to their thoughts and ideas about the approach to policies and programs that attempt to dissuade individuals at risk of radicalization or counterradicalization would go a long way toward establishing trust and a mutually beneficial relationship between the United States and those Muslims capable of steering potential extremists away from the jihadist cause.[24] Another important element to consider when targeting states, groups, and individuals for moderation promotion efforts is that the message disseminated by the United States and its allies must be tailored to specific locations and cultures. There is no magic formula that will enable Western countries to win the support of all moderate Muslims across the international system. Islamic cultures can differ greatly from nation to nation and from region to region. Peculiar cultural sensitivities can have a tremendous effect on the amount of influence the United States and its allies are able to exert in a given location. When reaching out to moderate Muslim groups and leading Muslim individuals around the world, it is critical to attempt engagement with as broad a swathe of the global Muslim community as possible. Trying to convert Islamic extremists is likely to be extremely difficult, if not completely impossible, and while no doors should be permanently closed to them, the extremists themselves should not be the primary focus of U.S. and allied engagement efforts.

A 2007 Rand research brief proposed targeting five specific groups of Muslims for engagement: liberal and secular Muslim academics and intellectuals; young, moderate religious scholars; community activists; women's groups engaged in gender equality campaigns; and moderate journalists and writers.[25] Some groups and individuals will be receptive to engagement efforts, and some will not. What is important under the public diplomacy approach is that channels of communication and support are open and easily accessible so that those individuals who are receptive to engagement efforts have a means through which they can communicate. The message promoted by the United States and its allies must consist of two parts: an alternative narrative and a counternarrative. The alternative narrative should be one that focuses on inclusion in the prosperity enjoyed by America and Western nations while being careful not to overreach in a way that provokes the anger and resentment already so prevalent in many Muslim societies. It must give Muslims a credible substitute for the violence and hatred offered by Islamic extremists. The counternarrative should have as its focus the discrediting of the extremists' radical message. It has to include sound ideological, political, historical, and theological reasons why the extremist vision is flawed and why following that vision is not in the best interests of Muslim societies. Both the alternative narrative and the counternarrative must be aimed where they can yield the greatest results: extremist recruiting venues, educational programs, moderate Muslim leaders in need of a platform from which to compete with the radicals and their message of hate for those who don't subscribe to their views, and those within the Muslim community who can shape Muslim opinion away from the extremist cause and toward moderation.

A final point that needs to be made is that the message put forth by the United States and its allies must be transmitted through Muslim outlets to the greatest extent possible. Western media and Western government information sources have woefully little credibility in the Muslim world and are unlikely to be taken seriously by the audiences being targeted to receive the West's message. A Muslim face on the West's vision is essential to any information operations effort that seeks to reach out to moderate Muslim populations. In the end, American public diplomacy is about communicating the intent and global vision of the United States in a way that advances U.S. national security to the greatest extent possible. It is not an effort to make Muslims feel good about the United States and its citizens or the dominant role America plays in the contemporary international security system.

Treating the war of ideas as an actual war would mean the United States and its allies would target for destruction those elements that promote Islamic extremism, including communications mediums, rank-and-file Islamic fighters, and extremist leaders whenever and wherever they could be found. The senior figures in radical Islamist organizations are exceptionally competent at disseminating propaganda through the use of audio and video messages and Internet technology. The United States is the most technologically advanced nation in the world. Even though extremist websites regularly switch network servers and employ advanced security measures to decrease their vulnerability, the United States government has the technological means available to seriously degrade the information operations capability of radical Islamic organizations and to block, even if only partially and temporarily, their extremist message from reaching potential recruits, supporters, and sympathizers. Rank-and-file fighters and their leaders are being relentlessly pursued through law enforcement efforts and on the battlefield in places like Iraq, Afghanistan, Pakistan, Yemen, Africa, and the Philippines. The detaining and killing of Islamic extremist fighters and leaders will continue unabated for the foreseeable future, and the United States and its allies must be prepared to stay on the offensive to minimize the possibility of being forced into a defense of the American homeland or the European continent. Treating the war of ideas as a real war cannot be done in isolation from the public diplomacy approach. The two are intimately connected. Killing those individuals who belong to the Islamic extremist movement is not enough. If their ideology is going to be marginalized to the point where the risk to Americans and others is substantively reduced, the overall effort must include a positive alternative message that offers a more prosperous, stable, and secure future than the one being offered by the extremists and a counternarrative that debunks the claims made by the radicals. The commitment required of the United States and its allies, in terms of both effort and time, cannot be overstated. Multiple factors, including growing youth populations in Muslim states, repressive Muslim governments, weak economic conditions, and Islamist influence in education and in everyday life, will ensure Islamic extremism does not go down without a long, difficult, and most likely, very bloody fight.

The Role of Public Opinion

The effect of the information element of national power on the American public and on the publics of U.S. allies, partners, and non-U.S.-friendly states is profound. A twenty-four-hour news cycle creates a pervasive information environment in which media coverage, both good and bad, can impact political decision making domestically and abroad in response to the opinions of the citizenries involved. Public opinion in U.S.-allied countries can affect the degree of support the United States receives in a given campaign or operation. In Germany, for example, significant public opposition to the war in Afghanistan limits the role of German military forces operating under NATO control and consequently limits the ability of the NATO commander on the ground to effectively and efficiently employ all of the forces at his disposal. Germany is not an isolated case by any means, especially when talking about the contributions of NATO's European members, but serves here as a useful example of how public opinion can affect national policy. The German public and the publics of the United States and other countries are bombarded with a constant stream of information from combat zones that over time affects public sentiment about the actions the United States and its allies are engaged in during this global conflict with Islamic radicals. Therefore it is essential that the United States work with allied and partner governments to tailor informational messages that will help to win the support of the various publics with a stake in this conflict.

It is critically important in dealing with these nations that the United States clearly articulate its own national interests and the means it intends to use to secure those interests so that timely and accurate information can be provided to concerned national populations. The provision of this information will enable other governments to explain to their publics how the national interests of their nations align with those of the United States, increasing the likelihood of public support in those countries. There must be a concerted push for international cooperation, the promotion of globally accepted standards for combating Islamic terrorism, and an aggressive effort to increase global engagement in areas ripe for exploitation by Muslim radicals, all supported by carefully tailored information programs designed to educate populations who are able to influence government decisions. In countries dealing with Islamic extremism within their borders, the attitudes of domestic publics can affect the formation of terrorist groups, the willingness of individuals to engage in terrorism, the level of public support given to terrorists, the actions that can be taken by government forces, and the willingness of citizens to provide information that could help combat the terrorist threat.[26] When providing assistance to foreign governments fighting Islamic extremists internally, winning hearts and minds with positive information that counters the propaganda efforts of the extremists is of much greater importance than the neutralization of individual terrorists who can be easily replaced by an extremist group's recruiting machine.

While public opinion in other nations is a matter of great importance to American policymakers, the opinions and attitudes of the United States' own citizens are even more critical to the formulation of U.S. national policies designed to combat the Islamic extremist threat. Despite the horror Americans felt in the immediate aftermath of the 9/11 attacks, with the resultant thousands of innocent civilian casualties on U.S. soil, the seriousness of the threat posed by Muslim radicals is difficult for the average American to understand after a decade without a similar attack on the homeland. There have, of course, been thwarted plots and failed attacks, but none of those have the sort of impact a successful mass-casualty-producing attack does. Traditionally, Islamic terrorism has been considered a Middle East phenomenon, far removed from America's shores and certainly not an existential threat to the United States along the lines of Nazi aggression or a nuclear-armed Soviet regime that controlled a significant portion of the European continent and had the ability to destroy American cities with little to no warning. The attacks on September 11, 2001, changed that notion briefly, but the sense of national concern about the threat posed by Islamic radicals has proved to be short-lived. Each year that passes without another major attack on the United States causes the degree of complacency among the American public to grow a little bit more. Public indifference is extremely dangerous because it leads to a lack of serious concern among the country's political leaders, who focus on those areas of policy that are of greatest worry to the people who elect them to their jobs—their constituents. If the American public is more focused on the economy, health care, or education than it is on the threat posed by Islamic radicals, then those elected to represent the public in Washington will understandably follow suit. The U.S. government can, through the concentrated employment of the information element of national power within the United States, provide Americans with knowledge about the continuing threat to the nation and the need for diligence and proactive action by the entire country.

The United States' geographical distance from the wars in Iraq and Afghanistan and the counterterrorism efforts in the Horn of Africa, the Philippines, and elsewhere mean there is little attention paid by information and news outlets to the global fight against Islamic extremism unless that fight is going poorly. The old saying, "If it bleeds, it leads," rings true in the contemporary international media environment. Sensational attacks that result in large numbers of casualties and significant amounts of damage are more likely to draw viewers to network and cable news shows and to Internet feeds than is the slow, methodical work of nation building, counterterrorism, and counterinsurgency. The extremists understand this and consequently target the national will by trying to convince Americans that any good reasons for being involved in the Muslim world are greatly outweighed by the costs in both blood and treasure of that engagement. To counter this effort by the extremists, the United States government must actively engage the American public with a strong information program that can mobilize domestic support for the fight against Islamic radicalism. With Americans dying daily at the hands of Muslim terrorists in Afghanistan, and, to a lesser extent, in Iraq, this can prove to be a hard sell for the nation's leaders to make. American citizens expect their armed forces to win the country's military conflicts quickly and with as little cost as possible. It is extremely difficult for the government to maintain public support in protracted armed engagements that bleed the country's youth and treasury. Americans can endure casualties if they believe the United States' vital national interests are at stake, there is a probability of success, and the fighting will be over in a short period of time. If these conditions are not met, public opinion can shift quickly and dramatically, limiting the ability of the country's elected leaders to act decisively and effectively to confront groups and individuals targeting the United States.

In theory, news stories with graphic or sensational images should not influence the long-term national policy decisions of America's elected leaders. The world of national-level decision making is not well suited to handle emotional influence. The reality, though, is that news stories do influence the men and women in the federal government who are responsible for making important national security policy choices. The reporters and photographers providing the media products that influence American public opinion cannot possibly record everything going on at a given moment or during a particular event, which means any news report presents only a portion of the larger story. Something is always left out, and that something could very well be critical to informed thought, debate, and decision making. Therefore, it is extremely important for the government to be able to influence the information that is provided to the American public. Shaping perceptions through the effective use of the information element of national power can directly impact the overall strategic environment and affect the level of public support for U.S. actions worldwide. The ineptitude demonstrated thus far by the United States in the information operations arena must be reversed immediately or the entire endeavor to minimize the risk posed by Islamic extremism could be lost. Overwhelming national power means nothing if the public prevents that power from being employed effectively against those who would do the United States and its citizens harm. America and its allies are losing the information battle, and they are losing it badly. Islamic terrorists regularly produce

6

The Military Element of National Power

SINCE PRESIDENT BUSH DECLARED America would engage in a "Global War on Terrorism" in response to al Qaeda's 9/11 attacks, the United States has been the target of some relatively strong and sustained domestic and international criticism for its use of American military power in the Middle East. Such criticism may or may not be justified, depending upon one's philosophy regarding the utility of force and the proper employment of a nation's military power in pursuit of its national interests. Whether one agrees or disagrees with the way in which American military forces have been utilized abroad since 9/11, the military element of national power has proved to be an essential resource in the arsenal of American might, one that must be employed in certain situations as a vital part of any grand, comprehensive strategic response to the Islamic terrorist threat facing the United States and its allies. The use of military power, generally, is a measure of last resort or near last resort, one that is undertaken only after all other efforts have failed to achieve a desired result or seem destined to fail. There are some in the United States who believe military power should never be used under virtually any circumstance imaginable. In an ideal world that might be possible. But the realities of the current international security environment have demonstrated time and again that there are some very unsavory characters at work in the global system trying desperately to bring harm to the United States and its citizens and interests. There are and will continue to be situations in which individuals, organizations, or states cannot or will not be dissuaded from committing or sponsoring acts of violent terrorism, making the use of military power in some instances not only appropriate, but justified.

The level of military power enjoyed by any nation-state is based upon multiple quantitative and qualitative factors, including the size, composition, and organization of forces available for deployment, the amount and quality of equipment and weaponry on hand, the ability of the nation to sustain its military forces once they are deployed away from the homeland, the morale of the individuals that make up the ranks, the quality of leadership at all levels of the command structure, the amount of discipline instilled in the individual members of the armed forces, the budget allocated to the military establishment, the capability of the nation to project its forces worldwide, the training quality or level of competency of armed forces personnel, and the nation's philosophy on the employment of its military assets. When the military establishments of the nations of the international community are looked at in terms of capability and effectiveness, the United States' armed forces clearly stand apart from the rest of the pack. American troops are members of the most powerful and professional military organization the world has ever seen, capable of confronting and defeating virtually any armed opponent in combat in any domain—land, sea, air, or cyberspace. No other nation can even hope, at least in the near term and probably in the long term, to challenge the United States militarily in a conventional force-on-force conflict. Russia and China are pursuing such a capability in earnest, but they are not there yet. Russian and Chinese investments in military modernization will continue to require serious attention from Pentagon planners and presidential and congressional advisers for the foreseeable future, lest the United States be caught ill prepared for conflict with significant regional powers acting in ways contrary to U.S. national interests.

Of course, as the United States has come to realize in the years since the 1991 Persian Gulf War, conventional conflict is the type of armed struggle least likely to be engaged in by U.S. military forces in the contemporary international security environment. Traditional nation-state conflict, in which masses of men and equipment face off in conventional forms of combat, is unlikely to occur on the scale it has in the past. The days of global warfare between nation-states are probably over, although regional conventional conflicts with the potential for U.S. involvement are likely to occur with unsettling regularity. Instead of another world war, the United States can expect to see an increasing number of irregular conflicts—so-called fourth-generation warfare fights—like Afghanistan and Iraq for the next several decades at a minimum. The term *fourth-generation warfare* is used to describe the most recent evolution in military strategy and tactics.

First-generation warfare, which dominated the beginning of the modern era, featured massed groups of fighting men in organized armies using line and column tactics like those characteristic of the American Civil War and earlier conflicts. Second-generation warfare saw the introduction of significant technological advancements in weaponry, like the rifled musket and the machine gun, which saw its first really effective usage in World War I. Second-generation warfare moved away from line and column tactics and was based instead on fire and movement. World War II and the Korean conflict were both second-generation warfare armed contests. Third-generation warfare was based primarily on speed of maneuver, with military forces seeking to bypass enemy firepower instead of engaging in direct force-on-force combat. A good example can be found in U.S. General Norman Schwarzkopf's "end-run" flanking maneuver around Iraqi military forces during Operation Desert Storm, the 1991 Persian Gulf War to liberate the tiny Arab nation of Kuwait from its seizure by Iraqi military forces. The latest evolution of warfare is the fourth generation, which is characterized by irregular or asymmetric methods used by a weaker power to negate advantages enjoyed by a stronger power, as in the post-9/11 conflicts in Afghanistan and Iraq. This fourth-generation of warfare features small, highly mobile forces fighting in an undefined area of operations that often includes large numbers of civilians and other noncombatants. There is no front line where armies face off, and there is no safe rear area for noncombat forces or support personnel in units not designed for direct engagement with the enemy. Large formations of troops and advanced weapons platforms are no longer the dominant factors in warfare, and the support of the population is instead the critical issue.[1]

The Decision to Use Military Power

The decision to use American military power is never taken lightly by the nation's elected leaders, or at least it shouldn't be taken lightly. The military element of national power is generally considered to be the most controversial and emotion-filled element, with no other element of power arousing the most intense passions of supporters and critics alike. Many people within the United States and abroad believe U.S. foreign policy since the 9/11 terrorist attacks has been too focused on the use of the military element of power and that America should reduce its military presence not just in the Middle East, but in all foreign lands. Despite the misgivings of some well-meaning citizens, the use of military power has been absolutely essential to the successes the United States has enjoyed thus far in the transnational fight against Islamic terrorists. Proactive, aggressive military measures employed over the last decade have undoubtedly contributed to the prevention of another 9/11-type attack on the U.S. homeland. Military

power must sometimes be used to protect U.S. national interests and to ensure the safety and security of America's citizens at home and in countries
far from the nation's shores. Other elements of power can and should be
employed before resorting to military power. If the other elements of power
fail, though, the United States must be able to fall back on its military might
to help secure the nation's vital and important national interests.

There are multiple scenarios in which the United States might employ its
military forces, whether unilaterally, within an alliance or temporary coalition, or through an agreement crafted in a multilateral organization like the
United Nations or the North Atlantic Treaty Organization. American political leaders could utilize U.S. military forces in a deterrent role to prevent an
actor from taking an action by convincing the actor that the cost is not worth
any potential gain or benefit; in a compelling role to force an actor to cease
an action that has already begun; in an acquisitive role to take territory or
resources; in an intervention role; in a counterintervention role; in a collective action role with other states; or in a support role to enhance the effectiveness of American diplomatic efforts abroad.[2] Sometimes it is possible for
the United States to influence the behavior of other states merely by locating
American military power in close proximity to a targeted nation. The presence of an American carrier strike group just off a country's coastline sends
a powerful and unmistakable message that carries with it the potential for
consequences of the gravest kind. Such a presence is rarely dismissed as irrelevant by a targeted state.

The decision to employ the United States military in pursuit of U.S. national interests is, as already stated, a very serious one that can carry with it the
direst of possible consequences for those on the receiving end. No other element of national power involves as much risk as the military element. Even a
successful operation has the potential to damage relations with other nations,
including allies, or to cause injury or death to American military personnel
involved in the operation's execution. The president of the United States, in
his capacity as commander-in-chief of America's armed forces, has no greater
responsibility than to exhaust all other reasonable options for resolving
disputes with other nations before putting America's sons and daughters in
situations in which they could be injured or killed. Outside of the president's
authority to employ military forces for a limited period of time without the
consent of the Congress, the legislative branch, too, has a responsibility to
ensure the other elements of national power have been given sufficient time,
opportunity, and resources to work and that the desired outcome cannot be
achieved without the use of American military power before agreeing to fund
any military action or before granting the president an authorization to use
the instruments of U.S. military power.

In the mid-1980s, Defense Secretary Casper Weinberger crafted what came to be known as the Weinberger doctrine, a series of six principles for the employment of U.S. military forces that still, with some modification, influence America's elected officials considering the employment of those forces in response to contemporary international security situations. First, Weinberger said, the United States should not commit its forces to combat unless the vital interests of the nation or its allies are clearly at stake. Second, if the decision to commit forces is made, the United States should commit those forces wholeheartedly or not at all. Third, both the military forces committed to combat and the political leadership making the decisions should have clearly defined objectives that lay out what, specifically, the military establishment is supposed to accomplish. Fourth, as conditions inevitably change, military and political objectives and the forces employed to achieve those objectives should be reassessed and adjusted as necessary, no matter how often that may prove to be. Fifth, the support of the American people and their representatives in Congress must be reasonably assured before military forces are committed to any type of armed action. Last, the Weinberger doctrine says the employment of American's military forces should be a measure of absolute last resort.[3]

Former secretary of state and former chairman of the Joint Chiefs of Staff General Colin Powell refined the Weinberger doctrine into what has been popularly labeled the Powell doctrine, adding requirements for plans to employ military power to include the overwhelming use of force and an exit strategy before making the decision to commit U.S. military troops to combat engagements.[4] These two provisions were no doubt influenced by General Powell's service in Vietnam, where the United States committed its forces incrementally over a period of several years and without a concrete plan for the termination of hostilities and the subsequent withdrawal of America's military personnel. Not all situations in which U.S. military forces are committed will result in combat, as the Weinberger and Powell doctrines imply. The escalation of a given security situation to combat, though, is always a possibility when military forces are involved in the resolution of an international security challenge being dealt with by the United States. It is because the possibility of combat exists that the decision to employ U.S. military forces must be a deliberate and carefully considered one.

The Pros and Cons of Using Military Power

The deployment of American military forces anywhere in the international system evokes both positive and negative reactions, typically very strong ones, both domestically and among the populations of the countries that make up the global community of nations. More than a few people in the United States and elsewhere believe America is too quick to exercise its overwhelming military power and that when military forces are employed, the United States does so with an extremely heavy hand that lacks precision and often results in unnecessary civilian casualties, or in military parlance, "collateral damage." Whether perceptions of the use of U.S. military power are accurate or misplaced, the prevailing international opinion, especially in the wake of the wars in Afghanistan and Iraq and ongoing special operations and unmanned drone aircraft strikes in Pakistan, Yemen, and other global hot spots, is one of too much force used much too quickly, without adequate consultation with U.S. allies and partner nations and without sufficient regard for potential unintended consequences.

Perceptions about the use of U.S. military power are important, as are the opinions of citizens in the United States and abroad. Perceptions and opinions aside, though, there are several advantages associated with the use of the military element of national power. First, the use of military power, even in a deterrent role, is a state activity of the most serious kind. Because it is serious, it demonstrates in an unequivocal way to the American public and to the rest of the world the resolve of the United States and may act as a forcing function that prompts other governments to step up to the proverbial plate and take more responsibility in the global fight against Islamic terrorism. Second, a successful military strike can disrupt terrorist operations in progress or degrade the ability of terrorists to conduct planned operations at some point in the future. Third, the fact that the United States has a powerful and technologically advanced military that can target terrorists and their sponsors anywhere in the world, and that the country will not hesitate to use military power when it is deemed necessary by American political leaders, may deter future attacks.[5] A side benefit of the use of American military power is that the results of military action are often immediately visible, providing military planners and civilian policymakers with the ability to instantly assess the success or failure of their recommendations and decisions. The ability to quickly assess the results of an action or series of actions facilitates adjustments that can help the United States achieve its objectives at the least possible cost. Even more critical is that the results of military action are also visible to allied and nonallied countries and nongovernment groups and individuals who can instantly see what the United States is willing and able to do and make adjustments to their actions in response.

Of course, there are also disadvantages associated with the use of American military power in the fight against transnational Islamic radicals. The terrorist enemy faced by the United States and its allies today is widely dispersed across the entire international landscape, operating in small, highly mobile and hard to find units or cells that spend more of their time hiding in the shadows than they do out in the open where they can be easily targeted by overwhelming American firepower. Large-scale, conventional U.S. military power tends to be ineffective against this type of enemy force, especially when the terrorists live, train, and plan their operations among civilian populations, some of whom actively or passively support the terrorists and their religious, social, and political goals. Additionally, much of the international community does not approve of the world's lone remaining superpower wielding its overwhelming military might when and how it sees fit, often without regard for the opinions of others in the international system. A heavy reliance on the military element of power could cost the United States the cooperation and support of other nations who might otherwise be willing to work with American leaders to combat the extremist threat through nonmilitary means. Another disadvantage of using U.S. military power against Islamic terrorists is that the individuals and groups most often targeted generally have little in the way of critical infrastructure and equipment that is worth destroying. Is anything of substance really accomplished by taking out safe houses and rudimentary training camps in remote areas or by killing the low-level fighters who tend to be the ones to actually engage in hostile actions against American forces? The facilities used by terrorists are easily replaced, as are the ordinary foot soldiers most likely to be vulnerable to direct U.S. military action. Finally, there is virtually no support from Muslim countries, the very places most likely to attract the United States' attention in the contemporary international security environment, for a strong U.S. military presence on their soil or just outside their borders, especially a presence as significant as that which has been used in Iraq and Afghanistan. These countries generally do not want substantial U.S. military assistance, at least not overtly, and direct action or a physical presence by U.S. military forces is likely to be counterproductive at best, possibly leading some who otherwise would not be so inclined to join the fight between Islamic radicals and the United States and its allies on the side of the extremists.

Preemptive and Preventive Uses of Force

One of the more controversial aspects of the debate over the use of U.S. military power concerns preemptive and preventive uses of force. Preemption refers to the first use of military force when it is believed an attack by a nation-state or nonstate actor is imminent.[6] Preemptive military action is widely considered to be an act of self-defense, even though it involves a first strike against another state or against a nonstate actor. The use of preemptive military force requires extremely good intelligence if both domestic and international support are going to be maintained following an attack, a lesson the United States learned the hard way in its ouster of Saddam Hussein's dictatorial regime and the subsequent military occupation of post-Saddam Iraq. Preventive military action, in contrast, is the use of force when it is believed military conflict, while not necessarily imminent, is nonetheless inevitable.[7] A good way to think about preventive military action is to use the old saying, "Better safe than sorry." Preventive military action is simply the taking of steps designed to stop a growing threat, as the Israelis have hinted at doing in response to Iran's continued defiance of the international community over its suspected nuclear weapons program. Of course, such action runs the risk of creating greater instability than existed before the action was taken. For example, it is widely believed that if Israel launched a preventive attack against Iran's suspected nuclear weapons facilities, the clerical regime in Tehran would respond in a number of troublesome ways, possibly including the use of Hezbollah terrorists to attack Israeli and Western targets worldwide, conducting covert actions designed to stoke sectarian violence in Iraq that would endanger U.S. personnel, providing greater levels of support for insurgent elements in Afghanistan, and potentially closing off the Persian Gulf at the Strait of Hormuz, disrupting much of the world's supply of critical energy resources. The chief differences between preemptive force and preventive force are timing and certainty about the imminence of the threat posed by the targeted state or nonstate actor. In an international threat environment featuring scores of state and nonstate actors behaving irrationally and dangerously, it is likely the United States will continue to maintain its right to keep both preemptive and preventive force options on the table in order to confront unpredictable and perilous enemies as far away from the American homeland as possible.

The Employment of the Military Element of Power

There are a number of ways in which the military element of national power can be employed as a critical component of the global effort to combat Islamic radicals. One of the most important ways can be found in the use of U.S. military power for the purpose of deterrence, particularly when the deterrent effort is directed at state sponsors of terrorism. Deterrence can be defined as the persuasion of an adversary that the consequences of a particular course of action outweigh any real or perceived benefits that might be achieved as a result of that course of action.[8] In other words, a nation-state using its military power as a means for deterring another nation-state is hoping to instill some measure of doubt in the targeted country's thinking about the value to be had in continuing or executing a particular behavior. Deterrence is a purely psychological matter. The goal is to cause the target of the deterrent effort to rethink what it is doing or planning to do. Given the overwhelming military superiority enjoyed by the United States, deterrence through the threat of military force can be an extremely valuable tool for American officials to use in the international security environment. Of course, the target of the deterrent effort gets a vote in determining whether or not deterrence is going to succeed. Not all state and nonstate actors can be deterred because deterrence requires a rational adversary capable of conducting sound cost-benefit analysis that will ultimately inform the decision to continue or abandon an objectionable behavior. It is not hard to argue that some of the relevant actors in the global struggle with Islamic radicalism, like the leaders of al Qaeda and its associated and affiliated movements, are anything but rational. Additionally, for deterrence to be successful, it must be backed by both the capability and the will to use military force if deterrence fails to achieve the sought-after objective. Bluffing is not a realistic option. If the threat of force is made in an attempt to deter a particular actor, the threatening party cannot simply back down from the threat without losing all credibility with the targeted actor and with outside observers in the international system.

An especially important and controversial use of the military element of power that will likely be employed extensively for the foreseeable future is the training of host nation security forces to better enable other countries to combat terrorist elements threatening them, the United States, and U.S. allies and partner nations. The training of host nation security forces is a complex endeavor usually involving assistance with organizing, training, and equipping those forces as well as accompanying them on combat missions to provide critical support until they are capable of conducting independent operations. Joint American and host nation operations are essential. It's like teaching a child to ride a bicycle. Parents generally do not take the training wheels off until the child is ready to try riding the bicycle on his own. Even then, parents will likely still provide a guiding hand on the seat until the child gets going more or less independently. Similarly, the key to successful host nation security force training efforts is a "lead by example" model that gradually transitions full responsibility for the conduct of security missions to the forces being trained. The cycle involves U.S. forces taking the lead initially, then conducting joint operations with host nation security forces to build proficiency, and finally moving from joint operations to overseeing, supporting, and mentoring the host nation security forces.

The training of host nation security forces will be particularly critical in Afghanistan and, to a lesser degree, Iraq over the next decade as the United States looks to transition those combat and security missions to Afghan and Iraqi police and military personnel. The training of Iraqi forces has been underway significantly longer than has the training of Afghan security forces, which did not begin in earnest until 2008, seven years after the U.S.-led invasion. It is the training of these two national forces that is at the center of the controversy concerning this specific use of American military power. Both Afghan and Iraqi security forces have proved themselves to be especially difficult to train in counterterrorism and counterinsurgency operations. Corruption has been a significant problem, as has infiltration by individuals opposed to the U.S. missions in both countries, causing concern among American citizens and government officials about the value of the host nation security force training effort. Progress has been slow, but there has been progress nonetheless.

Security forces in Iraq have made significant gains in recent years, enabling the drawdown of most U.S. military personnel from the country in accordance with a U.S.-Iraqi status of forces agreement that calls for all American troops to depart by the end of 2011. American military personnel levels in Iraq have decreased from a peak of more than 160,000 to just fewer than 50,000, with the remaining forces focused primarily on training and advising Iraqi troops and providing logistics assistance to the Iraqi government. In Afghanistan, the United States and NATO have spent billions of dollars training Afghan security forces, increasing the size of the Afghan National Army (ANA) from 97,000 to 144,000 and the Afghan police from 95,000 to 116,000.[9] Increases in size, however, do not tell the whole story. Nearly 90 percent of the recruits brought into the Afghan security forces are illiterate, making training in even the most remedial tasks exceedingly difficult. Additionally, attrition rates are far above where they need to be if a trained and ready Afghan force is going to be able to defend the central government without depending on significant levels of international assistance.[10] The U.S. Government Accountability Office reported in early 2011 that as of the previous September, not a single Afghan National Army unit was assessed by U.S. trainers as capable of conducting independent operations. The same report said only two-thirds of ANA units were assessed as being effective with limited support from coalition forces.[11] Such reports contribute significantly to the concerns of those in the United States who are wary of U.S. host nation security force training efforts as a means for getting American troops out of Afghanistan.

American strategies in both Iraq and Afghanistan are wholly dependent on these struggling host nation security force training efforts. A failure to sufficiently train Iraqi and Afghan security forces makes total withdrawal from those countries nearly impossible without significant risk to the U.S.-

backed Iraqi and Afghan governments. Training host nation security forces to a degree of proficiency that allows adequate protection of the national government takes a long time and cannot be rushed, no matter how desperately the American public and its elected leaders want to hand over security responsibilities. Forcing the pace in developing host nation security forces can result in more damage over the long term than benefit in the short term. The training of Iraqi security forces has been ongoing for the better part of a decade and eventually will facilitate the full withdrawal of all American troops. In Afghanistan, the security force training project has only been in place a few years and still has a long way to go. At least one estimate projects the Afghan government will need around $6 billion each year for the foreseeable future in order to provide its police and military personnel with salaries, fuel, repair parts, uniforms, and equipment.[12] With an annual revenue stream of only $1 billion per year and expenditures of more than $3 billion per year without including the costs of maintaining competent and reliable security forces, the Afghan government will need large amounts of international aid for a long time to come.[13] The American public will expect U.S. allies and partner nations, especially those in Europe, to contribute a fair amount of the required aid.[14]

The United States government's reliance on a training strategy rife with seemingly insurmountable difficulties has prompted many to question the wisdom of continuing the host nation security force training efforts in both Afghanistan and Iraq. There can be no doubt, though, that the training of Afghan and Iraqi police and military personnel is absolutely essential if the governments of Afghanistan and Iraq are going to survive after American forces withdraw. Outside the two primary conflict theaters in which American troops are currently engaged, U.S. military forces will be called upon to train the host nation security forces of countries where the United States is not involved in kinetic operations, the purpose being to increase the capacity of other nations to deal with the extremist threat without relying on the presence or active involvement of U.S. combat forces. This type of security force training mission is typically undertaken by United States Special Forces and is currently under way in countries across the international system.

Security cooperation is another instrument of the military element of national power that can help U.S. allies and nations cooperating with the United States to better prepare for the threat posed by radical Islamists. Security cooperation activities are defined by the Department of Defense as interactions with foreign defense organizations designed to build defense relationships that advance U.S. interests, grow allied and friendly military capabilities for self-defense and multinational operations, and provide American military forces with peacetime and contingency access to a host nation.[15] Activities that fall under the heading of security cooperation generally include multinational military exercises, multinational training, military-to-military contacts like conferences, senior officer visits, port visits by naval vessels, staff talks, military exchange programs, counterpart visits, multinational military education, and nation assistance activities like foreign internal defense, weapons of mass destruction counterproliferation efforts, security assistance programs, and humanitarian and civic assistance activities.[16]

Employment of the military element of national power will at times require the armed forces of the United States to engage in direct combat operations against armed and hostile opponents. Some of the harshest criticism directed at the United States in the years since the September 11, 2001, attacks has been directed at the use of U.S. combat power in Afghanistan and Iraq. The presence of hundreds of thousands of American military troops in two Islamic nations has been characterized as severe and unnecessary by U.S. friends and foes alike. The United States will, despite calls from many nations and from some elements of the American public to withdraw, necessarily remain militarily engaged in at least some capacity in both Afghanistan and Iraq for many more years to come. U.S. military forces will also be introduced to other global hot spots that surface as new crises develop during this era of persistent conflict. Aside from direct combat operations, U.S. military forces could also find themselves engaged in peacekeeping or peace enforcement operations or in support of insurgent elements or counterinsurgent forces, depending upon the country where the insurgent activity is taking place and the relationship the United States has established with that country.

Special operations forces trained in irregular warfare will become increasingly important for critical missions like reconnaissance, advising the security forces of other nations, and the selective targeting of high-value terrorist targets. The military targeting of individuals is an extremely sensitive and controversial topic. Moral arguments aside, there are valid reasons why the United States should maintain as an option the targeted assassination of individual terrorist leaders. Targeted killing can be defined as the planned killing by a state of specific individuals who belong to irregular armed groups in conflict with the state.[17] Targeting specific persons forces key terrorist individuals to devote critical and limited resources to their own protection. Any amount of time and effort spent on individual survival is time and effort taken away from planning and conducting terrorist attacks against the United States and its allies. The successful targeting of key terrorist individuals also inflicts damage on extremist organizations by eliminating important leaders and disrupting the command and control of the organization's subordinate elements. Cutting off the head, so to speak, will not kill this particular Islamic extremist snake. But it will create chaos and confusion in the ranks and in the power structures of Islamic terrorist organizations who suffer the loss of key figures essential to the groups' overall effectiveness. The targeting of individuals can be accomplished through the dispatch of Special Forces "hit teams," precision aerial strikes facilitated by strong on-the-ground intelligence, or the employment of armed unmanned aerial vehicles like those used extensively along the Afghanistan-Pakistan border. The benefits of targeting specific high-value individuals are too great for such targeting to be excluded from the options available to U.S. policymakers seeking to provide some measure of security for American citizens in the global fight against Islamic extremism.

Other tools or instruments of the military element of national power that can be employed in the global effort to combat Muslim radicals include sanctions enforcement, security of the homeland, ballistic missile defense, and force projection. The international community has demonstrated time and again that it is incapable of coming together in support of really stringent economic sanctions directed at the world's worst security problems. Too often nations put their own financial interests ahead of what is best for the international community as a whole and sanctions regimes, in general, that make it through forums like the United Nations Security Council tend to be watered down to the point where they are essentially not worth the paper they are written on. Even those few sanctions resolutions that do have some teeth are often ignored by key states for financial reasons, diminishing or negating the effect of the sanctions entirely. Given these realities, it is likely the United States will increasingly use its military power to enforce sanctions regimes unilaterally or in coordination with the relatively few nations that have demonstrated a serious commitment to global security and stability. When it comes to the security of the American homeland, the military forces of the United States have a clearly limited support role. Homeland security missions can include combat air patrols over America's skies (as was done after the 9/11 attacks), maritime defense, border security, and disaster response. The primary emphasis when U.S. military forces are employed domestically is on support to civilian authorities and first responders at all levels of government. Ballistic missile defense, or BMD, can be used by the United States to protect itself and its allies from the growing missile threat from openly hostile states like Iran and North Korea and from nonstate actors like the Lebanese-based terrorist group Hezbollah that have a demonstrated surface-to-surface missile capability. Given Hezbollah's intimate ties with Iran and its proven ability to conduct operations outside of the Middle East, it is both logical and appropriate for U.S. government officials to be concerned with a potential missile threat from Hezbollah operatives in the not-too-distant future. Iran, the world's leading state sponsor of terrorism, is actively pursuing a long-range ballistic missile program that could one day soon threaten U.S. personnel and allied states throughout the Middle East and in Europe, especially if Iran develops the ability to equip those missiles with nuclear warheads. North Korea is a known proliferation threat for ballistic missile technology, and the possibility that North Korean missile know-how or even North Korean missiles could end up in the hands of a terrorist organization seeking to target the United States is a real and dangerous threat that must be included in U.S. security planning. Finally, an important component of the military element of national power is the ability of the United States to project its forces around the world, either in a show of force for deterrent purposes or as a means for quickly responding to crisis situations that may require immediate military action. The United States cannot exert much influence over areas or situations which it cannot reach with its military might. The ability to project American military forces around the world, whether on fixed bases of operation in other nation-states or on U.S. naval vessels in international or allied waters, allows the United States to demonstrate its commitment to global security, its support of allied and nonallied nations cooperating with U.S. efforts, and its willingness to deploy its powerful military assets worldwide to combat the threat posed by Islamic radicalism.

The military element of national power is a critical tool in the United States' fight against Muslim extremists seeking to inflict harm on America, its citizens, and its national interests across the international system. The first priority of the nation, given the threat demonstrated to America's citizens on September 11, 2001, is the neutralization of those states, groups, and individual actors posing an immediate and direct danger to the United States and its allied and partner nations. That means, in the near term at least, military power will be employed frequently and sometimes forcefully as far from America's shores as possible. Allowing the terrorists to strike first is not an option that is acceptable to either the American public or the U.S. government. Every effort must be made to eliminate the possibility of another 9/11-type mass-casualty-producing attack on the American homeland. This is no easy task, which is why, ideally, most of the fight against Islamic terrorism will occur at a significant distance from the continental United States, with diplomatic, economic, intelligence, information, and law enforcement activities working in conjunction with the military effort in the short term and eventually taking the lead in the long term.

7

The Economic Element of National Power

THE ECONOMIC ELEMENT OF NATIONAL POWER consists of the financial tools or resources available to the United States in its effort to influence the behavior of nation-states and nonstate actors within the international system. This element of power can be significantly affected by the economic health of the nation, which is critical to determining how frequently and how effectively the United States can employ its arsenal of economic resources. The financial tools that make up the economic element of power can be used to influence behavior by providing incentives or rewards for desirable policies and actions from other nation-states or nonstate actors, or by inflicting punishment for behaviors deemed undesirable by the United States and contrary to U.S. national interests. Common tools or instruments of the economic element used as incentives or to reward behavior favorable to the United States include measures like trade agreements and economic aid packages that foster investment, development, and the growth of markets. The most common punitive or coercive instrument of the economic element is the imposition of sanctions designed to restrict the targeted country or nonstate group from the benefits of engagement in the broader global economic system. The overall economic health of the United States has a direct impact on the ability of the federal government to employ the economic element of national power in pursuit of the country's national interests. An economically weak United States is less able to leverage tools like trade relationships, sanctions, humanitarian and economic development aid, and other measures than is a United States experiencing a steady, vibrant, and growing economy with a stable market and a low unemployment rate. The strength or weakness of the U.S. economy is determined by a number of factors, including the industrial capacity of the nation, the economic policies implemented by the federal government, the availability and supply of the nation's natural resources, the size and ability of the American labor pool, the overall level of technology in the labor market, the strength or weakness of the U.S. dollar, the inflation rate, and the level of gross national debt.

Constructive Financial Tools

Since its emergence as a global power with influence across the breadth of the international system, the United States has promoted worldwide prosperity and economic interdependence by working to increase free and open trade among all nations and by providing financial aid to countries struggling to develop their national economies. In 2008, international trade accounted for more than 30 percent of the United States' gross domestic product (GDP), and more than fifty million Americans were employed by companies engaged in international trade.[1] Free and open trade helps the United States in its battle with Islamic radicalism by improving the overall quality of life for people around the world through the reduction of trade barriers, which leads to more open markets, more consumer choice, and lower prices for goods and services. Improving the economic quality of life in developing and struggling nations can reduce or eliminate entirely the dire conditions that can contribute to population support for Muslim extremist ideology. It has been estimated that the successful reduction of barriers to international trade could potentially lift almost a half-billion people out of poverty worldwide over the course of a decade.[2] Improving the quality of life in the developing world through international commerce helps to enhance the national security of the United States by reducing the number of potential terrorist breeding grounds available to Islamic extremists who like to claim the economic misfortunes of many non-Western states are a direct result of economic exploitation by the United States and its allies and partner nations. Free and open trade among the countries of the international system fosters national economic development and reduces the likelihood a country will become a failed state susceptible to dominance and manipulation by Islamic radicals who prey on the poor and disenfranchised seeking security and prosperity for themselves and their families.

There are three basic points of view when it comes to the disbursement of U.S. economic development aid. The first viewpoint essentially believes the United States uses foreign aid as a form of bribery that seeks to gain global support for U.S. actions in the international system and increase the popularity of the United States abroad. The second view holds that the United States provides economic aid to other countries as a charitable deed. In other words, the U.S. government, on behalf of American taxpayers, is sending money overseas out of the goodness of American hearts simply to help those who are less fortunate. Finally, the third viewpoint sees U.S. foreign aid as a strategic investment designed to increase the capacity of countries in the international system that have interests aligned with or similar to those of the United States.[3] Each of the three points of view has some degree of validity to it. The United States does use foreign aid as a means for improving its image and gaining foreign support. Foreign aid disbursements are well publicized, and the U.S. government makes it clear to those receiving the aid and to others in the international system where the aid is coming from. The United States also disburses foreign aid as a form of charity. Americans know their quality of life is far higher than that of the majority of the international system, and they generally expect their government to act on their behalf to help those who are less fortunate around the world. The most critical use of foreign aid, though, is as a strategic investment designed to increase the governance capacity of nations across the international system. The more capable other nation-states are in providing for the safety, security and prosperity of their populations, the less likely it is the United States will have to intervene militarily at some point to stop an Islamic extremist threat nurtured by desperate populations living in dismal economic conditions in a state that is failing or has already failed.

The disbursement of U.S. economic development aid to poor and struggling countries, like the promotion of free and open trade, improves the overall quality of life for the people of the nations receiving the aid and reduces ill will directed at the United States. Any comprehensive U.S. grand strategy for combating Islamic extremists must include economic policies that help poor countries grow and develop their economies, thereby increasing their ability to successfully participate in the global marketplace and reap the benefits of globalization and global economic interconnectedness. Economic development aid helps to counter repression and ultimately facilitates the development of societies less likely to provide support for radical Islamists seeking disenfranchised and despondent individuals to join their cause. Assisting other countries with their economic development reinforces the United States' diplomatic efforts in places susceptible to Islamic extremism, counters the extremists' message with tangible counterpoints that improve people's lives, and reduces the likelihood the United States will have to employ its armed forces in countries struggling politically, economically, and socially. Economic development aid can be directed at specific programs and areas of the targeted economy that will reduce any potential appeal Islamic radicals might have.[4] Specific focus areas could include support for free and fair elections, the promotion of economic freedom, investment in a country's people through education and health services, the impartial administration of law, the promotion of human rights, support for free media, tolerance for different religious faiths, and police and military units that do not engage in human rights abuses against the populations they are supposed to protect with fairness and impartiality.

While economic development aid is an important component of the overall American effort to combat Islamic extremism in destitute and developing countries, it is important to note that economic aid alone may be an insufficient remedy in nation-states with conditions already ripe for exploitation by Muslim radicals.[5] Aid to these countries will need to be accompanied by competent and effective government institutions that act responsibly and are accountable to the people of the nation. Otherwise, all the money in the world may not keep the Islamists from taking advantage of struggling societies with weak or corrupt governments that have the potential to become safe havens for those who subscribe to radical Islamist ideology. Opponents of the disbursement of U.S. foreign aid often cite the existence of poor governance capacity as a reason for keeping American tax dollars from flowing overseas, adding there is no direct correlation between developmental aid and a nation's economic growth, aid sent to a poor policy environment does not work and compounds a nation's economic troubles by contributing to already problematic debt, and even aid conditioned on specific market reforms has a dismal history of failure.[6] In other words, if the conditions for economic growth are not already present in a country targeted for U.S. economic development aid, then no amount of aid will make an appreciable difference in the country's economic growth and development. The track record of such aid is an important consideration for those charged with being good stewards of America's taxpayer-provided dollars. But even if the net effect of economic development aid on growth and future prosperity is in dispute, the provision of such aid by the United States has the potential for an always desirable benefit in that it is likely to bolster the image of the American people and their government with foreign populations. Improving America's image across the international system ultimately reduces the level of animosity directed at the United States and lessens the likelihood of popular support for an attack on the U.S. homeland or U.S. and allied interests abroad.

Economic Sanctions

When thinking about the punitive economic tools available to the United States for use against state and nonstate actors, the most common measure or instrument that comes to mind is the imposition of an economic sanctions regime. Economic sanctions are coercive but nonviolent measures one country or a coalition of countries can use against another country or nonstate actor to inflict some measure of economic pain designed to force a change in behavior by the targeted actor. Sanctions can be country based or they can be list based. List-based sanctions typically target specific individuals instead of sovereign nations. The United States uses economic sanctions primarily against countries engaging in behaviors that run counter to U.S. goals and objectives in the international arena, although a recent trend in sanctions imposition is toward list-based regimes because of the difficulties inherent in securing effective multilateral sanctions against nation-states that are increasingly economically interdependent within the global system. When it comes to Islamic terrorist activity, the United States pursues economic sanctions against states that practice terrorism as a matter of national policy and against countries that provide both direct and indirect support to terrorists without such support constituting official state policy.

Economic sanctions can generally be grouped into six categories: restrictions on trade, limits on technology transfers, the withholding of foreign economic assistance, the suspension or denial of export credits and guarantees, restrictions on foreign exchange and capital transactions, and restrictions on economic access.[7] Specific actions that can be taken by the United States include the freezing of individual or state assets, the adoption of embargoes or boycotts, the imposition of quotas, tariffs, or export controls, the suspension of foreign economic or development aid, and restrictions on air or ship traffic. Blocked or frozen assets can be used for leverage during negotiations with states supporting terrorism, and embargoes or boycotts can serve as a force to disrupt terrorist operations like the smuggling of weapons and other equipment necessary for the execution of violent terrorist acts. Quotas, tariffs, export controls, and restrictions on airborne and maritime vessels can make it more difficult for terrorism-sponsoring nations to conduct business in the international marketplace, and the withholding of foreign aid can put pressure on governments sponsoring terrorism or providing passive support to terrorists to change the specific behaviors the United States finds objectionable.

Economic sanctions generally have the most effect when they are imposed multilaterally, with a majority of the international community participating in sanctions enforcement, rather than by a single country or even a small number of countries uniting to impose a sanctions regime. Recent years have shown that it is extremely difficult for the United States to get other nations on board with the imposition of tough sanctions for destructive behavior by either states or nonstate actors. In a world made increasingly interdependent by the forces of globalization, it is not an easy feat to convince states to take an action that will have a negative financial impact on their treasuries. Even when a sizable number of states do agree to adopt an economic sanctions regime, the actual measures agreed upon are generally weak and more for the sake of appearance than for actually convincing the targeted state to change its undesirable behavior. Perhaps the best example of the difficulty often experienced in trying to secure multilateral sanctions can once again be found in the case of Iran's suspected nuclear weapons program. The United States and its European allies have been trying for years within the confines of the United Nations Security Council to impose meaningful sanctions on Iran in order to force the government in Tehran to comply with international demands to stop the enrichment of uranium and open fully Iran's nuclear facilities to inspectors from the Vienna-based International Atomic Energy Agency, the UN's nuclear watchdog. At every turn, stringent measures that might have a real and lasting effect on Iran have been blocked by both China and Russia, two nations with significant financial interests in Iran that would suffer economically under a meaningful multilateral sanctions regime. Instead of joining in the effort with the United States and the European Union to curb Iran's nuclear ambitions, China and Russia have repeatedly forced the most restrictive proposals to be abandoned in favor of weak measures that have thus far had little to no impact on the Iranian government, its policies, or its defiance of the international community and the United Nations Security Council. Even those few sanctions measures that have been imposed on Iran have been ignored and subverted by key state and nonstate actors with deep financial ties to Iran's economy.

The imposition of economic sanctions results in costs to both the country or countries imposing the sanctions and the country or countries targeted by the sanctions. The costs incurred can include economic losses for the imposing party, disputes with other nations over the use and severity of sanctions, and the creation of hardships for the citizens of the targeted country, because it is the ordinary people and not the targeted government that generally feels the impact of economic sanctions regimes most severely. A number of governments from Havana to Khartoum and from Tehran to Pyongyang have demonstrated time and again that they are able to insulate themselves and their security forces from the impact of financial measures taken against them, especially when those measures are weak and only halfheartedly enforced by countries with a financial stake in avoiding stringent sanctions. There are three general limitations when it comes to the use of economic sanctions designed to reduce state support for terrorism. First, in many instances, it is not clear what standards the targeted state is supposed to meet or whether standards that might already be in place have been met to a degree sufficient to satisfy the party imposing the sanctions. Second, economic sanctions have historically demonstrated limited utility in reducing the capability of a targeted state actor to provide support for terrorists and the violent acts they commit. Finally, as already mentioned, it is often a difficult task to get other nations to go along with an economic sanctions regime, in part because the U.S. policy of automatically imposing sanctions on countries listed as state sponsors of terrorism is not consistent with the policies of most other nations in the international system, and in part because countries are increasingly interconnected and interdependent as a result of the forces of globalization.[8]

The use of economic sanctions as a tool for reducing terrorist activity and state support for terrorism has limited overall practical value. The potential for changing state behavior certainly exists, but generally that potential is realized only when dealing with states that are economically weak and when attempting to change behavior concerning policy matters of relatively minor national importance to the targeted state. When a state's vital national interests are on the line, it is unlikely economic sanctions will force a reconsideration of national policy by the targeted state, especially when there is seldom a shortage of nations willing to bypass any sanctions regime that might be imposed. Vital national interests are nonnegotiable, and targeted states will take all measures within their power to defend them. Dependence on foreign trade, national economic strength, the level of international support, and the importance of the targeted behavior all play a part in determining the effect economic sanctions will have on a targeted country. Ultimately, economic sanctions have the potential to increase the financial, diplomatic, and domestic political costs a government must absorb if it wants to continue an objectionable behavior. There is no guarantee, though, and indeed it is extremely unlikely, that the behavior in question will be changed. So why do some nations choose to impose economic sanctions on other countries, knowing that historically such measures fail to achieve the desired results? The unfortunate reality is that economic sanctions allow the imposing country or countries to *appear* to be taking decisive action without actually *doing* anything of substance. If economic sanctions are in progress or if economic sanctions are being considered by a group of nations in response to some objectionable behavior, an argument can always be made that more time is needed before considering more severe measures like the use of military force.

While sanctions are generally used to target states that directly or indirectly support terrorist activities, punitive economic measures can be and often are taken against nonstate actor extremist individuals and organizations. Executive Order 13224 allows the United States government to block the assets of individuals and groups that either commit terrorist acts or pose a significant risk of committing terrorist acts.[9] The effectiveness of such measures, though, is degraded by the complex nature of the financial networks used by terrorist groups to secure funding for their campaigns of violence. Islamic terrorist organizations fund their terror operations through unofficial banking mechanisms (the *hawala* system), support from host populations and foreign donors, state sponsors, illegal activities like theft crimes, kidnappings for ransom and drug trafficking, legitimate front companies (used fairly extensively by Osama bin Laden to finance al Qaeda's terrorist operations), and support from various charities and nongovernmental organizations. Additionally, some Islamic terrorist groups conduct fund-raising activities during religious pilgrimages to the Muslim holy city of Mecca in Saudi Arabia.[10] Cutting off all funding for Islamic terrorists is virtually impossible, given the large number of sources from which such funding is derived. Still, the reduction of funding for terrorist operations by any amount, no matter how insignificant it may seem, reduces the ability of extremists to execute attacks against the United States, its people, and its global interests. The bottom line when it comes to the use of economic sanctions against either state or nonstate actors is simply this: the goals or objectives of any sanctions regime must be realistic, focused, and limited; the sanctions employed must be applied fully from the beginning rather than being implemented incrementally over time; and, finally, the support of as many nations as possible from across the international system must be secured if the sanctions are going to be effectively enforced.

The Economic Health of the United States

The role the United States plays in the contemporary international system is critical to global security and worldwide economic growth and development. It is reasonable to think a majority of the nations that make up the international community expect the United States, as the world's lone superpower, to take a proactive and responsible leadership role in the international effort to combat Islamic terrorism. In order to fulfill that leadership role effectively, it is imperative that the United States has a strong economy that facilitates the employment of all the elements of national power, especially the economic element of power. A strong economy allows the United States to provide economic development and humanitarian aid that undermine the ability of Islamic extremists to exploit potential terrorist breeding grounds, and it facilitates the ability of the United States to impose economic sanctions on those states that provide material or other support to radical terrorist organizations. A vibrant American economy also provides the budget resources necessary for maintaining and employing what is currently the strongest, most competent, and most technologically advanced military force the world has ever seen. That military force, whether employed in the form of small, specialized teams conducting targeted missions or large battle formations conducting decisive conventional combat operations, is absolutely critical in the global fight against Islamic extremists. Its success and effectiveness are largely dependent upon the ability of the United States government to provide it with sufficient levels of funding for research and development, acquisition of materiel, training, and the execution of critical operational missions.

Conversely, a weak U.S. economy diminishes the ability of the federal government to provide assistance to other nations in need and to weather the domestic effects of lost financial opportunities that result from the imposition of economic sanctions against countries acting in ways contrary to the national interests of the United States. A weak U.S. economy diverts away from the dangers of Islamic radicalism the attention of both American citizens and their political leaders, who understandably choose to focus less on external threats to the country and more on pressing domestic matters during times of economic difficulty. It is extremely tough to get anyone to concentrate on anything but the economic health of the country when individuals are concerned about their ability to pay their mortgages or provide food and other essentials for their families. Finally, a weak economy in the United States limits the pool of financial resources available to the government to fund critical defense budget priorities that are regularly employed in the fight against Islamic terrorists. Perhaps the most worrisome aspect of reduced defense budgets is the potential impact on military investment in future war-fighting capabilities. Long-term investment in military and defense capabilities is a critical budget item that must be sufficiently funded in order to ensure the continued supremacy of the United States' armed forces, both in the current fight against Muslim radicals who have targeted and will continue to target the U.S. homeland and American interests abroad, and for the future conventional and irregular conflicts that will inevitably occur with little or no time to prepare for them. A world-class military force cannot be maintained on the cheap.

Equipment and weapons platforms are two of the most significant expenditures in the military budget, and both are largely dictated by the type of force the United States wishes to field. Given the wide range of potential scenarios in which U.S. military forces could be employed, questions concerning the structure of the American military have understandably arisen. Some within the defense establishment have argued American military forces should be structured in a manner that best enables them to deal with the types of asymmetric threats encountered by U.S. troops in Afghanistan and Iraq. This group generally believes the days of traditional force-on-force conflict between massed armies are a relic of the past and the future of warfare lies in the failed and failing states and ungoverned or undergoverned areas where transnational terrorists seek safe haven. Others believe the current asymmetric conflicts that are stressing America's armed forces are important and will continue, but should not drive the long-term focus of the Department of Defense. This group believes the best course of action is a return to planning for large-scale traditional wars between nation-states with an emphasis on the conventional combat capabilities of America's armed forces. Such a focus would, they argue, allow America's military establishment to be fully prepared for the challenge of a resurgent Russia or a globally focused China if either chooses to act in a way that requires a military response from the United States.

Not surprisingly, the focus of the American military right now is on the irregular threat posed by small groups of terrorists using guerrilla tactics to negate the overwhelming conventional advantage enjoyed by U.S. military forces. This is the immediate challenge, one that is currently being dealt with by American military troops in Afghanistan and Iraq and in less visible areas of conflict where U.S. advisers and Special Forces trainers are providing assistance to host nation governments battling Islamic radicals within their borders. But the conventional threat to the United States has not disappeared. China and Russia continue to expend great sums of money on the modernization of their armed forces, and both are working feverishly to close the military capability gap with the United States. The potential for conventional state-on-state conflict in the not-too-distant future cannot be discounted outright and as such must be planned, trained, and budgeted for in order to reduce the level of long-term risk to the country. These competing priorities demand a balanced and flexible military force capable of confronting both conventional and asymmetric threats in the contemporary international security environment. Such a force cannot be had without significant investment in current and future military resources.[11] There is a danger, though, in attempting to achieve this type of balanced force. A military designed to counter multiple types of threats risks being a jack-of-all-trades but a master of none, to use an old saying. It is impossible for America's armed forces to train on every potential combat task to a degree that would ensure a satisfactory level of mastery. The likely outcome of a balanced general-purpose force is that the United States would have a competent and effective military able to execute a wide variety of tasks across the spectrum of potential conflict but that would not be as dominant as if it specialized in a specific type of warfare.

The wars in Afghanistan and Iraq have stressed the military forces of the United States, in terms of both personnel and equipment, almost to the breaking point. If America's armed forces are going to one day regain the level of personnel and equipment readiness that existed prior to the commencement of the Bush administration's "Global War on Terrorism," high levels of funding will be required for many years, probably decades, into the future. Equipment worn, damaged, or destroyed during combat operations in harsh desert and mountain environments will need to be repaired, refurbished, or replaced. In addition, funding for advanced weapons platforms designed for conventional force-on-force conflict in future armed engagements will still be necessary because the United States will have to possess the resources required to face conventional foes like China and Russia if a security situation involving one or both of those countries develops unexpectedly. Researching, buying, testing, and fielding of equipment and weapons require significant levels of monetary investment. The current level of military funding, about 4 percent of the nation's gross domestic product, is insufficient to meet the demands of the contemporary international security environment while simultaneously reconstituting the armed forces after nearly a decade of war and preparing for potential future contingency operations.

In 1965, in the middle of the U.S.-Soviet Cold War, defense spending as a percentage of the nation's gross domestic product (GDP) was just under 8 percent. In 1975, at the end of the United States' involvement in the Vietnam conflict, defense spending had dropped to slightly below 6 percent of GDP. By 2001, just before al Qaeda's 9/11 terrorist attacks on the American homeland, defense spending as a percentage of GDP had decreased to a paltry 3 percent, a sum reflective of the "peace dividend" the United States was experiencing since the end of the Cold War. In 2009, with hundreds of thousands of U.S. troops deployed around the world, many engaged in hostile action in Iraq and Afghanistan, defense spending as a percentage of GDP was only about 4 percent.[12] To maintain the worldwide qualitative advantage currently enjoyed by U.S. military forces, defense funding levels will have to be increased to percentages of GDP seen in previous periods of armed conflict. It takes considerable financial resources to maintain the world's best military force and to ensure that force is prepared to defend the nation against the threats it currently faces and the threats it cannot yet anticipate or fully prepare itself for. The financial investment in the United States' military capability must be robust and sustained over time if American troops are going to continue to get the best support and equipment available for the missions they are assigned to carry out and if the United States is going to continue to militarily come to the aid of allies and partners who find themselves in need of U.S. military assistance. If the United States intends to maintain its military superiority, it will have to find the economic resources for long-term, significant military investment with a funding level somewhere between 6 and 8 percent of GDP. Those financial resources will only be available if the United States is experiencing a healthy and robust economy that facilitates the full employment of U.S. economic power.

Some Final Thoughts

The United States has far and away the world's largest and strongest national economy with a GDP for the years 2008 and 2009 of about $14 trillion per year, easily surpassing the national economies of all other nations in the international system. Second and third behind the United States in terms of size of national economic activity are China and Japan, with gross domestic products of just over $4 trillion each.[13] The size and strength of the economy in the United States give policymakers and decision makers in Washington a significant amount of flexibility when it comes to the employment of economic tools or instruments designed to change the behavior of other states or non-state actors deemed detrimental to U.S. interests worldwide. Humanitarian and economic development aid foster international goodwill and bolster the image of the United States and its people abroad while improving the quality of life of other populations and helping to address the economic conditions that lead individuals and societies to support terrorist groups and their acts of extreme violence. Free and open trade with other states can be a powerful weapon against Islamic extremism, providing developing countries the opportunity to participate in an increasingly globalized and interconnected international economy and paving the way for a better quality of life in those nations not as economically privileged as the United States and many of its Western allies.

In seeking to use its economic power in a positive and productive manner in the international system, the United States should actively work to secure free trade agreements with as many nations as possible while focusing its economic development aid efforts on those fragile developing countries that demonstrate sound governmental practices, including the just application of law and respect for basic human rights. Hard choices will have to be made about which countries get American aid and which do not because there are simply not enough financial resources in the American treasury to satisfy the needs of the many nations seeking U.S. economic assistance. The selective use of economic aid is an absolute must. When considering the use of punitive economic measures, the United States would do well to remember that previous attempts, even when those attempts were ostensibly multilateral, have met with less-than-stellar results in most cases. For economic sanctions to be even marginally effective, the targeted country has to consider the behavior that brought on the sanctions to be of relatively minor importance to its national interests. Otherwise, no degree of economic sanction will have much effect. No nation, including the United States, compromises on its vital national interests—that's why they are referred to as vital. They are nonnegotiable. Another factor that impacts the effect of economic sanctions is the state of the economy in the targeted country. For sanctions to have any real and lasting effect, the economy of the targeted nation has to be relatively weak and susceptible to pressure from the sanctions being imposed. A nation with a strong and healthy economy will be able to withstand most economic sanctions that come its way. Finally, any attempt to impose a sanctions regime has to have broad international support or the targeted nation will simply bypass the country or countries imposing the sanctions in favor of trade with those states that choose to ignore the sanctions regime. For a good example, consider the case of American neighbor Cuba. Put in place in the early 1960s and subsequently codified into U.S. law, sanctions against Cuba are largely meaningless because they are regularly ignored by most of the nations of the international community. U.S. economic sanctions against Cuba have not only failed to achieve their goals, they have provided the Cuban government with a scapegoat that can be used as an excuse for Cuba's economic troubles. Only in cases of severe and deliberate aggression by a state can it be reasonably expected that most of the international system's key powers will sign on for any tough economic sanctions regime. For minor transgressions or behavior that threatens an isolated few states, self-interest in a globally interdependent economy is almost always going to win out over multilateral action that might financially impact states imposing sanctions regimes.

The economic element of national power is a critically important component of any U.S. grand strategy designed to combat the threat posed by Islamic terrorism, and a strong and healthy American economy is absolutely vital to the success of any economic measures undertaken by the United States. Current economic conditions at home and abroad, as well as rising U.S. gross national debt, limit overall American economic effectiveness in the contemporary international security environment. The economic future of the United States is likely to continue to be characterized by chronic budget

8

The Intelligence and Law Enforcement Elements of National Power

---

Discussions of the elements of national power often revolve around the four primary elements detailed in the preceding chapters: diplomatic, information, military, and economic. These elements are described here as primary elements because they are generally the most visible types of power employed by the United States, both in dealing with other nation-states and in dealing with nonstate actors like terrorists and the organizations to which they belong. Diplomatic overtures, information campaigns and outreach programs, kinetic and nonkinetic military operations, and positive and negative economic measures get a significant amount of attention in both domestic and foreign media because they can be exciting and because the results can usually be seen very quickly after the tools of those elements are employed against an international actor at the state or nonstate level. But there are also other, less sensational and less visible but equally important ways in which the United States and its allies can work to minimize the threat from transnational Islamic extremism. Two additional critical but low-key elements of national power can be added to the primary elements that make up the DIME acronym: intelligence operations and law enforcement measures. Finance is sometimes included in the list of elements of national power as well, expanding the acronym to DIMEFIL. This text, though, makes no distinction between economic and financial resources available to the United States in this era of persistent conflict.

Intelligence: Roles and Functions

Intelligence information about individuals, groups, or nations targeting the United States is one of the most valuable tools available to American policy-makers responsible for executing the national-level actions necessary for the safety of U.S. citizens during the fight against Islamic terrorism. It is important not only because it provides valuable data that may lead to the prevention of terrorist attacks or to the apprehension of individuals responsible for the planning or execution of terrorist attacks, but also because the other elements of national power depend on it to varying degrees for their success. When engaging in diplomatic efforts with states or nonstate actors, it is far easier to negotiate from a position strengthened by detailed and accurate knowledge of one's adversary than it is to negotiate with an inaccurate or incomplete understanding of the situation at hand. Public diplomacy and other information programs designed to win support at home and abroad require facts that are consistent with a wide array of cultural values and popular opinion. Military operations, too, are heavily dependent upon accurate and timely intelligence data for their success, and financial measures like sanctions and foreign aid for economic development require knowledge of the targeted entity's strengths, weaknesses, challenges, needs, and wants.

Obtaining actionable intelligence information that is both timely and accurate can be considered America's first line of defense in the fight against Islamic radicalism. Detailed data about the United States' enemies can be obtained in a variety of ways, including the collection of freely available open-source material, human intelligence gathering, signals intelligence, and imagery intelligence. Once collected, this data must be shared unreservedly among the various agencies and departments of the federal government responsible for intelligence analysis and dissemination to U.S. and allied government agencies and organizations, a necessity made disturbingly clear by the 9/11 al Qaeda attacks. Important intelligence information can also come from America's allies and partner nations through the sharing of gathered intelligence at all levels of government. Many countries have national interests that align with those of the United States, and even those that do not generally share U.S. national interests have a stake in fighting Islamic extremism. The threat from Muslim terrorists is not focused on just one or even a few nation-states. It is not targeted at just the United States, the West, or secular regimes in the Middle East. It is a global threat that knows no boundaries and as such requires the cooperation of all states in the international system, even those not currently threatened or those that do not anticipate being threatened by Islamic radicals in the near future. It is precisely because the threat is transnational in nature that the United States must work to cultivate broad intelligence networks which span the international landscape so that threats can be discovered and negated before they are able to inflict harm on the U.S. homeland or on U.S. interests abroad. The United States, as a global power with vital and important interests across the international system, must have the ability to monitor developing situations around the world if it is going to be able to adequately protect American citizens and U.S. interests from the dangers of Islamic extremism.

It is important to note that intelligence operations are very complex. Success in any intelligence endeavor is far from assured, largely because the collection and analysis of intelligence data is an inexact science. Accurate predictions about possible future events are particularly difficult to make, and the establishment of strong intelligence networks with trained and experienced analysts takes many years to accomplish. Even more difficult is the development of a strong workforce of human intelligence collectors with access to those personnel and organizations of most interest to the United States and its allies. Terrorist groups are, by their very nature, relatively small in size and dispersed in local and regional cells around the world, with few individuals possessing the type of actionable information that would allow the United States to stop future terrorist attacks before they happen. Those critical few individuals also tend to be the hardest of the hard core, the worst of a very bad lot of terrorist actors who see violence as the single best way to achieve their political and social objectives. The bottom line is that extremist individuals with the intelligence information most valuable to the United States are the ones least likely to give up that information. Understanding this reality, Western governments have undertaken efforts to establish human intelligence networks inside Islamic terrorist groups through the infiltration of individuals willing to provide valuable intelligence information to the United States and its allies. The infiltration of Muslim extremist groups is an extremely dangerous and difficult task, but the potential rewards of successful infiltration are significant enough to make the effort worth the risk. Infiltration cannot be done by just anyone. For a Western operative to be able to gain access to those terrorist players who would possess actionable intelligence information, that operative would have to be capable of blending in with local populations in appearance, language dialect, mannerisms, and cultural norms. It would be impossible for the average American or European citizen to gain access to al Qaeda or its franchises and affiliates, a reality that has led Western intelligence agencies to expand their hiring pools in order to attract recruits from ethnic groups outside of traditional focus areas.[1]

The most serious problem facing the intelligence community today is that many in the American public and in the United States government have no faith in its ability to collect, analyze, and disseminate timely and accurate intelligence data upon which the United States can act to thwart planned terrorist attacks. The fiasco involving intelligence information on Iraq's possession of weapons of mass destruction inflicted long-term damage to the intelligence community's reputation. That reputation has not fared any better in recent years as intelligence failures like the missed indicators pointing to the Christmas Day bomber, Umar Farouk Abdulmutallab, continue to surface. The process of collecting, analyzing, and disseminating timely and accurate intelligence information is a difficult undertaking that is hindered by significant bureaucratic challenges within governments across the international system. That does not mean it shouldn't be a priority for those charged with leading the United States and protecting American citizens from potential terrorist strikes. To the contrary, it should be the highest priority because sound, actionable intelligence can not only save American and allied lives if future terrorist attacks are thwarted, it can strengthen the other elements of national power while weakening the operational effectiveness of Islamic extremist organizations seeking to do harm to the United States and other nations. Even if U.S. intelligence collection and analysis operations do not provide accurate and actionable information that can be used to stop future terrorist attacks, any data made available to senior policymakers and decision makers in the federal government and allied and partner nation officials abroad still increases overall situational awareness and understanding of a very complex international security environment that produces constant threats to global peace and stability. Dozens of terrorist attacks against the United States and its allies have been thwarted since the 9/11 strikes in New York and Washington, D.C. Not one of those attacks would have been stopped without timely and accurate intelligence about the whereabouts and intentions of the would-be perpetrators. Continued investment in the intelligence community's ability to collect, analyze, and disseminate useful intelligence information will be essential if the future attacks that are undoubtedly being planned by Islamic radicals across the international system are going to be stopped before they can bring their death and destruction to the American homeland once again.

Law Enforcement Efforts and Detainee Operations

There is a strong sentiment among some in the United States and abroad, particularly in European nations, that the threat posed by Islamic radicalism is a matter best dealt with primarily through the work of law enforcement professionals with some assistance from diplomatic and intelligence personnel. Others feel the United States is at war with Islamic radicals who have to be confronted with the overwhelming military power of America's armed forces. Of course, the choice is not so clear cut, and those who focus on either of these two elements as the lead effort ignore the roles played in grand strategy by the other elements of national power. Law enforcement is certainly an essential component of the global fight against Islamic extremists who target innocent civilians in support of their political goals, but there are several problems inherent in an approach centered on law enforcement.

To begin, law enforcement is relatively ineffective as a primary anti- or counterterrorism tool in the contemporary global security environment because it is mostly punitive in nature and does not adequately address the prevention of future terrorist attacks. Prosecuting a terrorist and putting him in prison takes him off of the global battlefield, to be sure, but those individuals most likely to be caught and detained are the low-level operatives who execute terrorist plots and not the more senior individuals serving in key leadership and facilitator positions within extremist groups. The most important terrorist figures, those filling organizational roles that involve planning, resourcing (including funding), and the provision of operational or spiritual guidance are the individuals least likely to be arrested and prosecuted. Think also for a moment about the most extreme of the Muslim radicals, the suicide bombers who willingly sacrifice themselves in attacks carried out against both military and civilian targets. Does any rational person truly believe these aspiring martyrs will be deterred by law enforcement efforts that imprison other terrorists? These extremist individuals are not intimidated by the prospect of going to prison, even for life. It is because they *want* to sacrifice themselves in the name of their religion that they are impossible to deter.

Second, labeling terrorism as a criminal matter best left to law enforcement techniques essentially limits the ability of those personnel who are trying to protect American citizens and interests to the tools traditionally employed by law enforcement agencies. If law enforcement efforts are the priority, the other elements of national power, and especially the military element of power, will necessarily be relegated to supporting roles. Such secondary efforts typically receive fewer and sometimes inadequate resources for the missions they are tasked to accomplish. Diplomacy will still be important, to a degree, in the negotiation of agreements of cooperation or extradition with the law enforcement agencies of other nations, but the other elements of U.S. national power will be less effectively employed than if law enforcement resources were used to *complement* the primary elements of power rather than *be* the primary element of power. Limiting the options available to individuals charged with protecting the United States and its citizens unnecessarily hinders the application of the full range of U.S. national power in combating a complex and adaptive transnational threat that does not respect the just administration of law.

Finally, there are issues with the proper collection of evidence and chains of custody for the evidence that would be used to prosecute those accused of plotting or carrying out terrorist attacks. Evidence collection and chains of custody are regular features of domestic law enforcement cases, including some involving suspected or actual terrorist activity. The problem in the contemporary global security environment is that the majority of the actions taken by the United States against Islamic terrorists are not conducted on U.S. soil against American citizens, but against foreign nationals operating in lawless places overseas where traditional law enforcement agencies do not have a strong presence. In combat zones, like Iraq and Afghanistan, and in other places, like the Pakistan side of the Afghanistan-Pakistan border, Yemen, and Somalia, it is unrealistic to expect the collection and preservation of evidence, particularly by soldiers engaged with enemy forces on the battlefield, that may ultimately be used in a U.S. court of law.

Despite the problems associated with attempts to use law enforcement techniques as a primary effort in the campaign against violent extremism, there are valuable contributions that law enforcement can make when specific situations could require traditional police-type functions, such as when terrorist activity or suspected terrorist activity takes place on U.S. soil or when the suspected perpetrators are American citizens. Each case that presents itself has to be examined individually to determine the right path to take. Law enforcement contributions to the fight against Islamic radicalism can include the disruption of planned attacks through the arrest of terrorist suspects, the incapacitation of individual terrorists through the incarceration of those persons successfully prosecuted in legal proceedings, and the gathering of intelligence information during postdetention interrogations of terrorist suspects.[2] A careful distinction needs to be made, though, between traditional criminality and armed conflict. The two are not the same, even though the line between them may at times be blurred. Separate laws and separate procedures must be established and followed to effectively deal with instances of terrorist activity that may occur in the United States or in other countries in the international system.

Terrorist suspects picked up in the course of normal law enforcement operations can and generally should be prosecuted through American civilian criminal courts if the apprehended individuals are legal citizens of the United States. Foreign terrorists apprehended within the borders of the United States or abroad, though, in places like Iraq, Afghanistan, the Philippines, and anywhere else the fight against Islamic extremism might occur, should not be afforded the same protections as those provided to American citizens by the U.S. Constitution. Giving foreign terrorists constitutional rights and providing them with access to U.S. courts will not do anything to keep Americans safe. In fact, the granting of such rights and access could make Americans even less safe by compromising critical intelligence methods, endangering intelligence sources, or tipping off suspected terrorists through the presentation of sensitive evidence in open court proceedings. A basis for this fear can be found in the civilian trial of the 1993 World Trade Center bombers, when prosecuting attorneys were required to provide the defense's legal team with information on unindicted co-conspirators, including Osama bin Laden. Former attorney general of the United States Michael Mukasey, who presided over that trial, wrote that in just barely over a week, a copy of the list of alleged co-conspirators provided to defense attorneys made its way to bin Laden in Sudan, letting him know his connection to the case had been discovered and that he was subsequently under the watchful eye of the United States government.[3]

In wars of the past, foreign armed combatants were usually associated with states that had organized military forces carrying weapons in the open and wearing easily identifiable uniforms and insignia. In the post-9/11 international security environment, that is no longer the case. Islamic terrorists who do not conform to the traditional customs of war should not be treated as mere criminals or even as lawful combatants covered by the Geneva Conventions. Instead, they should be classified as unlawful enemy combatants subject to unique rules specially designed for the current threat environment. In fact, the language of international law specifically covers situations involving the treatment of individuals like the Islamic extremists threatening the United States and its allies and partner nations today. Dr. George Friedman, a former political science academic who founded the private geopolitical intelligence and forecasting firm Strategic Forecasting (STRATFOR), has written:

> The Geneva Conventions do not apply to them because they have not adhered to a fundamental requirement of the Geneva Conventions, namely, identifying themselves as soldiers of an army. Doing so does not mean they must wear a uniform. The postwar Geneva Conventions make room for partisans, something older versions of the conventions did not. A partisan is not a uniformed fighter, but he must wear some form of insignia identifying himself as a soldier to enjoy the conventions' protections. As Article 4.1.6 puts it, prisoners of war include "Inhabitants of a non-occupied territory, who on the approach of the enemy spontaneously take up arms to resist the invading forces, without having had time to form themselves into regular armed units, provided they carry arms openly and respect the laws and customs of war." The Geneva Conventions of 1949 does not mention, nor provide protection to, civilians attacking foreign

countries without openly carrying arms. The reasoning behind this is important. During the Franco-Prussian War, French franc-trieurs fired on Prussian soldiers. Ununiformed and without insignia, they melded into the crowd. It was impossible for the Prussians to distinguish between civilians and soldiers, so they fired on both, and civilian casualties resulted. The framers of the Geneva Conventions held the franc-trieurs, not the Prussian soldiers, responsible for the casualties. Their failure to be in uniform forced the Prussians to defend themselves at the cost of civilian lives. The franc-trieurs were seen as using civilians as camouflage. This was regarded as outside the rules of war, and those who carried out such acts were seen as not protected by the conventions. They were not soldiers, and were not to be treated as such.[4]

The first issue that must be addressed when it comes to the treatment of foreign terrorist suspects is the location where these individuals will be detained from the time of their capture through the disposition of their cases. The U.S. detention facility at the naval base in Guantanamo Bay, Cuba, has been the subject of heated debate within the United States and throughout the international system. President Obama promised Americans even before taking office that closing the facility would be a top priority for his administration. The number of detainees at the facility had dropped sharply during the last years of the Bush administration, and shortly after Obama's inauguration American officials embarked upon an intense effort to transfer the remainder of Guantanamo's detainee population to other countries that would be willing to take prisoners so that the infamous detention facility could be shut down. Some detainees were transferred to their home countries, some were transferred to third-party nations willing to host them, and some remained incarcerated in Cuba. Transfers to home countries and third-party nations have sometimes resulted in released individuals returning to the fold of radical Islamists waging war against the United States and the West. A 2010 report by the United States' director of national intelligence revealed that of the 598 detainees transferred out of the detention facility at Guantanamo Bay, 150, or 25 percent, were either confirmed or suspected of participating in terrorist activity after their transfer. Of these 150, thirteen were killed, fifty-four were recaptured, and eighty-three were unaccounted for at the time of this writing.[5]

The transfer of Guantanamo Bay's remaining detainees has proved difficult thus far, and resistance within the United States Congress and among several segments of the American population makes it unlikely the facility will be closed in the foreseeable future. The closure of the detention center, if it ever happens, will not restore America's tarnished image in the international community because a basic problem will still remain even after the prison's doors are shut: those apprehended as suspected terrorists must still be detained in some location until their cases are adjudicated. Any new location that is chosen will quickly become the new Guantanamo Bay. Detention centers in active combat zones are a possibility, but these, too, are understandably viewed with significant suspicion around the world, especially after the abuses at the Abu Ghraib prison just outside Baghdad in Iraq and reported issues of abuse at other detention centers in Iraq and Afghanistan. CIA-operated "black site" prisons in foreign nations where the United States is not conducting active combat or counterterrorism operations suffer from the same stigma attached to Guantanamo Bay and military prisons in America's combat theaters. Detention at a military confinement facility on a Department of Defense installation within the United States is both feasible and, some would argue, logical because military detention has historically been a key component of armed conflict. Maximum security "supermax" prisons in the United States are also a possibility, and one the Obama administration has advocated with its support for using the Thomson Correctional Facility in Illinois to house suspected terrorists until their disposition is ultimately determined. Hundreds of terrorists are already incarcerated in U.S. prisons, and no inmate has ever escaped from one of these fortresslike detention facilities. In short, there are multiple options available to U.S. policymakers when it comes to the detention of those accused of engaging in terrorist activity. No matter which option is chosen, if an alternative to Guantanamo Bay is chosen at all, the selected location will, as Guantanamo Bay did, become a magnet for international criticism of America's terrorist detention policy.

The second issue that must be addressed is the "how," or the rules by which foreign terrorist suspects will have their cases adjudicated. This is the core challenge facing the United States today when it comes to the ultimate fate of those terrorists who are captured and detained instead of killed during counterterrorism operations. Indefinite detention without charge, a practice embraced by both the Bush and Obama administrations, is a difficult concept to justify to Americans who hold due process under the law sacred, even in cases where the suspect or suspects are not U.S. citizens and are accused of barbaric acts of terrorism against innocent civilians. Indefinite detention violates traditional American beliefs about the fair and impartial administration of justice. It stands contrary to everything the United States is supposed to represent. Even the revised rules put in place by the Obama administration under its "prolonged detention" policy are insufficient.[6] Merely allowing periodic challenges to a suspected terrorist's incarceration does not change the fact that the United States government is holding indefinitely without charge certain individuals who cannot be prosecuted because the case evidence against them is too tainted to be used in legal proceedings and who cannot be released because they are considered too dangerous to be allowed to go free. If the United States is going to maintain the moral high ground in the fight against Islamic terrorists, it must let those who stand accused know what it is they are being charged with doing. The initial arraignment, at a minimum, should be made in a military court because the accused are individuals who engaged in armed conflict against others, an activity generally reserved for military forces. Following the presentation of charges, terrorist suspects should be afforded some basic rights that most Americans would probably not disagree with, including an impartial judge, access to legal representation, access to the evidence to be used against them (including at least an unclassified or redacted version of classified evidence), the ability to call witnesses to testify on their behalf, restrictions on the use of any evidence against them that was obtained in violation of U.S. law and, if convicted of the charges presented against them, a limited appeals process that ensures the disposition of their case is the correct one.

If the president and Congress cannot come up with a satisfactory set of rules for the prosecution of foreign terrorist detainees, another option that might be possible is the adjudication of cases in the International Criminal Court (ICC) at The Hague in the Netherlands, provided terrorism-related cases were added to the court's mandate. The ICC has been described by one prominent former Naval War College professor as the "logical descendant" of the court at Nuremberg that tried Nazi officials for war crimes after the conclusion of World War II.[7] Using the ICC for legal proceedings involving terrorism suspects would probably be good for bolstering America's image with the rest of the world as the broader international community would likely embrace the United States' use of a multinational forum as a means for combating the Muslim extremist threat. It would be absolutely essential, though, before agreeing to use the ICC, that U.S. officials secure in advance exemptions for American decision makers, military forces, and intelligence personnel in order to prevent frivolous attempts to prosecute Americans by those who might disagree with the actions the United States takes to protect itself from the Islamic radicals seeking to do it harm.

Law enforcement efforts can greatly contribute to the United States' national strategic plan for combating Islamic extremist violence. Whether it is pre-event surveillance and intelligence sharing domestically or with allied and partner nations, extradition agreements that keep pressure on terrorists and deny them safe havens across the international system, or postevent investigative work at home and abroad that leads to the apprehension and prosecution of terrorist suspects, law enforcement is a necessary and important tool in the U.S. arsenal of resources available for an era of persistent conflict with radical Muslim terrorists. Ultimately, though, the role of law enforcement is limited by a simple reality: Islamic radicals are engaged in armed battle with U.S. military forces and American citizens and interests in multiple countries across the international system. Every country in the world is a potential battleground in this fight. Treating terrorist violence primarily as a criminal matter results in only one party to the conflict playing by an established set of rules, and that puts the United States and its citizens at a serious disadvantage.

Security of the Borders

Any discussion of law enforcement as a component of the fight against Islamic radicalism has to include the issue of U.S. border security. The borders of the United States are the first physical line of defense against those seeking to bring death and destruction to America through terrorist attacks on the U.S. homeland. The defense of those borders, a critical and complex national security challenge, must be a top priority if U.S. government officials are going to protect American citizens from extremists who are relentless in their efforts to infiltrate the United States. This is no easy task, and the size and scope of the challenge are daunting. The long land and sea borders of the United States make it virtually impossible to completely seal off the flow of terrorists trying to enter the country. At the end of fiscal year 2010, the U.S. Border Patrol had varying degrees of control over only 873 miles of the nearly 2,000-mile-long border with Mexico. Of those 873 miles, 129 (15 percent) were classified as "controlled" and the other 85 percent (744 miles) were classified as "managed."[8]

Given the difficulties involved in maintaining control of the United States' long borders, there can be only one realistic objective. The goal cannot be to stop all immigration, legal or illegal. Such a move would prove disastrous to the economy because legal immigrants remain a vital component of America's economic strength. America was built in large part by immigrants looking for employment, refuge, or new opportunities in life, and there should be a place in the United States for those who wish to properly enter the country in pursuit of a better future for themselves and their families. More than seventy million immigrants have come to the United States since the early 1800s, and as long as America remains a land of opportunity and promise, more will seek to do so.[9] Rather than seeking to keep all foreigners out, as some have proposed, the goal of U.S. government action at the borders must be focused on stopping those terrorist individuals who are planning to do the United States harm before they can get to their targets and execute their attacks, while simultaneously keeping the option of legal immigration open to those who can help America grow and prosper.

The desire of some in the United States to close the borders entirely is understandable when one thinks about just how many undocumented immigrants have already made their way into the country. As of 2010, there were more than eleven million illegal immigrants living in the United States.[10] Equally troubling is the rising level of drug-related violence spilling across the Mexican border into American towns. Many see the U.S.-Mexico border region as nothing short of a war zone, and they have hard data to back up their view. Mexican drug violence claimed more than twelve thousand lives in 2010, and more than thirty thousand have died in the drug wars since 2006.[11] Some of that violence has migrated to the United States' side of the border, putting American citizens in the country's Southwest in grave danger.

Sealing the borders entirely, though, is an impractical task and an undesirable one. It is impractical because the resources necessary to fully seal the borders, in terms of both personnel and funding, would be enormous and would greatly strain the U.S. budget. It is undesirable because the U.S. economy requires a steady supply of immigrant labor and because free and open trade between the United States and other nations requires borders that make the American market accessible to merchants by land, sea, and air. If the nation's borders are too difficult to penetrate, international trade partners will look for other consumers for their products, resulting in a loss of commerce for U.S. businesses and a loss in tax revenue for the federal government. The focus should not be on the extremes, sealed borders or very liberal immigration policies, but on finding the right balance of legal immigration, controlled through the coordination of efforts by the states and the federal government, and border security to allow adequate cross-border movement of people and goods while providing the maximum amount of protection possible to American citizens and critical American infrastructure.

Former president George W. Bush increased the size of the Border Patrol from eleven thousand agents to more than seventeen thousand, added more than six hundred miles of physical barriers, including fencing, increased the use of unmanned aerial vehicles to track individuals violating the borders, and deployed more than one hundred new radiation monitors at ports of embarkation.[12] The administration's efforts slightly improved the security of the borders, but they are not even close to being sufficient in scope if the United States is going to get a firm understanding of what and who is entering the country. At least one estimate of resource requirements says fully manning the borders of the United States would take more than five million security and management personnel.[13] The Obama administration must continue to improve border security by building on the measures taken by the Bush administration so that the federal government can maximize its ability to protect the American people from potentially catastrophic terrorist attacks. The horrific events of September 11, 2001, should have been a border security wake-up call for the United States, yet it seems that American officials in Washington have not gotten the message. Access to the United States should be a privilege, not a right. Virtually unchecked mass immigration is foolish and dangerous in the contemporary international security environment, and sealing off the United States from the rest of the world is unrealistic and cost prohibitive. Border security needs to be structured in a manner that allows refuge for those genuinely suffering persecution and that provides a place of opportunity for those who legally help to meet the labor demands of the U.S. economy. The most important priority, however, must always be the prevention of terrorist infiltration into the country.

Protecting the American Homeland

The Department of Homeland Security was formed in the aftermath of the 9/11 attacks with five core missions: preventing terrorism and enhancing security, securing and managing the borders, enforcing and administering immigration laws, safeguarding and securing cyberspace, and ensuring resilience to disasters.[14] No matter how much the federal government might try, there is no possible way to secure every potential target within the United States that Islamic terrorists seeking to inflict harm on America and her people might consider valuable and worth attacking. Bridges, mass gathering sites like sports stadiums and shopping malls, mass transportation systems, monuments of historical importance, government office buildings, airports, and a host of other possible soft targets are easy to locate, easy to conduct surveillance on, and easy to attack. A general risk management framework developed by the libertarian Cato Institute outlined simple guidance for those officials charged with protecting the homeland to help them assess risks to the country, take steps to reduce the chances of an attack, and, in the event an attack is successfully carried out, mitigate the consequences.

The first step in the process is to establish what needs to be protected. Not all potential targets can be protected, so careful analysis and prioritization must be part of the target identification process. Once the potential target is identified, security planners have to determine what they are trying to protect the object from. In other words, what is the threat? Third, the likelihood of each identified threat coming to fruition has to be evaluated, along with the consequences associated with each threat's transition from possibility to reality. Next, an assessment of the actions being taken in response to each threat has to be conducted. And, finally, once the countermeasures for each threat are examined, new risks associated with the countermeasures have to be identified.[15] Cato's checklist is an uncomplicated and straightforward framework that can help government officials and ordinary Americans evaluate threats to the homeland, prioritize protection measures, and develop appropriate preventive procedures to help protect precious lives and critical infrastructure.

Before a terrorist attack is carried out on American soil, the federal government can assist state and local governments, who are typically the first to respond to an incident, by providing important threat and vulnerability information and by helping to coordinate and synchronize prevention and protection measures across the country. In the event a terrorist attack is successfully executed against the homeland, it is imperative that federal officials stand ready to quickly and effectively support local and state officials, with all the resources available to the United States government, in the response effort. A failure to act decisively could cost the country severely in both treasure and blood. The key to effective pre- and postevent success is regular and substantive consultation with any individual, group, agency, or government that has a part in protecting the United States or responding to the successful execution of a terrorist attack on American territory. Those charged with safeguarding the citizens of the United States and critical U.S. infrastructure cannot work in isolation within their respective federal agencies, the nation as a whole, or internationally. Prior coordination and planning between the federal government, state and local governments, and U.S. allied and partner countries is absolutely essential to effective crisis management and the United States' ability to protect the nation and its citizens from the Islamic extremist threat.

9

A Complex and Dangerous World

T HE UNITED STATES EMERGED FROM THE COLD WAR as the world's only remaining superpower, the undisputed global leader in an increasingly complicated and dangerous international security environment suffering from the effects of the Soviet Union's rapid disintegration. Instability, insecurity, and low-intensity conflict once held in check by the dominance of the American and Soviet superpowers were unleashed in places around the world that would quickly become the primary security focus of U.S. and Western government leaders. The complicated security environment that emerged after the Cold War was aptly described by many in the defense community as one of volatility, uncertainty, complexity, and ambiguity.[1] It was a global system conducive to the establishment of multiple safe havens for radical Islamist groups like al Qaeda and other nonstate actors with newly acquired influence and power in embattled, failed, and rogue states where the rule of law and security were woefully inadequate or completely absent. The danger and uncertainty of the 1990s continued into the twenty-first century, where threatening state and nonstate actors were and continue to be in abundant supply. Much of the international community was thrust into varying degrees of turmoil in the wake of the Soviet Union's collapse and the insecure, hostile, and unpredictable mess that emerged during the next decade promises to endure for the foreseeable future. Islamic extremist groups seeking to spread their intolerant and hateful ideology have no shortage of options when it comes to choosing bases of operation in this chaotic security environment. States or territories within a state inhabited by desperate populations suffering from weak or nonexistent governmental controls are particularly attractive because they offer significant freedom of movement and operation for the planning and execution of terrorist attacks.

In pursuing the country's vital, important, and peripheral national interests and in seeking to ensure security and stability in a volatile and uncertain global security environment in which Islamic extremists are targeting the United States and its allies, U.S. government officials must be prepared to confront a wide range of threats in multiple places across the international system simultaneously by taking military and nonmilitary action as far away from the American homeland as possible. The United States will unavoidably be involved in a seemingly never-ending series of international security actions during this era of persistent conflict. Those actions will range from full-blown combat missions in distant and hostile lands to providing various forms of diplomatic, information, military, economic, intelligence, and law enforcement assistance to allied and nonallied governments facing internal and external threats from Islamic radicals. The most immediate areas of focus will necessarily be the primary battlefield in Afghanistan, where American military forces are engaged in decisive combat operations against multiple opposition groups, and the effort to fully transition security responsibility to host nation security forces in post-Saddam Iraq. More than one hundred thousand of America's sons and daughters remain in harm's way in both those countries, and some form of American assistance to both will be required for decades still to come. Even while focused on Afghanistan and Iraq, though, the United States will be forced to exercise its national power in other places across the international system as part of a comprehensive global effort to combat the transnational Islamic extremist threat. The rest of this chapter is devoted to an examination of those global hot spots most likely to be focused on by the United States and its allied and partner nations in the coming years, beginning with the U.S.-led efforts in Afghanistan and Iraq.

The Afghanistan Problem

When the United States invaded Taliban-controlled Afghanistan in late 2001, it did so in pursuit of three specific strategic objectives: the destruction of Islamic terrorist training facilities, the capture of key al Qaeda senior leaders, and the removal of the Taliban regime from power.[2] These goals were to be achieved through the execution of military operations broken up into four phases. In the first phase, the United States and its allies would move military forces into the region surrounding Afghanistan and negotiate arrangements allowing a U.S.-led coalition to operate from or through the airspace of neighboring countries. Next, air and Special Operations Forces would attack targets considered critical to the viability of al Qaeda and its host, the Taliban regime. Third, the United States would remove the Taliban from power and destroy al Qaeda's Afghan safe haven. Finally, in the concluding phase, American military forces would transition from major combat operations to a security and stability mission in support of a new Afghan government.[3] Removing the Taliban from power and destroying al Qaeda's terrorist base of operation turned out to be relatively easy tasks for the world's most powerful and lethal military force. The quick battlefield successes enjoyed by the United States led the UN Security Council to establish an international framework for Afghanistan in December 2001 for economic, humanitarian, and security aid from the international community to be provided to an Afghan nation that had essentially been at war for more than a generation. Not long after the Security Council's action, the International Security Assistance Force set up operations in the capital city of Kabul to help the fledgling Afghan government begin the process of rebuilding its country.

The forces opposed to a new Afghanistan are diverse and extremely complex. The term *Taliban* is often used, as it is here, as a catch-all word, primarily for reasons of simplicity, to describe what is in reality a conglomeration of multiple opposition groups, each with its own interests and objectives, battling American, coalition, and host nation forces supporting the Afghan government. The Taliban itself consists of two primary factions or councils, called *shuras*. Both are believed to be based in Pakistan, with one in Quetta (led by Mullah Omar) and the other in Peshawar. Other major forces opposing the U.S.-led coalition include the Haqqani network in North Waziristan, Hezb-i-Islami Gulbuddin (HiG) in eastern Afghanistan, Tehrik-i-Taliban Pakistan (TTP), Lashkar-e-Taiba (LeT), sometimes called Jamaat-ud-Dawa (JD), Jaish-e-Mohammed (JeM), Sipah-e-Sahaba, Laskhar-e-Jhangvi (LeJ), the Islamic Movement of Uzbekistan (IMU), the Islamic Jihad Union (IJU), and several foreign organizations and criminal networks that provide varying levels of support to the primary opposition groups in Afghanistan.[4] The total number of enemy forces facing the United States and its NATO allies in Afghanistan proper and along the Afghanistan-Pakistan border is estimated to be around sixty-two thousand, only three hundred of whom are suspected of belonging to al Qaeda prime.[5]

In the years since the 2001 invasion, the United States and its allies have steadily lost ground to the Taliban, remnants of the al Qaeda prime organization, and other hostile groups operating in Afghanistan. Each year that passes proves to be more deadly than the one that preceded it. Violence is spiraling out of control, and the situation on the ground is unsustainable over the long term. The level of hostile activity in Afghanistan has increased by 300 percent since 2007, with improvised explosive device (IED) attacks up 82 percent and civilian casualties up 53 percent since 2009.[6] Significant increases in the number of U.S. and allied troops on the ground in 2009 and 2010 made some headway in southern Afghanistan and around Kabul, but enemy activity remains strong and shows no sign of decreasing. This, of course, is not a consensus view. An independent study conducted in 2010 concluded that the Taliban reached the peak of its resistance the previous year, in 2009. Citing an analysis of fighting data in the 398 districts that make up Afghanistan's 34 provinces, the report says incidents of violence affected 70 districts in 2007, 99 districts in 2008, 180 districts in 2009, and 133 districts in 2010.[7] The study cautioned its finding cannot be used to draw a definitive conclusion about whether the United States and NATO are winning the fight in Afghanistan but instead suggested that some force or combination of forces has caused the Taliban to reduce its operational activity. Whether the Taliban has reached its peak or not, the reality on the ground is that U.S. and allied troop levels approaching one hundred fifty thousand soldiers did not prevent the level of violence in the first six months of 2010 from increasing 70 percent above the level it was at during the first six months of 2009.[8] By virtually every measure available, the United States and its NATO allies are losing the fight to the extremists, a reality not likely to improve significantly by the end of 2014, the target date for transitioning security responsibilities to the Afghan government first put forth by Afghan president Hamid Karzai and subsequently adopted by the United States and its coalition partners. Of course, the target date for the withdrawal of coalition forces is negotiable and could shift based on an assessment of security conditions on the ground in 2014, something the United States has already hinted is a possibility.[9] Withdrawal deadlines during times of conflict are nonsensical. Imposing set deadlines that are not based on conditions tend to embolden enemy forces who are unlikely to make concessions to an opponent who is scheduled to withdraw and encourage outside actors who may take advantage of a perceived opportunity to gain power or influence in the wake of NATO's departure.

A Western presence of any significance beyond 2014, though, is highly doubtful, whether conditions on the ground warrant a withdrawal or not. U.S. and allied goals have shifted since 2001, and the new strategic end state lends itself to a gradual transition that transfers security responsibilities from the United States and its partner nations to Afghan military and police forces as soon as is realistically possible. U.S. strategic objectives in Afghanistan now include denying al Qaeda safe haven, denying the Taliban the ability to overthrow the Afghan government, and strengthening the capacity of Afghanistan's security forces and government so that they can assume full responsibility for the future of their country.[10] The specific military goals presented to the Obama administration in late 2009 included reversing the momentum of the Taliban, preventing the Taliban from gaining access to and control of critical population and production centers and lines of communication, disrupting Taliban activity and influence outside secured areas, preventing al Qaeda from once again gaining safe haven in Afghanistan, reducing the capabilities of the Taliban to such an extent that the Afghan government is able to manage the threat, increasing the size and competency of the Afghan National Army and Afghan National Police, and improving the capacity of Afghan leaders to govern.[11] As 2014 approaches, the focus of U.S. and NATO forces will increasingly be on building the capacity of Afghan security personnel so that a gradual transfer of responsibility can take place. There will be no drawdown of any significance for Western military forces in the near future, though. With major combat operations expected to continue until at least 2014, any reduction in U.S. forces, which make up the bulk of the allied effort in Afghanistan, will be purely for show. Other NATO forces may downsize, but the current contribution levels of those forces mean any such reductions will be minor relative to the broader military presence. After 2014, the maintenance of any significant foreign troop presence in Afghanistan will be nearly impossible politically, in the United States and in the European countries of NATO. Wavering public support in the United States and abroad will make it increasingly difficult for political leaders in all coalition nations to keep combat troops in Afghanistan engaged in a stalemate or losing effort against Islamic radicals who recognize they are engaged in a war of political attrition. Measurable progress will have to be demonstrated in the very near term if the current trajectory is going to be reversed.

The Taliban, too, expect Western military forces to depart Afghanistan in the next few years and have begun preparations for their return to power. Taliban plans for a postcoalition-supported Afghan government, first published in late 2010 in the Taliban's *al-Somood* magazine and then posted in early 2011 on the Taliban's *Voice of Jihad* website, call for the establishment of an Islamic emirate instead of a caliphate. The difference between the two is a matter of scope, with an emirate being regionally focused and a caliphate being globally focused. The Taliban's emirate would be headed by the Amir al-Mu'minin, or commander of the faithful, who would appoint a high shura council to draft laws and regulations based on Islamic principles. Subordinate to the high shura council are the main committees that would assume the duties and responsibilities of current Afghan government ministries. The main committees under a Taliban emirate would include military, preaching and guidance, culture and information, political, education, financial, prisoners and orphans, health, and foreign establishments committees. Each of Afghanistan's thirty-four provinces would be administered by a governor appointed by the commander of the faithful in consultation with the high shura council.[12] The Taliban know the staying power of the United States and its Western allies in Afghanistan is limited, and they are laying the groundwork for future governance in anticipation of their success in removing from power the Western-backed leadership in Kabul after NATO departs the country.

The primary reasons for the dismal state of affairs in Afghanistan include a resurgent Taliban, a weak and corrupt central government, inadequate Afghan security forces, a halfhearted commitment by many NATO member states, a fearful and distrustful Afghan population, and a lawless region along the border with Pakistan that makes it virtually impossible to prosecute the conflict to a conclusion that is satisfactory to the United States and its allies. The Taliban has made a strong comeback in several of Afghanistan's provincial regions, and the movement's influence and reach are steadily expanding. Taliban fighters have regrouped and rearmed themselves since being driven from power in 2001 and have over time allied themselves with various disaffected portions of the population within Afghanistan that provide them with safe haven and critically needed operations and logistics support. They are increasingly confident, and they have demonstrated an ability to conduct frequent and sustained attacks against coalition forces, the central government, and the Afghan population. They have proved themselves to be adaptive and resilient, and they have steadily worked to increase their level of control in the south and east of the country. They enjoy a fair but nonmajority amount of local support, strong financing from a lucrative drug trade, and the patience and resolve to fight a war of attrition against the political will of the United States and its NATO allies.

The Taliban knows that time is on its side, that it can pursue a "run out the clock" strategy, and that foreign military forces will eventually withdraw. They always do. There is a reason why Afghanistan is known as the "graveyard of empires." No occupation force has ever won there. In the end, Afghanistan is more important to the Taliban than it is to the United States and its coalition allies. For the Taliban, Afghanistan is the birthplace of the modern Islamist movement, where it all began for bin Laden and other Islamic extremists who took on and defeated the Soviet superpower more than two decades ago. In Kabul, the central government has lost the confidence of the Afghan people, if it ever really had it, because of rampant fraud and corruption and an inability to exert its authority outside of the capital in the impoverished rural areas of the country. A popular saying to come out of Afghanistan since the new government was established claims, "Where the road ends the Taliban begins."

Such a statement is an accurate reflection of the central government's inability to reach out to the areas of Afghanistan most in need of assistance. The Afghan government has demonstrated time and again that it is not serious about cleaning up corruption, and no amount of pressure from the United States or NATO is going to change a culture in which bribes and quid pro quo deals are a normal part of societal life. As long as it is business as usual in Kabul, the people of Afghanistan who are most in need will continue to look elsewhere for the security and social services they need.

The Afghan National Army and National Police, while growing in both size and capability, are years away from being able to conduct operations independent of coalition military support. Even if a basic level of counterinsurgency and counterterrorism capability is achieved, Afghan security forces will continue to rely on U.S. and NATO military assets for desperately needed logistics support, operational and tactical advice, training, funding, equipping, and airpower. Within the NATO alliance, the problems are not much better. NATO forces in Afghanistan are limited in their effectiveness as a result of inadequate troop contributions from member states, national caveats that severely restrict the types of missions NATO units are permitted to engage in, a lack of support among the populations of troop-contributing nations, disparate military capabilities, and a dysfunctional chain of command in which some forces have to get permission from their national governments before participating in certain types of missions, typically offensive operations that are likely to result in significant numbers of casualties. There are, of course, exceptions to this blanket statement about NATO forces. The military units from Great Britain, the Netherlands, Denmark, and Canada have certainly done their fair share of fighting and dying alongside their American counterparts. In general, though, NATO forces have tended to be as much a hindrance as a help in the fight against the extremists. Nearly half of all nations contributing military forces to ISAF have imposed geographical or mission-related caveats that limit the ability of the international coalition to effectively deploy and utilize its personnel and equipment assets.[13] Any military unit that cannot be used when and where the commander on the ground deems necessary, without conditions or national caveats attached to its employment, is worthless to that commander and to the mission he is charged with accomplishing.

With the Taliban increasingly active throughout Afghanistan, the central government unable to provide security or essential services, Afghan security forces weak and ineffective, and coalition forces seemingly unable to make any significant and sustainable progress in reducing violence or expanding reconstruction efforts, the Afghan population has become increasingly fearful and discouraged about its future. Wary of the political will of the United

States and its allies to stay in Afghanistan for the long haul, and mindful of the fact that the central government in Kabul has proved unwilling or unable to provide basic services and security, the population has increasingly gravitated away from the U.S.-led coalition and the central government and toward Afghanistan's tribal warlords and, to some degree, the Taliban. These challenges have put the United States and its coalition partners in an extremely difficult position. Each of these challenges, though, pales in comparison to the problem posed by the lawless border area between Afghanistan and neighboring Pakistan.

The Critical Role of Pakistan

It is widely believed that shortly after U.S. military forces entered Afghanistan, Taliban and al Qaeda leaders relocated to the Federally Administered Tribal Areas (FATA) on Pakistan's side of the Afghanistan-Pakistan border, known as the Durand Line. One of the poorest regions in the world, the FATA is a breeding ground for Islamic terrorists associated not only with al Qaeda, but with radical groups in multiple countries across the international system. The FATA region is home to Lashkar-e-Taiba (LeT), Jaish-e-Mohammed (JeM), and the Tehrik-e-Taliban Pakistan militant group, an extremist organization that wants to turn Pakistan into a religious state and that is believed to be responsible for the assassination of former Pakistani prime minister Benazir Bhutto in 2007.[14] The FATA has a literacy rate of just 17 percent, compared with Pakistan's national average of 40 percent, and a per capita income of just $250, with nearly two-thirds of the region's population living below the poverty line.[15]

The reasons for Pakistan's FATA problem include a failure to reintegrate mujahideen fighters after the Soviet withdrawal from Afghanistan in February of 1989, a failure to provide basic social and economic resources and services to the region's population, and a failure to institute desperately needed reforms in the region at the political and administrative levels.[16] Taliban and al Qaeda fighters take advantage of the lack of effective governance in the tribal areas to conduct cross-border attacks against Afghan and U.S.-led coalition forces and then return to the Pakistani side of the border with little retribution (other than a few unmanned aerial drone strikes) from the United States, NATO, the Afghan government, or Pakistan. Additionally, al Qaeda prime's top leadership personnel continue to seek refuge among FATA's population, undoubtedly waiting for an opportunity to regroup and strike another 9/11-type blow at the United States or other "nonbeliever" nation. Finally, Islamic radicals and the Pakistani Taliban use the tribal areas as a staging ground for an active insurgency against the fragile Pakistani government.

This lawless border area arguably holds the greatest growth potential in the world for Islamic extremist ideology. There is no escaping the fundamental reality that the Federally Administered Tribal Areas along the Afghanistan-Pakistan border are critical to the ultimate success or failure of the U.S.-led effort in Afghanistan and to the future stability of Pakistan. Since it is unlikely this region will be brought under control in the near term, it is unlikely the West will prevail in Afghanistan. The link between Afghanistan and Pakistan cannot be stressed enough. Pakistan's Inter-Services Intelligence Agency (ISI) supported the Taliban with training, equipment, and other assistance during and after the group's rise to power in Afghanistan in the mid-1990s, and it is widely believed that many ISI senior leaders still maintain close contact with and provide support to Taliban leaders today, despite the removal of the Taliban from power. Maintaining ties to the element most likely to regain control of Afghanistan in the event of a U.S. and NATO withdrawal makes perfect sense for the ISI. Hedging its bets in Afghanistan is a logical course of action because stability and security in Afghanistan directly impact stability and security in Pakistan, making it necessary to lay the groundwork for eventual cooperation with whichever party is ultimately left standing after ISAF is gone.

In addition to the growing instability in neighboring Afghanistan and in the Federally Administered Tribal Areas, Pakistan's government institutions and leadership are having considerable difficulty with basic democratic principles, an ongoing economic crisis, continuing tension with longtime foe and nuclear neighbor India, and a rampant corruption problem that undermines public confidence in the government's ability to see Pakistan through these troubling times. Perhaps most worrisome, though, is an ongoing Islamist insurgency within Pakistan's borders that puts the country in very real danger of becoming a failed state in possession of nuclear weapons. Insurgent terrorist violence in Pakistan has increased more than 700 percent in just the past five years, threatening the very survival of one of the world's nuclear-armed regional powers.[17] In Pakistan's commercial capital, Karachi, more than one thousand people were killed in 2010 alone.[18] A failed Pakistani state would be a disaster for the U.S.-led mission in Afghanistan and the region in general and would give al Qaeda and other extremists access to new and valuable resources, including, potentially, nuclear weapons. If the United States and its allies are going to prevent Afghanistan from once again becoming a safe haven for terrorists and a launching pad for international terrorist attacks that put American citizens and American interests in danger, the extremist problem in Pakistan will have to be addressed concurrently with the problem in Afghanistan. The two countries cannot be dealt with in isolation from each other. Recognizing the importance of increasing Pakistan's ability to survive its current turmoil, the U.S. Congress in 2009 approved more than $7 billion in non-military aid over a five-year period in order to bolster Pakistan's economy and strengthen its government institutions.[19] Aid of this magnitude should not be unconditional, however. Pakistan has not been a particularly strong or reliable partner in the United States' effort to defeat the Taliban and al Qaeda and to stabilize Afghanistan. The U.S. government should make it clear to Islamabad that a continued failure to adequately address American concerns in the region could result in increased unilateral U.S. action within Pakistan's borders or a stronger U.S. focus on Pakistan's longtime rival, India.

Keeping Iraq on the Road to Recovery

There has been considerable disagreement in the United States and abroad over the reasons and justifications for the U.S.-led invasion of Iraq on March 19, 2003. Douglas Feith, former undersecretary for policy in the Bush administration's Defense Department and a key proponent of the war with Iraq has written, "Saddam Hussein was a threat to U.S. interests before 9/11; the threat of renewed aggression by Hussein was more urgent after 9/11; all reasonable means short of war had been tried unsuccessfully; the risks of leaving Hussein in power outweighed the risks associated with his removal; and Americans after 9/11 had a lower tolerance for such dangers."[20] Feith's justifications are not far off the mark. Saddam Hussein's Iraq was an aggressive and dangerous regional state actor, initiating two wars against neighboring countries Iran and Kuwait, providing a safe haven for international terrorists like Abu Nidal, and employing chemical weapons of mass destruction against Iraqi Kurds in the late 1980s and against Iranians during the Iran-Iraq War. Containment measures put in place after the 1991 Persian Gulf War were inadequate and losing support across the international community. The United States could not maintain no-fly zones over northern and southern Iraq indefinitely because the monetary costs and the risks to American airmen were simply too high, and the continuance of economic sanctions, which had done little to undermine Saddam during the twelve years they had been in place, was becoming increasingly difficult as nation-states looked to cash in on Iraq's vast oil reserves. It is very likely that Saddam and his top advisers were merely waiting out the international community knowing at some point they would be able to execute their weapons programs unobstructed by outside nations led by the United States and its Western allies. In the immediate aftermath of the 9/11 attacks, there was, as Feith suggests, a general belief within America, and particularly at the top levels of government, that the United States could no longer afford to stand idly by while potential threats to American national security matured in other countries. The American public wanted the threat from Islamic extremism and other rogue actors dealt with as far from American shores as possible, and that meant taking the fight to those who threatened the United States and its interests wherever they might be. Putting these reasons aside, though, there was also ample justification for including Iraq in any truly "global" fight against Islamic terrorism.

Iraqi documents recovered after the U.S.-led invasion in early 2003 were examined by the Iraqi Perspectives Project (IPP) of the Institute for Defense Analyses in an effort sponsored by the United States Joint Forces Command, a Department of Defense functional combatant command headquartered in Virginia. Functional combatant commands focus on specific tasks like transportation (U.S. Transportation Command) or special operations (U.S. Special Operations Command). Geographic combatant commands focus on global areas of responsibility, like Europe (U.S. European Command) or Africa (U.S. Africa Command). The IPP review concluded Saddam's Ba'athist regime maintained a viable terrorist capability and the willingness to use that capability, right up to the point where it was removed from power by the U.S.-led coalition during Operation Iraqi Freedom. Analysts who reviewed the captured Iraqi documents found that Saddam's government frequently cooperated with a wide array of terrorist groups when it believed those groups could in some way help advance Iraqi interests; that the Iraqi regime had ties to various Palestinian terrorist organizations; and that state sponsorship of terrorism was such a regular practice for Iraq under Saddam Hussein that the Iraqi government established a formal monitoring and accountability system for the recruiting, training, and resourcing of terrorists.[21] While Saddam was unquestionably an active supporter of terrorist violence in general, it has never been established that he was involved in the planning or execution of the 9/11 attacks or that his regime was formally affiliated with al Qaeda or Osama bin Laden during the run-up to the 2003 U.S. invasion. In 2004, after Saddam had been removed from power, Jordanian-born terrorist Abu Mus'ab al-Zarqawi changed the name of his Islamist movement from the Monotheism and Jihad Group to al Qaeda in Iraq (AQI), also known as al Qaeda in Mesopotamia, and joined forces with bin Laden and al Qaeda prime.[22] Bin Laden and his deputy, Ayman al-Zawahiri, considered U.S.-occupied Iraq a critical front in al Qaeda's war with the West and openly supported, at least rhetorically, Zarqawi's efforts to combat U.S.-led coalition and Iraqi forces. After Zarqawi was killed by a U.S. airstrike in 2006, Egyptian-born Abu Hamza al-Muhajir, also known as Abu Ayyub al Masri, took over al Qaeda's Iraq affiliate until he, too, was killed by U.S. and Iraqi forces in early 2010.

The United States and its allies have made considerable progress toward the stabilization of Iraq since early 2007, when President Bush ordered a "surge" of U.S. military forces to the country in response to rising levels of violence and a rapidly deteriorating political situation in Baghdad. At the time Bush ordered additional troops to Iraq, dramatic claims were made about the president's decision to "escalate" a violent crisis that was already spinning out of control. In reality, though, the so-called surge was not outside of the historical norm established over the previous four years. Troop levels in Iraq after the invasion in 2003 had regularly increased and decreased in response to changing security conditions throughout the country or in anticipation of critical national-level events like elections. The "surge" was no more than the latest addition of troops designed to bring the level of violence in Iraq back down to a manageable level. In the years since President Bush changed the American strategy in Iraq, the number of attacks against coalition and Iraqi forces and against Iraqi civilians has dropped dramatically. There were 8,233 incidents of violence in Iraq in 2010, down from 11,203 in 2009 and significantly lower than the 67,727 incidents that occurred in the Iraq War's deadliest year, 2007.[23]

Virtually every metric tracked by the United States has shown significant improvement, and casualty levels for coalition and host-nation security forces have fallen dramatically. Iraqi security forces continue to grow in size and capability, although significant challenges still remain, and al Qaeda in Iraq has been practically destroyed, though the group still maintains the ability to pull off a few spectacular mass-casualty-producing attacks on occasion.[24] Political accommodation among the three main ethnic groups, Shia, Sunni, and Kurd, while still painfully slow, is showing signs of improvement. The Iraqi government is increasingly taking full responsibility for security in Iraq's provinces, and the results achieved by the Bush administration's strategic and tactical adjustments, in conjunction with the "Anbar Awakening" by Sunnis fed up with al Qaeda's brutal tactics and the stand-down of Muqtada al Sadr's Mahdi Army Shia militia, have thus far proved to be both positive and sustained. There are, of course, periodic spikes in the level of violence in Iraq, but that is to be expected as groups opposed to the Iraqi government are vying for power and influence in anticipation of a U.S. military withdrawal. There is no question, though, that the trend lines are continuing to show improvement. If conditions in Iraq continue to improve, the U.S. and Iraqi governments will be able to continue the transition of responsibility set out in the status of forces agreement negotiated between the Bush administration and Baghdad and inherited by President Obama. If the trend lines are reversed, the United States could keep its military forces in Iraq significantly longer if the Iraqi government asks for continued support.[25]

Even if progress continues and U.S. military forces are able to withdraw from Iraq as planned, the United States will still be involved in Iraqi security and political affairs for many years to come. Ethnic and sectarian differences over power sharing in the central government and the distribution of oil revenues still simmer and have the potential to impede continued progress toward a secure and stable Iraq that is allied with the United States. Problematic actors like the anti-U.S. cleric Muqtada al-Sadr are expanding their influence across the Iraqi government. Al-Sadr is an Iranian loyalist, and his strengthening position in Iraq weakens U.S. influence and opens the door for troublesome meddling by Tehran. The overall level of violence in Iraq, while down, is still cause for concern. Iraqi security forces will require several more years of coalition support before they are capable of fully independent operations, and Iraq's neighbors will continue to seek increased regional influence by interfering in Iraq's internal affairs. At a minimum, significant logistics assistance will need to be provided by U.S. forces because of a continuing lack of support capability within Iraq's Ministry of Defense, despite an investment of more than $20 billion by the United States since the 2003 invasion.[26] Additionally, stand-off support from unmanned aerial vehicles and possibly ship-launched cruise missiles will be critical to Iraqi security force efforts to combat armed antigovernment groups. For the United States, the near-term focus will be on the attainment of realistic objectives that support long-term U.S. interests in the Middle East, including the containment of Iranian influence, the denial of Iraq as a safe haven for international terrorists, and the reduction of violence in Iraq to a level that does not threaten the stability of the Iraqi government, neighboring states, or the broader Middle East region. A complete disengagement from Iraq would prove disastrous to U.S. national interests, increasing Iranian influence in the country and across the broader Middle East.

What ultimately happens in Iraq will have significant consequences for the entire Middle East for decades into the future. If some form of democracy survives, however imperfect it may be, the regional status quo will face a serious challenge as the populations of neighboring countries suffering under dictatorial regimes look at Iraqis as they cast votes for candidates of their choice and say, "Why not us?" By the same token, a failure to defeat democracy's opponents in Iraq, whether they are Islamic extremists or homegrown insurgents loyal to Muqtada al Sadr or the Ba'ath Party, would serve to validate the use of terrorist violence as a political tool and would embolden Islamic terrorists worldwide to continue using violent attacks in pursuit of their political, economic, and social goals. Vital U.S. interests are at stake in Iraq, including the global effort to combat terrorism, the stability of the broader Middle East, and the maintenance of U.S. global leadership and credibility within the international community. Leaving Iraq before setting the conditions for sustainable security and stability would be a historic mistake that would likely return to haunt the United States in the not-too-distant future.

The Threat from Failed and Failing States

While the United States will remain strongly committed to and focused on Afghanistan and Iraq for many more years, failed and failing states around the world cannot be ignored if there is going to be any hope of establishing a relatively safe, secure, and stable international security environment that restricts the ability of Islamic radicals to establish safe havens from which to plan and execute their acts of terror. A failed state can be defined as a state that no longer has the ability to sustain itself politically and economically.[27] Typically, the rule of law is absent and the government, if one exists at all, lacks substantive authority, exercises little control over its territory, population, or outside forces acting within the state's borders, and no longer enjoys the traditional state monopoly on the legitimate use of force. Where a government does exist, it is generally incapable of allocating state resources or providing basic services to the people, and it generally lacks legitimacy within the international system. In most cases where a failed state exists, the government has ceased to function in any meaningful capacity at all. Somalia and Afghanistan are both good examples of failed states. A failing state is simply a country that is well on its way to failed state status if something is not done to change its downward trajectory.

Failed and failing states are ideal safe havens for Islamic extremists who are able to exploit weak or nonexistent governments and fearful populations to ensure their ability to plan, organize, and train for terrorist operations. Counterinsurgency and counterterrorism expert Dr. David Kilcullen has theorized that extremist groups like al Qaeda use a four-phase process to establish themselves in failed and failing states. During the first phase, which Kilcullen calls the "infection" phase, al Qaeda or an affiliated or associated movement establishes itself in a remote, ungoverned, or conflict-affected area. In the second, or "contagion" phase, the extremist group expands its level of influence and begins to have an effect on its host location, other countries within the region, and, sometimes, other regions in the world either directly with violence or indirectly through the use of propaganda dissemination and media influence. During the third phase, the "intervention," outside forces like the

United States and its allies begin to take overt or covert steps to stem the power and influence of the extremist group. In the fourth and final phase, the "rejection," the host population rebels against the presence of outside forces by aligning with the extremists against the foreign elements, solidifying the group's grip on the area.[28]

American citizens concerned about their safety and security in an increasingly volatile and unstable world experiencing an era of persistent conflict need look only at Afghanistan for an understanding of why the United States must take seriously the threat posed by terrorist exploitation of failed and failing states. Prior to the 9/11 attacks on the American homeland, Afghanistan was, by any reasonable measure, a classic failed state with the potential for causing a serious security challenge in the international system. U.S. decision makers in Washington, though, considered the Taliban-ruled al Qaeda safe haven to be a relatively minor foreign policy problem with little impact on the overall national security of the United States. Once the Soviet Union had withdrawn, Afghanistan went to the bottom of the list of U.S. foreign policy priorities. It took the worst terrorist strike in U.S. history to awaken the American public and its elected leadership to the horrific consequences of ignoring the failed and failing states where Islamic terrorists seek refuge. These states do not simply disappear when they are ignored by major powers, but instead foment regional instability that cannot be disregarded as a distant problem for neighboring states to deal with on their own. The stability of faraway countries that seem insignificant to the United States warrants attention, even if there is not a vital or important U.S. national interest at stake in a given failed or failing state. As a global power with transnational concerns in an increasingly globalized and interconnected world, the United States cannot avoid being affected in some way by what goes on in virtually every other country or region in the world. Make no mistake, the prospect of taking on the failed and failing state security challenge in the international system is an intimidating one. These unruly lands are complicated, messy, and often dangerous environments that involve many years of engagement and high levels of investment. Denying sanctuary for extremists, though, is the absolute best way for the United States to prevent Islamic radicals from gaining the capacity to once again strike America on its home turf. Failed and failing states are not going to fix themselves, and they are not going to go away. In fact, recent trends like the global economic crisis, rapid population growth, environmental degradation, globalization, competition for natural resources, the wide availability of weapons, and the growth of Islamic extremism are likely to result in growing numbers of failed and failing states throughout the international system.[29] While other foreign policy problems may be deemed more critical or of a higher immediate priority, failed and failing states are a problem the United States, its allies, and partner nations ignore at their own peril.

The Growing Danger in Africa

Much of the African continent is in serious crisis. Extremely poor by any standard, African states trail most nations in the world in categories of human well-being (life expectancy, infant mortality, etc.) and suffer from high rates of poverty, oppression by autocratic regimes, limited or unreliable security and law enforcement elements, weak judicial systems, and massive government corruption. Across the continent, per capita income in 2006 was only $1,727, barely up from $1,715 a quarter century before.[30] Dire conditions create situations in which many African nations are ripe for exploitation by Islamic extremists who have been looking to expand their influence and secure new bases of operation since being forced from Afghanistan in late 2001. Muslim radicals have been interested in gaining a foothold in Africa for decades, and the need for new sanctuaries has grown tremendously as extremists have been rooted out of their traditional operating areas and forced to find new safe havens from which to plan and conduct their acts of violence. Muslims are believed to make up nearly half of Africa's population, a fact not lost on Islamic radicals seeking an African foothold from which they can expand their operational base.[31]

Osama bin Laden was active in Sudan in the mid-1990s before turning his focus to Afghanistan, and al Qaeda militants attacked the United States' embassies in Nairobi, Kenya, and Dar es Salaam, Tanzania, in 1998. Al Qaeda in the Lands of the Islamic Maghreb (AQIM), which operates out of the West African nations of Mali and Mauritania after being forced out of Algeria by government counterinsurgency efforts, has been an affiliate of al Qaeda prime since 2006, when it joined bin Laden's terrorist network and changed its name from the Salafist Group for Preaching and Combat. AQIM started as a localized Algerian insurgency in the early 1990s before reaching out to al Qaeda proper and increasing its activity level in multiple West African nations, including Morocco, Algeria, Tunisia, Libya, and Mauritania. Funded by kidnappings and drugs, AQIM has conducted attacks against Western interests in Africa and has declared a desire and intent to target the West outside of the continent, although some analysts believe the group uses terrorism as a cover for criminal activities focused on revenue generation.[32] Whether AQIM is interested in a criminal enterprise in West Africa or is looking to expand its terrorist operations to include attacks beyond the Maghreb, the United States has realized it cannot afford to wait until such a capability manifests itself in the form of an attack on the American homeland before it acts. Operation Enduring Freedom–Trans Sahara provides U.S. military support to the Trans Sahara Counter Terrorism Partnership Program with efforts focused on security and cooperation with partner nations Algeria, Burkina Faso, Morocco, Tunisia, Chad, Mali, Mauritania, Niger, Nigeria, and Senegal.[33]

The United States has also become concerned in recent years with increasing radical Islamic influence in the failed state of Somalia, which has gone through more than a dozen governments in just the past two decades. The last several years, in particular, have seen considerable gains for Islamic extremists in Somalia, with the Islamic Courts Union (ICU) capturing the capital city of Mogadishu in 2006 before falling from power after Ethiopian military forces entered the country to battle Islamic militants in late 2006. The ICU was followed by al Shabaab ("the Youth"), the Courts Union's former militant wing, which is still operating in Somalia today. While other Islamic extremist groups are active in Somalia, including Ahlu Sunna wa al Jama'a, Hizb al Islam, and al Qaeda in East Africa (not an official al Qaeda prime franchise), the al Shabaab organization poses the greatest threat to Somalia's Western-backed Transitional Federal Government (TFG). Al Shabaab controls significant amounts of territory in the southern and central regions of the country, while the TFG is confined to a few locations within the Somali capital. The leaders of the al Shabaab movement claim to be affiliated with al Qaeda, although the depth of that affiliation is the subject of much debate in defense and foreign policy circles. Officials in Yemen allege that al Shabaab members have made their way to Yemeni refugee camps set up for displaced Somalis and that the militant group has established links with and transferred arms to al Qaeda in the Arabian Peninsula.[34] There are indications al Shabaab has, at a minimum, adopted al Qaeda–style terrorist tactics, including the use of suicide bombers, perhaps as a means for gaining recognition, support, and formal designation by al Qaeda prime as an official al Qaeda franchise. Furthermore, al Qaeda recruiters are reportedly active in Somalia seeking new fighters, including children, to join the jihadist movement. A 2010 report by ADNKronos International claimed al Qaeda operatives have used a twenty-eight-minute video designed to attract young children to their cause. The report says the video shows dozens of children five to seven years old participating in a quiz show run by international terrorists in which toys like plastic weapons are awarded as prizes.[35]

Whether the group is growing closer to al Qaeda or not, al Shabaab, which hosts foreign fighters from several nations in the international system, including Yemen, Afghanistan, and Pakistan, subscribes to the same radical ideology as al Qaeda prime and serves as a prime example of the growing danger of

Islamic extremism in struggling African states. Somalia's permissive operating environment, porous borders, political instability, proximity to the Middle East, and lack of a strong central government offer Islamic terrorists seeking to conduct their attacks on a global scale a potentially ideal safe haven from which to organize, train, and launch terrorist operations. The weak Transitional Federal Government, supplied by the United States with weapons, intelligence, and logistics assistance, is supported by the African Union Mission in Somalia (AMISOM), a small force of several thousand peacekeepers that has been defending the TFG from al Shabaab since early 2007.[36] Without AMISOM, the TFG would likely collapse. Given the continuing strife in Somalia, it is likely that AMISOM, authorized by the United Nations Security Council, will remain engaged in Somalia for some time to come.

The Somali government is unstable and dysfunctional, and its inability to pay its soldiers has resulted in mass desertions, defections, and arms sales to al Shabaab and other militant groups.[37] If international assistance stops or is curtailed even slightly, Somalia will be ripe for the establishment of a transnational Islamic extremist base of operations. Designated a foreign terrorist organization by the United States, al Shabaab has not yet demonstrated a capability to attack targets outside of Africa but has demonstrated an ability to carry terrorist operations beyond Somalia's borders, creating a new threat for the other nations of East Africa to worry about. Al Shabaab claimed credit for coordinated twin bombings against soccer fans attending a World Cup match in Kampala, Uganda, that killed scores of people and wounded dozens of others. The Kampala attack, al Shabaab's first successful international terrorist operation, likely targeted Uganda for its support to the African Union's AMISOM peacekeeping force in Somalia. Uganda and Burundi, which has also been on the receiving end of threats issued by al Shabaab, are the only two African nations contributing military forces to the AMISOM operation. As al Shabaab's ability to conduct international terrorist attacks is strengthened over time, it is not far-fetched to believe the group could seek to expand its operations to include U.S. and Western targets in East Africa and beyond.

Recognizing the growing importance of East Africa in the fight against transnational Islamic extremism, the United States established in 2002 the Combined Joint Task Force–Horn of Africa (CJTF–HOA) at Camp Lejeune, North Carolina. The task force initially conducted operations from a U.S. Navy ship positioned just off Africa's coast before setting up camp in Djibouti City, Djibouti, in early 2003. CJTF–HOA works with African governments to improve partner country security capacity through a variety of missions, including the training of African militaries in counterterrorism and counterinsurgency tactics. The task force also conducts a series of humanitarian missions in Horn of Africa countries, including the building of schools and medical facilities and the conduct of medical assistance visits to targeted nations.[38] CJTF–HOA is a two-part effort designed to increase the capacity of African nations to combat extremism while simultaneously working to win the support of the populations in targeted countries through humanitarian work that directly impacts the people of key African states. In early 2007, the United States followed up the CJTF–HOA effort with the creation of U.S. Africa Command (AFRICOM), a geographic combatant command led by a four-star general officer with responsibility for all Department of Defense activities on the African continent.[39] One of AFRICOM's primary missions is the conduct of military-to-military activities that build the security capacity of African nations. The more capable African countries become at handling the growing threat from Islamic extremists seeking safe havens on the African continent, the less likely it is the United States will have to engage in armed conflict on behalf of those nations.

Africa's trouble spots and potential Islamist breeding grounds far exceed the resources available to the United States, especially with ongoing major operational commitments in Afghanistan and Iraq. A significant problem for AFRICOM, aside from a general lack of resources, has been the hesitance with which African nations have greeted the military command. Fears of a new round of Western colonialism and the belief that an overt U.S. presence in Africa would invite Islamic extremist attacks have made it difficult for the United States to find an African nation willing to host the AFRICOM headquarters. Unable to establish operations on the ground in its area of responsibility, AFRICOM has been forced to base its operations out of Stuttgart in the Federal Republic of Germany in Europe. Some have suggested AFRICOM's headquarters should be moved to the United States.[40] Stationing AFRICOM personnel in North America, however, would put the combatant command's headquarters farther away from its area of responsibility than it already is, making it even more difficult to proactively address Africa's many complex security challenges. Proponents of locating AFRICOM's headquarters in the United States like to cite U.S. Central Command's (CENTCOM) Florida headquarters, thousands of miles away from its area of operation in the Middle East. In making their argument, they overlook or ignore CENTCOM's robust forward headquarters in Qatar, which enables the command to monitor its area of operations from within the region it is responsible for. No such forward option has been made available to AFRICOM. Every effort should be made to limit the distance AFRICOM has to negotiate in order to effectively execute its responsibilities in Africa. The command's challenges are significant, and given the continuing missions in Afghanistan and Iraq along with the United States' many other global commitments, there is simply no way American leaders can address all of the real and potential trouble spots in Africa that need U.S. attention. Prioritization of effort will be critical. With vital national interests like the elimination of terrorist networks and safe havens, the prevention of weapons of mass destruction and arms proliferation, and the maintenance of safe and accessible trade routes, it is likely the United States will be involved in African affairs for many decades to come. That involvement will have to be managed carefully if American efforts in Africa are going to be effective in securing U.S. goals on the continent.

The Israeli-Palestinian Conflict and Lebanon

The Middle East has been at the top of the list of U.S. security concerns for several decades and promises to continue to require the attention of the United States for the foreseeable future. Key U.S. interests in the region include sustaining America's access to available energy resources and preventing the emergence of a single dominant regional power. The ongoing conflict in Iraq, the ever-present threat to American ally Israel from Islamic terrorism originating in the Palestinian territories and Lebanon, Iran's state sponsorship of terrorist activity, and the continuing impasse over Iran's suspected nuclear weapons program all have the potential to cause increased levels of instability and chaos in the region. Entrenched autocratic regimes, the repression of political dissent, and severe social oppression have fostered extremism directed not only at governments in the region, but at the United States and its allies as well. Sustained and often violent instability, coupled with the threat of a showdown between the West and Iran, puts reliable access to regional oil supplies in serious jeopardy. Much of the world depends on oil resources drawn from the countries of the Middle East and, as global demand for oil continues to grow, access to that oil will become increasingly important to the United States and its allies and partner nations.

With Iraq seemingly on the road to recovery after nearly a decade of war that followed a quarter century of dictatorial brutality at the hands of Saddam Hussein's Ba'athist regime, the ongoing terrorist threat from the Palestinian territories and Lebanon necessarily moves up in priority in the United States' effort to combat Islamic extremism in the Middle East. The Palestinian Gaza Strip has been ruled by the terrorist group Hamas since the summer of 2007, just a year and a half after Hamas defeated rival Fatah in the January 2006 Palestinian Authority general legislative elections. Fatah, a secularist group that used to be the dominant faction within the Palestine Liberation Organization, controls the Palestinian West Bank. Formed out of the Egyptian Muslim Brotherhood, Hamas is an Islamist group that has consistently refused to recognize Israel's right to exist and is believed to be responsible for the deaths of hundreds of people as a result of a constant barrage of terrorist attacks against innocent Israeli civilians, including women and children. Sharp divisions between Fatah and Hamas have prevented the formation of a unified Palestinian front capable of negotiating the core issues of contention—control of Jerusalem, Jewish settlement building in Palestinian areas, mutually acceptable borders, and the disposition of Palestinian refugees—with Israel on behalf of all Palestinian people. Major differences between the Palestinian political movements have led to continual conflict between Fatah and Hamas, with Fatah at least claiming a desire for peace with Israel, although its actions often do not match its rhetoric, and Hamas continuing its terrorist assault on the Jewish state with regular attacks launched from Gaza. Ultimately, those interested in peace in both Israel and the Palestinian territories see the conflict as nothing less than a fight for survival, making compromise for the sake of lasting peace an exceedingly difficult prospect, even if Fatah and Hamas could join together so that Palestinians could speak with one voice. Unless Hamas abandons terrorism and accepts Israel as a legitimate state entitled to exist in the Levant, there will be no peace in the Middle East. Similarly, unless Israel shows restraint when it responds to Palestinian aggression and genuinely works toward a negotiated settlement that leads to the formation of a viable Palestinian state, there will be no peace in the Middle East. And as long as there is no peace in the Middle East, there will remain significant potential for Islamic extremism from Gaza to spread beyond its current limits and ultimately threaten the citizens and interests of the United States.

In Lebanon, the terrorist group Hezbollah, or "Party of God," has been increasing its power and influence since it was first formed in response to an Israeli invasion in 1982. Hezbollah enjoys significant public support in Lebanon because of its continued resistance to Israel and because its extensive social assistance network provides basic health and education services to the Lebanese people that the Lebanese government cannot or will not provide. Hezbollah maintains close ties with both Syria and Iran and has planned, conducted, or been linked to multiple terrorist attacks against U.S., Israeli, and Western targets, including the 1983 bombing of the Marine barracks in Beirut that killed nearly three hundred Americans. Hezbollah has already demonstrated an ability to reach beyond Israel, executing attacks in Saudi Arabia and Argentina, and is believed to have cells in the United States, Europe, Canada, and South America. With its global presence and its ability to conduct violent attacks against soft targets that are almost impossible to defend, Hezbollah is a terrorist threat the U.S. government must be prepared to take action against, preferably before Hezbollah attacks American citizens or infrastructure within the borders of the United States. As is the case with Hamas, there can

be no peace in the Middle East as long as Hezbollah sees value in using terrorist violence to advance its political, social, and religious goals. Continued and
active U.S. involvement in the Middle East peace process, perhaps through a
functionalist approach that focuses on areas of common interest and defers
the more difficult items of contention until some small victories on the road
to peace have been won, will be critical to finding any sort of solution, no
matter how fragile, to the Arab-Israeli conflict.

The Islamic Republic of Iran

The Islamic Republic of Iran, by any reasonable standard, is a rogue state
that poses a serious international security challenge for the United States, its
allies, and Sunni Arab secular governments in the Middle East. Consistently
defiant of the international community, openly hostile to neighboring states,
and seeking to be the indispensable and dominant power in the region, Iran is
an active supporter of terrorist proxies in Lebanon, the Palestinian territories,
Iraq, and Afghanistan. Because Iran provides military advice and training,
significant financial support, advanced weapons systems, and ideological
support to groups like Hamas, Hezbollah, Palestinian Islamic Jihad, and various Iraqi militias, the clerical regime in Tehran is considered by the United
States to be the world's leading state sponsor of terrorist violence. The use of
proxy groups to conduct acts of terrorism offers Iran multiple strategic advantages, including power projection, influence, deterrence, and flexibility.[41]
In addition to its state sponsorship of terrorism, Iran's suspected pursuit of
a nuclear weapons capability is cause for great concern for the international
community as a whole, and especially for the United States, Israel, Arab states
in the Middle East, and the nations of Europe. The dispute over Iran's nuclear
program has been a dominant characteristic of the international security environment for nearly a decade, since an exiled Iranian resistance group first
revealed to the West in 2002 Iran's progress toward development of a nuclear
weapon. The quest for an Iranian nuclear capability can be traced to the 1950s
and President Dwight Eisenhower's Atoms for Peace program, when Western
nations assisted Iran in its efforts to develop nuclear power until the Iranian
Revolution in 1979.[42] After an Islamic clerical regime took power in Tehran
following the revolution, aid from the United States and its allies was largely
cut off, forcing Iran to eventually turn to other countries for whatever assistance it could get before Russia began investing in Tehran's nuclear program
in the mid-1990s.

While Iran insists its nuclear program is strictly for peaceful civilian energy
purposes, there are valid reasons to believe Iran would be interested in acquir-

ing a nuclear weapons capability. The possession of such a capability would fundamentally alter the balance of power in the entire Middle East in Iran's favor, negating the nuclear fail-safe currently enjoyed by Israel. A nuclear-armed Iran would also likely be treated differently by its neighbors and by the international community as a whole than a non-nuclear-armed Iran would be treated. It's a simple reality that those countries in possession of nuclear weapons hold a different status in international relations than those countries that do not possess nuclear weapons. Iran could, and probably does, view entrance into the club of nuclear nations as a matter of national pride and state power, and it is easy to understand why Iran might be motivated to seek nuclear weapons, given the rough and volatile neighborhood it lives in. But a nuclear-armed Iran is not in the best interest of the broader international system, and there are compelling reasons for the United States and the rest of the international community to do everything possible to prevent Iran from becoming the next nuclear-armed nation. The effort to stop Iran's nuclear progress will be an uphill battle. In the Middle East, Arab governments increasingly concerned about growing Iranian power and influence are at odds with the attitudes of their respective publics. In a survey conducted in early 2008, Shibley Telhami found that nearly half of the Arabs he polled believed a nuclear-armed Iran was more positive than negative for the region, and a full two-thirds of Arabs polled believed Iran had a right to pursue its nuclear program.[43]

Recognizing that Iran has been hostile toward the United States since the 1979 Islamic Revolution, the United States has pursued through the UN Security Council a series of sanctions regimes against the Iranian government and specific individuals and security forces believed to be involved in Iran's nuclear program. The quest for tough and meaningful sanctions against Tehran has been met with tepid support from key Security Council members. China and Russia, both with extensive financial interests in Iran that would be affected by stringent sanctions, have thus far balked at any truly significant measures that might inflict enough pain on the Iranian government to cause a reconsideration of the path it has seemingly embarked upon. One measure Iran would likely have no choice but to respond to would be a blanket ban on the import of refined petroleum products. Iran has large quantities of oil but lacks the capacity to refine it in quantities sufficient to meet growing domestic demand. But the banning of imports of refined petroleum products is not even under consideration by the Security Council. Instead, the UN has been forced to pass multiple rounds of weak sanctions regimes that have had little real impact on Iran's nuclear ambitions or its refusal to work with the international community to resolve the nuclear issue. United Nations Security Council Resolution 1929, the latest UNSC sanctions resolution on Iran, passed in mid-2010 with twelve of fifteen Security Council member votes. The resolution expanded the arms embargo on Iran to include more conventional arms and equipment that could be used for nuclear proliferation and missile development, authorized UN member states to search vessels suspected of hauling illicit cargo to Iran, and placed more stringent restrictions on Iran's financial sector.[44] The United States, unhappy with the measures passed by the Security Council, followed up this UN action with the Comprehensive Iran Sanctions, Accountability, and Divestment Act of 2010 (CISADA) that expanded unilateral U.S. sanctions targeting Iran's energy and banking industries.[45] The United States also announced at the end of 2010 new sanctions against Iranian shipping.[46] These measures, however, have not prompted Iran to reconsider what it describes as its right to develop its own full nuclear capability. Instead, Iran continues to promise multiple rounds of negotiation that have already dragged on for years and that have thus far not produced any Iranian concessions.

Despite the difficulties involved, the United States must be prepared to continue taking the lead in the global effort to counter Iran's irresponsible behavior in the international system. Unless confronted immediately and in a consequential way, Iran will continue to exacerbate the state of instability that characterizes the Middle East and will continue to threaten the interests of the United States and its allies in the international security environment. Iran's support for international terrorism is a significant problem, to be sure, but the more immediate concern for the United States and its allies is the Islamic Republic's continued defiance of the international community over its suspected nuclear weapons program. No one knows for sure how a nuclear weapons capability would affect future Iranian behavior in the Middle East region or internationally, but the behavior of other states could prove to be much more significant. Middle East countries without nuclear weapons might decide it is in their national interest to pursue such weapons, if for no other reason than to counter an Iranian nuclear weapons capability. According to at least one estimate, no fewer than fourteen Middle East states, including Syria, Yemen, and Saudi Arabia, have in just the last few years declared their intention to develop civilian nuclear programs.[47] Israel, often the target of bellicose Iranian rhetoric, could feel compelled to take unilateral action against Iran's nuclear program, including the targeting of key scientists and infrastructure, to maintain the current balance of power in the region and to ensure that no Iranian nuclear attack could be launched against Israeli territory. Precedents for such preventive action by Israel are readily available in the 1981 Israeli strike that destroyed an Iraqi nuclear reactor and the 2007 raid by Israel on a suspected Syrian reactor. There is also the very real possibility that Iran's ties to various regional and global terrorist organizations could result in Iranian nuclear weapons making their way into the hands of Islamic terrorists either deliberately or accidentally.

Iran poses a long-term strategic threat to the United States and its Middle Eastern and Western allies because of its sponsorship of radical Islamist ideology and terrorist violence and its continued pursuit of a suspected nuclear weapons program. Tools or instruments of power available to the United States and the broader international community include UN and non-UN sanctions, interdiction operations targeting suspect cargo shipments bound to or from Iran, nuclear technology export controls, security assurances for Iran's Sunni Arab neighbors and Shia-led Iraq, aggressive diplomatic efforts, and the use of military force. While the potential disadvantages of a military strike on Iran's nuclear facilities could be significant, one thing is certain—the last time the United States suspected Iran had stopped work on a nuclear weapons capability was in 2003, when more than one hundred thousand U.S. military troops were operating in neighboring countries Afghanistan and Iraq. The threat to use force demands attention and as such is an option the United States should not, under any circumstances, remove from its list of possible courses of action. Employment of the instruments of national power against Iran will take significant time and a great deal of patience and sustained effort, as well as considerable coordination between the United States and other nations concerned about Iranian behavior and Iran's destabilizing effect on the Middle East and the larger international community. This is not a short-term endeavor, and time is very clearly on Iran's side.

Extremism in Saudi Arabia

Perhaps no country in the Middle East has the reputation Saudi Arabia has for being a breeding ground for Islamic extremism. The Saudi kingdom is the birthplace of Islam and the site of two of the Islamic faith's most sacred shrines, in Mecca and Medina. Fifteen of the nineteen 9/11 hijackers were Saudi Arabian citizens, and many believed in the aftermath of the 9/11 attacks that the Saudi Arabian government should have been squarely in the United States' crosshairs for retributive action. Historically, the Saudi government has done very little to combat extremism within its borders, generally choosing instead to look the other way as radical sermons and an intolerant educational curriculum spread extreme messages of hate and violence directed at Israel and the West. In recent years, however, the Saudi government has begun to take more aggressive steps aimed at reducing the Islamic extremist threat within the kingdom's borders. Aggressive offensive operations by Saudi security forces have resulted in the death or capture of scores of al Qaeda–linked terrorists and the disruption of terrorist plots aimed at overthrowing the Saudi government. While the ruling al Saud family appears to have recognized, finally, the dangers associated with allowing Islamic extremism to exist unchallenged on its territory, there is still much work to be done to reverse the influence of Islamic radicalism in Saudi society. An extremist takeover of Saudi Arabia would put at risk the economic security of oil-importing nations around the world, something the United States and the international community cannot afford to let happen. Pressure will need to be consistently maintained on the Saudi government to keep up its counterterrorism and anti-extremist efforts, to reform its educational system, and to steadily move toward a more inclusive government that could relieve some of the pressure from disaffected groups within the Saudi population.

The Crisis in Yemen

Another Middle East state causing great concern among the nations of the international community is the Republic of Yemen on the Arabian Peninsula. A weak economy, high unemployment, a poor and illiterate population, and a shortage of natural resources make Yemen a highly desirable location for Islamic extremists seeking a safe haven from which to operate. Oil resources, which account for roughly two-thirds of Yemen's revenue and the vast majority of its income from exports, are expected to be completely exhausted within a decade.[48] Oil production decreased from 460,000 barrels per day in 2002 to less than 350,000 barrels per day in 2007.[49] The people of Yemen are not happy with the status quo, and the government in Sana'a has a tenuous grip on power and limited control over the population. Without immediate and significant international assistance, the Yemeni government will be completely helpless in the face of imminent threats from an insurgency in the north, a secessionist movement in the south, and a growing al Qaeda presence throughout the country. Lacking the resources necessary to hold the country together in the face of numerous security challenges, no Yemeni government is safe. The conditions in Yemen are favorable for al Qaeda in the Arabian Peninsula (AQAP) as it seeks to advance its goal of establishing a strict Islamic state in a strategic location within the Middle East.

AQAP is the local al Qaeda franchise, formed in early 2009 with the merger of the Yemeni and Saudi Arabian al Qaeda groups and headed by individuals once imprisoned at the U.S. terrorist detention facility at Guantanamo Bay, Cuba. Its membership includes recruits from across the international landscape, including North America and Europe.[50] Yemen's al Qaeda franchise also plays host to radical cleric Anwar al-Awlaki, a preacher of violent jihad against the West who has been linked to multiple Islamic terrorists that have targeted the U.S. homeland and America's allies, including Fort Hood gunman Nidal Malik Hasan, Christmas Day bomber Umar Farouk Abdulmutallab, and others. Al-Awlaki, who is a natural-born U.S. citizen, has been designated a legitimate target for assassination because of his ability to effectively and efficiently spread al Qaeda's ideology to English-speaking Muslims across the international system. In early 2009, al-Awlaki published his *44 Ways to Support Jihad*, outlining the responsibility of every Muslim to either directly or indirectly support violence against nonbelievers.[51]

Even before al-Awlaki became the face of al Qaeda on the Arabian Peninsula, Yemen had a significant history of terrorist activity directed at U.S. interests overseas. Terrorist attacks against the United States in Yemen include several strikes on American oil facilities, a failed attack on the USS *Sullivans* in 2000, a successful suicide bombing on the USS *Cole* in 2000 in which seventeen sailors were killed when a motorboat packed with explosives rammed into the side of the American warship, and a 2008 attack on the U.S. embassy in Sana'a. Yemen-based attacks on U.S. personnel and facilities will continue unless something substantive is done to change the country's downward slide toward failed-state status and to reverse the gains being made in Yemen by Islamic extremists. The Obama administration has significantly increased direct U.S. economic and military aid to Yemen, but the amount allocated is unlikely to be sufficient to radically change the current trajectory. The international community's other major players will have to get involved, and soon, if Yemen is going to survive and if al Qaeda is going to be denied a much-sought-after base of operations in a critical region of the world. In the meantime, the United States will need to continue to provide Yemen with funding, weapons, military equipment, and assistance from the CIA and U.S. Special Operations Forces while trying to marshal international support to save Yemen from the disastrous consequences of state failure.

AQAP's leadership believes outside aid, especially if it originates in the United States, could help the group achieve its objective of establishing an Islamic state on the Arabian Peninsula. An AQAP strategy called *Yemen to the United States: I Sacrifice Myself for Your Sake*, released in early 2010, says U.S. financial and military aid could drive a wedge between the Yemeni government and its people, clearing the way for an AQAP takeover.[52] U.S. assistance to a Middle East government always carries with it the risk of alienating the receiving country's citizens because of the poor reputation the United States has among Arab populations. Whether that risk will be realized or not, though, is unknown. What is known is that in the short term the stability of the Yemeni government and its capacity for dealing with security threats within the country's borders must be addressed. In the long term, if less than a decade can be considered long term, a way must be found to increase the ability of the Yemeni state to provide for the needs of its citizens in the face of rapidly dwindling natural resources. There is no way to ignore, wish away, or avoid the coming crisis in Yemen, and the sooner the United States and the international community undertake concrete measures to ensure Yemen's stability and security in an already volatile and dangerous region, the better off America and its allies will be.

Indonesia and the Philippines

In Southeast Asia, where the al Qaeda terrorist network has been active for many years, the threat from Islamic radicals is particularly worrisome in Indonesia, which has the largest Muslim population in the world, and the Philippines, which has struggled for years with Islamists seeking to carve out a Sharia-governed state independent of Philippine authorities in Manila. The geography of these two countries provides Muslim radicals with ideal safe havens for hiding and training militant fighters. Thousands of small and remote islands and vast jungle areas make border control virtually impossible and allow for the relatively easy movement of personnel, equipment, and money. In Indonesia, a Muslim-majority democracy that can serve as an example for the rest of the Islamic world, the most significant threat comes from Jemaah Islamiyah (JI), a militant Islamic terrorist group that also has operational cells in Singapore, Malaysia, Thailand, and the Philippines. JI is believed to have received funding from al Qaeda, and some of its operatives reportedly underwent training in al Qaeda camps in Afghanistan prior to the U.S.-led invasion in 2001. Jemaah Islamiyah is strongly suspected of being responsible for the 2002 nightclub bombing in Bali that killed more than two hundred people, including some American citizens. In the Philippines, the Moro Islamic Liberation Front (MILF) and the Abu Sayyaf Group (ASG) pose the greatest Islamist danger to the Philippine government. Radical Islamic militants from both the MILF and the ASG have had some success winning support among the poorer inhabitants of the Philippines who feel neglected and discriminated against by the Filipino government.

Significant progress against the threat from Islamic radicalism has been made in both Indonesia and the Philippines, but the fight against Muslim extremism in these island archipelagoes is far from being over. Since the 2002 Bali bombing, the Indonesian government has made a concerted effort to get its Islamic extremist problem under control, although Muslim tolerance of Christians in Indonesia continues to be a challenge.⁵³ The complacency of the past seems to have been rejected as the government in Jakarta has come to understand the threat it is facing from the global Islamic extremist movement. In the Philippines, U.S. assistance in the fight against terrorism has been instrumental in Manila's battle with Islamic separatists operating in and around the southern islands. The United States' Operation Enduring Freedom–Philippines strategy of providing low-visibility support while working to legitimize the Filipino government and Filipino armed forces could serve as a model for future counterterrorism efforts across the international system. The terrorist threat in Southeast Asia has been significantly reduced in recent years, but it has not been entirely eliminated. Support from the United States and the broader international community will continue to be critical to Southeast Asian nations working to reduce the region's Islamic extremist problem.

North Korea and the Proliferation Problem

While there is no credible evidence to suggest North Korea directly or indirectly provides support to Islamic radicals, there is a very real possibility that North Korean ballistic missile or nuclear technology could end up in the hands of extremists targeting the United States and its allies and partner nations. North Korea is a known proliferator of weapons technology, and the cash-starved regime in Pyongyang will pursue any course of action that might help keep the Stalinist government in power. Changing North Korean behavior has been a significant challenge for the United States and the West. All previous efforts, to include international isolation, economic sanctions, diplomatic negotiations, designation of North Korea as a state sponsor of terrorism, humanitarian aid, and economic incentive programs, have failed. Occasionally, the North Korean regime demonstrates a willingness to work with the international community to address weapons proliferation concerns, but gestures of goodwill are often short-lived and designed to secure some measure of concession from the major powers in the international system. As soon as North Korea gets what it wants, the cooperation ends.

Ramping up the pressure on Pyongyang is the most logical way ahead if the risk of extremists obtaining unconventional weapons technology from North Korea is going to be mitigated. A policy of "aggressive isolation" advocated by one prominent Asia expert would put North Korea back on the State Department's list of state sponsors of terrorism for its suspected arms sales to Hamas and Hezbollah and for its suspected assistance to Syria's nuclear program, freeze North Korean assets overseas, impose severe travel restrictions on

North Korean officials, develop a robust missile defense program in Southeast Asia, and increase the level of resourcing for the Proliferation Security Initiative's nuclear activities.[54] Of course, increasing the level of pressure applied to North Korea could cause the government to collapse, sparking a humanitarian crisis that would send a flood of refugees across the borders of China and South Korea. Increased pressure could also provoke a violent reaction from Pyongyang if the North Korean regime felt threatened enough to lash out at regional allies of the United States or at American interests in the region. There is no way to know for sure what North Korea's reaction to increased pressure would be, but what is known is that the current international effort to rein in North Korea's weapons proliferation activities has been an abject failure. Maintaining the status quo does nothing but increase the likelihood that extremists will find a way to secure North Korean assets or technology that could be used to target the United States and its allies.

Europe's Muslim Problem

Islamic extremism has become a significant national security problem for European governments faced with declining native populations, a continued influx of Muslim immigrants from the Middle East and Africa, and more frequent Islamic terrorist plots and attacks since al Qaeda struck the U.S. mainland in 2001. The threat from Islamic extremists in Europe is real, and it is growing. Various terrorist networks across the continent are using European nations as sources of desperately needed funding, new militant recruits, and critical logistics support. Muslims are immigrating to Europe in large numbers, and there are serious questions about the willingness and ability of European governments to welcome these immigrants and to assimilate them into European society, not to mention the reluctance of Muslims to integrate fully into the European system. France has the largest number of Muslim inhabitants, with about five million, followed by Germany with more than three million and the Netherlands with about one million.[55] Denmark, Austria, Switzerland, the United Kingdom, and Italy also have significant numbers of Muslims within their populations, and a rise in terrorist activity linked to Islamic extremists in recent years is causing concern among European governments about increasing radicalization among European Muslims. Since the bombings in Madrid and London, Europe has developed a greater sense of urgency in its efforts to deal with Islamic radicals, efforts that will require the cooperation and assistance of the United States if Europe is to be prevented from becoming a launching pad for terrorist strikes against the U.S. homeland.

The contemporary international security environment is a volatile and dangerous one, with no shortage of global hot spots requiring the attention of the United States and its allied and partner nations. The wars in Iraq and Afghanistan, failed and failing states in Africa and the Middle East, rogue nations like Iran seemingly intent on sacrificing peace and stability in exchange for power and influence, a reduced but still dangerous Islamic extremist presence in Southeast Asia, and a rapidly growing threat from Muslim radicals in Europe all must be addressed proactively and aggressively if the United States is to prevent another 9/11-type attack on its soil.

10

The Long Road Ahead

C AN THE UNITED STATES EVER REALLY WIN the global battle with al Qaeda and other radical Islamist groups that make up the broader AQAM network? That is the question increasingly on the minds of American citizens, political leaders, military personnel, and U.S. allied and partner nations after a decade of persistent conflict with Muslim extremists who continue to target the United States and other countries with violent acts of terrorism designed to advance their political, economic, and social goals. The simple answer is "no," the United States cannot win, at least not in the way most people think of when it comes to concepts of victory or defeat in armed conflict. In traditional notions of war, one party "wins" when the opposing party either capitulates or is beaten into submission, with the winning party then able to impose its political will on the losing party. For example, the United States "won" its war of independence with England, achieving its political goal of self-governance, no longer beholden to the British crown. Similarly, Union forces "won" the American Civil War, forcing the Confederacy to accept President Lincoln's political goal of preserving the United States as a single nation. But America's current struggle is different.

The fight against Islamic radicals is not a battle or war that will end in a traditional "win" or "loss" for the United States and those nations that choose to help America in this global campaign. There will be no negotiated settlement, pact, or treaty that allows non-Muslims or even Muslim non-radicals to live side by side in peace with the extremists, and there is virtually no chance Islamic radicalism and the terrorist violence it promotes will just fade away and cease to be an influential ideology that draws despondent

Muslims to its ranks. There will likely always be some individuals, particularly those who believe in the principle of abrogation when it comes to the interpretation of the Koran, that seek to spread their Islamic faith through the use of force. The principle of abrogation holds that when Koranic verses contradict each other, those verses appearing later in the text supersede those verses that preceded them.[1] In the Koran, verses claiming Islam is a religion of peace and tolerance appear near the beginning and are abrogated or annulled by later verses that call on Muslims to compel non-Muslims, through force if necessary, to convert to the Islamic faith. The principle of abrogation is critical to the Islamic extremist movement because it provides Muslim radicals with an Islamic justification for committing acts of terrorism that result in injury and death for nonbelievers and for Muslims who are deemed to have strayed from the path of true Islam. As long as the principle of abrogation is accepted within Islamic societies as a divine authorization to engage in violent acts of terrorism, there will be Islamic extremist brutality directed at the United States, the West, and Muslim governments aligned with the West. Understanding this reality, the United States must work to develop a comprehensive strategic framework that allows America and its allies and partners to reduce the threat of extremist violence to a level that minimizes the disruption of daily life and reduces as much as possible the risk of damage to U.S. and allied interests abroad. This is a fight that will last at least a generation or more and may never end. The sooner that certainty is accepted, the sooner those countries in the crosshairs of Islamic extremism will be able to develop and employ effective responses focused on the long-term management of the problem through the employment of all the elements of national power.

The road ahead will not be an easy one, in the American homeland or anywhere within the international system. The years to come promise to be especially difficult for secular Arab regimes in the Middle East and for the nations of Europe, both of which are in closest proximity to the bulk of the extremist threat. Serious progress against the danger posed by Islamic radicals during this era of persistent conflict begins with an understanding of the enemy and the harm he is capable of inflicting upon the populations he targets. The Muslim extremists targeting the United States and its allies and partner nations today and for the foreseeable future are intelligent, educated, adaptive, creative, and cunning individuals who know how to find and exploit our weaknesses with devastating consequences. They have the advantage. They are willing to wait out U.S. efforts in Afghanistan and Iraq, knowing that eventually the political will of America's leaders will falter, forcing a withdrawal of U.S. military and civilian personnel from both countries. They have an abundance of possible safe havens in failed and failing states in Africa and the Middle East, and they do not place the same value on human life as most individuals in the international system. They are well financed, well armed, well led, and well trained, and they generally get to choose the time, place, and manner of conflict with those who stand in opposition to them. Of course, some terrorist groups targeting the United States and its allies can and will be destroyed. But it is not likely that Western efforts to eradicate *all* such terrorist groups will be successful. The elimination of one extremist organization is likely to be met with the creation of another, ready to take the eliminated group's place among the ranks of the world's radical Islamists. Still, given that some of these terrorist organizations will in fact be eradicated, it is worth noting, in general, how these groups tend to meet their ends.

Extremist organizations of various types have come and gone throughout history, with some lasting just months and others surviving for decades. A Rand Corporation study of more than six hundred terrorist groups that existed between 1968 and 2006 found extremist organizations have generally ended for two major reasons: members of the group decided to adopt nonviolent tactics and work for change through the political process, or local-level police and intelligence agencies arrested or killed important members of the groups. The study also found that military force has seldom been the main cause of a terrorist group's downfall (only 10 percent of the studied groups ended as a result of military action), and very few terrorist groups have been successful in realizing their goals (a mere 7 percent).[2] These findings are not particularly surprising and have been supported by the experiences of American military and civilian personnel operating in Afghanistan, Iraq, and elsewhere. The United States has learned after a decade of conflict with Islamic radicals that some of the greatest progress has been made through the incorporation of disgruntled parties into the political process, as in the case of Sunni insurgents in Iraq, and that local-level intelligence and police forces are far more acceptable to host populations than are foreign military forces, even if the host nation forces are challenged by corruption and sometimes engage in abuses of the law.

Of particular concern is a finding in the Rand study that religious terrorist groups, like al Qaeda and several other Islamic extremist organizations targeting the United States and the West, typically take longer to eliminate than other types of terrorist groups. This finding reinforces the likelihood that the United States will remain engaged, at least for the foreseeable future and probably for at least a generation or more, in a fierce struggle against a committed opponent who will not be easily defeated or limited in his ability to inflict harm against America and its global interests. The Rand findings also underscore the need for the United States to move to a more balanced approach involving all the elements of national power as large-scale combat operations in Afghanistan wind down over the next few years and as security and governance responsibilities in Iraq are fully transitioned to host nation security forces.

Understanding that the current fight against Islamic radicalism is likely to be a generational endeavor is the first step toward managing the Muslim extremist threat. This is a long-term project during which the United States and other nations will need to take a variety of actions involving each of the elements of national power if the terrorism problem is ever going to be successfully managed. The instruments employed within one element of national power will need to be coordinated with the instruments employed within the other elements of national power if they are going to be effective in helping the United States reduce the radical Islamist danger. No single element of national power can be successfully employed in isolation from the other elements. Likewise, an overreliance on one element of power, like the military element over the past decade, at the expense of the other elements of power will result in an inefficient and ineffective approach to a problem that has already demonstrated its deadly potential to cause the deaths of thousands of innocent civilians in vicious surprise attacks on American soil. As the United States reduces its combat commitments across the international system over the coming years, the nonmilitary segments of the federal government will have to assume greater responsibility than they have now. Military resources can only carry the nation so far. Eventually, kinetic operations will have to become more targeted and less frequently employed while the diplomatic, information, economic, intelligence, and law enforcement elements of national power become more actively involved in U.S. grand strategy.

The Diplomatic Element

In the months preceding the U.S.-led invasion of Iraq, President George W. Bush warned the United Nations that the international body risked becoming irrelevant in solving global security challenges if it failed to confront the dangers posed by Saddam Hussein's Ba'athist regime. After the United States entered Iraq with a coalition of dozens of partner states, toppling Saddam's dictatorial government in a matter of just a few weeks, Bush was criticized for abandoning stalled diplomatic efforts within the United Nations Security Council in favor of launching a first strike against what had been described as an imminent threat posed by the Iraqi regime. Bush defended his decision, in part, by arguing that diplomacy with Iraq and with the other nations of the

Security Council had proved to be a futile endeavor, and more than a decade of negotiation and containment backed by weak economic sanctions and the occasional targeted use of military force was failing as a means for gaining Iraqi compliance with international demands. The decision to walk away from potentially endless discussions over Iraq's weapons of mass destruction program was also due in large part to the belief among some Bush administration officials and many Americans that the 9/11 terrorist attacks had ushered in a new era in which the United States could not afford to wait for threats to materialize within America's borders before taking action. The possibility of preventive war was foreshadowed in Bush's 2002 *National Security Strategy*, which said, "As a matter of common sense and self-defense, America will act against such emerging threats before they are fully formed."[3] The United States had to aggressively and proactively go after those who threatened it before they were able to once again commit their acts of violence within America's borders.

The inauguration of Barack Obama as the forty-fourth president of the United States in January 2009 was accompanied by the promise of a new engagement effort across the international system that would put the diplomatic element of national power back at the forefront of U.S. foreign policy. In addition to expressing a desire to work diplomatically with all interested nations and making a concerted attempt to reset U.S. relations with a resurgent and increasingly aggressive Russia, President Obama reached out diplomatically to Iran, the world's leading state sponsor of terrorism and longtime American foe, and indicated negotiation with at least some elements of the Taliban was an idea worth further examination. Neither effort has thus far yielded any tangible results or advanced the prospects for peace and security in a complex and increasingly volatile international security environment. Iran continues to rebuff diplomatic offers from the United States and its allies, protected from stringent economic sanctions to a significant degree by United Nations Security Council permanent members Russia and China, and the Taliban elements that could make a difference in bringing peace to Afghanistan have repeatedly scoffed at the idea of dealing diplomatically with the United States, the Afghan government, or the European members of NATO.

Iran's lack of cooperation forced the Obama administration to explore other options with its allies and partner nations. After diplomatic efforts at the UN failed to achieve what the United States hoped for, unilateral U.S. sanctions against Iran were signed into law by President Obama and diplomatic pressure was increased on Iran's neighbors to boost their national and regional defense capabilities as a counter to Iran's growing power and influence. The Obama administration also worked diplomatically to strengthen the Iraqi government's ability to block Iranian influence and to serve as a strategic buffer to Iran, and to improve Israel's capacity to defend itself in a region increasingly hostile to its very existence as a nation. In Afghanistan, the Obama administration has pursued a strategy of working with U.S. allies to boost aid and support to the Afghan government while simultaneously taking steps to strengthen Pakistan's ability to combat Islamic extremists within Pakistan proper and along the contested Afghanistan-Pakistan border. The result of this effort has been an increasing amount of pressure on militant fighters operating in the border region, making it easier for the United States to battle the Taliban while working to improve Afghanistan's independent governance capability. The overall momentum in Afghanistan is still on the Taliban's side, but the United States' task has become a little more manageable since early 2009.

Regardless of which diplomatic options the United States pursues now or in the years ahead, it is critical that every attempt be made to enlist the support of both allied and shared-interest states in all international relations efforts and not just those where American military troops are committed or where there is a clear danger to the international community. The Islamic extremist threat is not of consequence to the United States alone, a point that needs to be stressed to all potential partner nations at every possible opportunity. Diplomacy works best when it is multilateral and when it targets stable nation-states with demonstrated governance capabilities. Given the generally ineffective historical performance of multinational organizations like the United Nations and NATO and the disparity in capability between the United States and other countries, including America's European allies, the United States should always maintain the right to undertake diplomatic efforts outside the framework of existing international institutions or unilaterally when U.S. government leaders determine it is in the national interest of the United States to take action on its own. Of course, this is a lot harder than it might appear. International events are already moving faster than the State Department can handle. Asking the secretary of state to undertake additional diplomatic efforts independent of the assistance provided in established multinational organizations would require a much greater level of resourcing than the State Department is currently allocated.

Recognizing that manning and funding levels were less than adequate for the challenges of the current international security environment, the State Department developed its first ever assessment of how it could, in conjunction with the U.S. Agency for International Development, become more efficient, accountable, and effective in the execution of its diplomatic responsibilities. The *Quadrennial Diplomacy and Development Review (QDDR) of 2010* recognized the need for increased civilian power at the State Department and called for significant changes in four areas of the department's operations: adapting to existing diplomatic realities in the contemporary operating environment, transforming international development by modernizing it and increasing its level of priority, preventing and responding to global conflicts and crises by improving civilian capabilities, and reforming existing business practices to enable better planning, procurement, and personnel.[4] Implementing changes to the State Department will require more dollars and more personnel from an already stretched federal budget and manpower system. The reforms are critical, though, if the United States is going to effectively utilize the diplomatic element of national power as military operations around the international system decrease in frequency and intensity and as other, less kinetic means for achieving U.S. national objectives become more important.

The Information Element

If the United States is going to win the war of ideas against Islamic extremists, the battle for the hearts and minds of average Muslims everywhere, it will have to develop a credible message that gives ordinary Muslims around the world an alternative to the perverted ideas put forth by radical Islamists, as well as a counternarrative that discredits their twisted vision and exposes them as the barbaric fanatics they are. Al Qaeda prime sees itself as the leading ideological force in a global movement seeking to unite the world under the banner of its radical version of the Islamic faith. Since it was forced to go into hiding after the U.S.-led invasion of Afghanistan, al Qaeda prime has become an ideological role model for like-minded Islamic terrorist groups, providing guidance and direction for al Qaeda affiliates and franchises and for local and regional groups that share the global vision of bin Laden and al-Zawahiri even while focusing on issues of noninternational consequence. Al Qaeda groups and cells have been identified in Iraq, the Maghreb in Western Africa, Saudi Arabia, Yemen, Somalia, Kenya, Tanzania, Uzbekistan, Afghanistan, Pakistan, the Philippines, Europe, the United States, and a number of other nations in the international system. These groups and cells look to al Qaeda prime for strategic-level leadership, ideological guidance, and moral support, and they spread al Qaeda's radical message to the Muslim communities in which they live and operate, gaining the sponsorship of some portions of the population and recruiting new fighters for their battle with those who do not subscribe to their world vision.

Muslim societies throughout the international system, in particular where al Qaeda and its ideology are present and active, must be the primary target of a broad U.S.-led information operations strategy that takes advantage of the reach of the Internet and traditional broadcast radio and television media. Since the terrorist attacks of September 11, 2001, the United States has been steadily losing the battle of narratives to the extremists. Al Qaeda proper and some of its more notable affiliates, especially al Qaeda in Mesopotamia (Iraq), have made extensive use of video footage showing Muslim casualties inflicted by U.S. military forces operating in Islamic countries. Such propaganda is part of a concerted effort to portray American and Western actions as a war against the Islamic faith in which all good Muslims are required to come to the defense of their besieged religion. Bin Laden's followers continue to re-lease audio messages exhorting Muslims everywhere to action and promoting the "war against Islam" theme. The United States and its allies have done an extremely poor job countering the al Qaeda–led extremist media campaign, a trend that must be reversed if the United States is going to win the war of ideas with the radicals.

The information operations way ahead for the United States targets two main groups: ordinary Muslims who might be swayed away from support for extremists and key Muslim figures that hold influence within Muslim communities. The first group is targeted with U.S. outreach programs, including humanitarian aid and media operations. The second group, key Muslims who can influence the larger Muslim population, including par-ents, religious figures, political leaders, and other persons who can help the United States delegitimize the extremist message being promoted by Mus-lim radicals, is targeted with information about America's benign intent and a counternarrative that rebuts claims made by the extremists. One other group deserving of mention as a secondary effort in programs reaching out to Muslim populations is the cadre of low-level Muslim foot soldiers en-listed to do the dirty work of extremist leaders. Senior figures who provide ideological guidance, funding, and planning for terrorist attacks will rarely, if ever, be swayed from their cause. Some of the grunt fighters recruited from normal Muslim families and looking for a good source of income from terrorist operations, however, may be open to changing their minds if a viable alternative to the extremist message and a better way of life are pre-sented to them. Amnesty programs could potentially prove beneficial with rank-and-file Islamic militants, but programs targeting these individuals should take a back seat to efforts directed at the two primary groups. When reaching out to any of these segments of Muslim society, it is critical for the United States to make every effort possible to put a Muslim face on the message being broadcast in order to maximize the message's credibility with the broader Muslim community. For example, the Sakinah campaign in Saudi Arabia uses Islamic scholars who are opposed to terrorist violence to interact on the Internet with individuals looking for religious information, a model that could be useful to the United States in its information outreach to Muslim audiences. Another good example for the United States is the Pakistani practice of posting graphic videos of extremist violence against Muslims on YouTube.[5] Such postings can help show the brutality and complete disregard for human life that is an essential part of Islamic extremist ideology. Finally, moderate Muslim scholars in the United States could be provided an online platform that helps discredit the extremist message and influence would-be terrorists to avoid the radicals' cause.

Another critical target of the information element of national power is public opinion, both in the United States and across the international system. To say the effect of the media on public opinion is profound would be a colossal understatement. The populations of the United States and other countries in the international community are bombarded with a steady flow of information through a twenty-four-hour news cycle that includes local and national news from major networks, cable news outlets, local and satellite radio broadcasts, print publications, and the Internet. This regular stream of information gives domestic and allied publics, and the publics in Muslim lands, an awareness of global events that can seriously impact the decisions of government leaders. Sometimes state leaders ignore public opinion, as former president Bush did when he sent tens of thousands of additional American military forces to Iraq in 2007 in spite of overwhelming public opposition to an increase in U.S. troop levels in that country. Strong public pressure, however, can force a government to take actions that will satisfy popular demand, as when Bush conceded to public wishes by negotiating a status of forces agreement with the Iraqi government that would remove all U.S. military troops from the country by the end of 2011 unless Baghdad asked the United States to stay and assist Iraqi forces beyond the negotiated withdrawal date. Antiwar sentiments among European publics led several nations allied with the United States to abstain from participation in the Iraq war and to limit involvement in Afghanistan to humanitarian and reconstruction missions. The power of public opinion can be overwhelming. It can dramatically affect the range of options available to political leaders seeking courses of action to ensure the protection of their citizens from Islamic extremists attempting to do them harm. It is imperative that information operations target domestic and allied publics and the publics of the broader Muslim community so that informed populations can better enable their governments to take effective action on their behalf.

The battle of narratives is one of the most critical of the global struggle against Islamic extremism and the target of the information element of national power, and it is a battle the United States and its allies are losing. Radical Islamists are gaining power and influence across the international system, and there is no shortage of potential safe havens for future extremist bases of operation. The continued presence of U.S. military forces in Afghanistan and Iraq and the ongoing diplomatic relations between the United States and secular Muslim countries in the Middle East, Africa, and Southeast Asia will provide a steady stream of propaganda to extremists seeking to enlist support from the populations they depend upon for safe haven and various forms of assistance. If the United States and its allies are going to be successful in reducing the threat of Islamic extremism to a level that is manageable and that poses as little danger to Westerners and non-extremist Muslims as possible, the battle of narratives will have to radically change course, and soon.

The Military Element

There is a perception among some in the United States and abroad that the military element of national power has been grossly overused in the years since the 9/11 terrorist attacks, largely at the expense of the other elements of power. Unfortunately for a war-weary American public, the end of the military element's dominance in the fight against Islamic extremism is not coming anytime soon, even as the United States finds it necessary to gradually move to a more balanced approach to the extremist problem in the years ahead. There will necessarily be significant military commitments to Afghanistan, Iraq, the Philippines, Somalia, Pakistan, Djibouti, Yemen, and other as yet unforeseen global hot spots for the foreseeable future. Afghanistan has been labeled the "good" war, a justified response, at least initially, by the United States to a barbaric strike on American soil that left several thousand innocent people dead in the rubble of the World Trade Center towers, the Pentagon, and a field outside Shanksville, Pennsylvania. The situation in Afghanistan, U.S. and European political rhetoric aside, has deteriorated to the point where a renewed commitment by the United States is likely to prove insufficient over the long term. It remains to be seen just how far away the long term will be. In Iraq, the security situation has improved considerably since the sectarian warfare of 2006 and 2007 that brought the country to the brink of civil war, but a U.S. military presence in some form, even if extremely limited and located outside of Iraq proper, will continue to be required for a considerable period of time, despite efforts by the United States to shift the security and governance burdens to the Iraqi government. Combat operations in Iraq are not over for American forces, no matter how many politicians say they are. Simply saying a brigade combat team is an "advise and assist" brigade does not change the reality that young Americans will continue to die in the cities and deserts of Iraq. The government in Baghdad is still extremely fragile and could easily collapse, and ongoing military support from the United States and other nations in the international system will be critical if Iraq is going to stay on a path toward a potentially stable and secure future.

In addition to the major efforts in Afghanistan and Iraq, the United States military will continue to be involved to varying degrees in targeted operations against Islamic extremists in failed and failing states and in stable nations susceptible to violence from radical Islamists. Not all military actions involve active combat operations in which American troops are put in danger of injury or death. Discrete military operations like unmanned aerial vehicle strikes are already increasing in number as the United States looks to reduce its overseas military footprint. A discrete military operation can be defined as a single or continuing use of military force designed to achieve a defined military and political goal by inflicting casualties or causing destruction, without seeking to conquer an opposing army or to capture or control territory.[6] Other military actions will be limited to combat support, logistics support, and advisory and training roles, especially in places like Indonesia, the Philippines, and the Trans-Sahara region in Africa. As the United States moves, eventually, away from active combat and toward a more measured and discrete use of military force, it will seek to maintain a forward presence in or near potential global hot spots so that crises can be addressed before they make their way to the American homeland. In an insecure and dangerously complex international security environment, diplomacy does not always achieve the results desired. In those instances when diplomacy fails, the United States military will have to possess the best personnel, equipment, and technology available if America's political leaders are going to effectively employ the military element of national power as a means for securing the nation's vital national interests.

The primary focus of the military element of power will remain in the near term centered on the threat posed by Islamic extremists. For the long term, though, it is important to remember that threats from states employing conventional military forces have not and will not disappear from the contemporary international security environment. It will be essential for the United States to find an appropriate balance in its military capabilities so that it can wage both traditional, state-on-state military operations against potential conventional foes and asymmetric, counterterrorist, and counterinsurgent irregular warfare actions against nonstandard opponents. The United States does not have the luxury of being able to ignore the growing military power of China and Russia because of a myopic focus on Muslim radicals. A balanced force capable of confronting a variety of challenges will be critical to the long-term security of the American people and U.S. national interests in the international system. Such a powerful and multi-functional force does not come without significant expense. To prepare its armed forces for any possible contingency while reconstituting its military personnel and equipment after nearly a decade of hard-core, active conflict, the United States will have to invest considerable financial resources in the human and materiel instruments employed as part of the military element of power. Simply finding efficiencies in military programs and reducing waste in the defense budget will not be enough.[7]

At a minimum, the United States should be prepared to invest between 6 and 8 percent of its gross domestic product on sustaining America's status as the world's preeminent military power. But the historical trend is not encouraging. Total federal spending on U.S. defense capabilities as a percentage of GDP has steadily decreased over time since the end of World War II. During that conflict the defense budget was nearly 35 percent of the nation's gross domestic product. During the Korean action just a few short years later, it had dropped to just below 12 percent. Defense spending during the Vietnam War slipped into the single digits to less than 9 percent, while the height of the Cold War under Ronald Reagan saw a further drop to only 6 percent of GDP. By the time the United States launched the Persian Gulf War in 1991 to oust Iraqi military forces from Kuwait, the U.S. military's budget had fallen to a level below 5 percent of GDP. In 2010, in the middle of a decades-long conflict with Islamic extremists who have demonstrated an ability to lethally attack the American homeland, the percentage of the United States' gross domestic product spent on its military forces was barely more than 4 percent.[8]

A significant number of weapons systems and equipment platforms, in particular airframes and naval vessels, are several decades old and will have to be replaced in the near term. This is going to be a very costly but necessary expense for the U.S. treasury. The most substantial outlay for the defense budget, however, will be the maintenance of a quality all-volunteer military force during a period of persistent conflict. The United States is currently involved in the longest armed struggle in its history as a nation. That struggle has stretched the nation's military almost to the breaking point, and armed forces personnel are feeling it the most. The strain on America's all-volunteer force, and the understanding that the fight against Islamic extremism will not end anytime soon, has prompted some in the United States to suggest it is time to bring back conscription as a means for providing manpower to the armed forces. Such a move would prove disastrous for the men and women who volunteer to serve their country in uniform. It is the quality of these individuals that has transformed the United States military since the end of the draft into the most formidable armed force in the history of the world. A volunteer military allows those individuals who want to serve their nation in uniform the opportunity to do so, and it allows the military establishment to be selective about who gets to enter its ranks and who does not. The men and women serving in the United States armed forces today are there because they want to be there and because their military has decided that it wants them to be there. Quality personnel are not cheap. The key to attracting and keeping men and women of high caliber in America's armed forces lies in the provision of compensation and benefit packages equal to or better than those found in the private sector. Personnel expenses will remain high, but they are necessary if the United States is to maintain its qualitative manpower advantage over the armed forces of other nations.

It is true that the American military is not large enough in terms of its troop strength to meet all of the demands being placed on it by U.S. government leaders without suffering a high degree of stress on its personnel and equipment. History has shown, though, that when the American people perceive a cause to be just, they will volunteer their service to the nation no matter the cost involved. Americans from all walks of life have done so in every conflict the United States has ever been involved in, and they are continuing to do so today in America's fight with Islamic extremists. Recruiting goals continue to be reached by all branches of the armed forces, although some extreme measures have been necessary to ensure that minimum manpower requirements continue to be met. Recalling reservists, imposing "stop-loss" to prevent critical specialties from exiting the force, lowering enlistment standards, raising the maximum enlistment age, offering sizable monetary bonuses, and providing waivers for unlawful activity have helped the military services reach their recruiting targets but have not degraded the overall quality of the force. These measures simply expanded the potential pool of applicants in order to get more people in the door at armed forces recruiting stations across the country. Those who enlist still have to complete basic military training and specialty skill training before they are able to join the operating force, and standards for those requirements have remained stringent.

The all-volunteer force has proved to be exceptionally capable and effective in major combat and counterterrorism operations while maintaining the ability to conduct other missions, like humanitarian and disaster relief or antipiracy operations, that might be directed by its civilian leadership. In the American military today, quality trumps quantity, and that is the way it should stay. This is not to say additional manpower is not desirable or needed.

Of course it is. But any talk of personnel expansion in the armed forces should be focused on those specialties with the greatest operational need and the best way to attract quality recruits to serve in those critical fields, not on increases in military manpower through the forced enlistment of individuals not eager to serve in uniform. Compulsory military service is not only incompatible with traditional American values and beliefs about involuntary servitude, it results in a lower-quality military force than that achieved with the current all-volunteer force model.

The military element of power is the most visible form of national power exercised by the United States. Hundreds of thousands of U.S. troops are forward-deployed in more than a hundred countries around the international system. The complex and fragile nature of the contemporary international security environment dictates that this will remain the case for decades into the future. Islamic extremism is far from dead as an ideology, and radical Muslims determined to inflict harm on the United States and its citizens will continue to use violent acts of terrorism as a means to strike a foe with vastly superior conventional capabilities. In some cases, the proper response to a global security situation or crisis will be a military one, and in some instances a preemptive or preventive strike may be necessary and justified. A substantial number of American forces will remain committed to Afghanistan and support requirements in Iraq will be necessary for many more years, even as the United States reduces its presence in those countries over time in favor of a more measured use of military power. The naval forces of the United States will continue to patrol the world's oceans and take action where necessary, such as in antipiracy operations along major maritime trade routes and interdiction operations of suspect cargo ships in international waters. American military personnel will be called upon to provide critical humanitarian assistance, training of foreign militaries, counterdrug operations, and counterterrorist or counterinsurgent missions in stable, failed, and failing states in every corner of the world. In short, the United States will not soon significantly reduce the size of its worldwide military presence.

As the demand for the various instruments of the military element of power holds steady or possibly increases, the need for significant investment in the defense establishment will become more critical. A professional and capable all-volunteer force with modern weapons and equipment is expensive but necessary if the United States is going to maintain its current superpower status in the international security arena. The need for a credible military option is as great as it has ever been, even as the United States tries to move away from a heavy use of force and toward the other elements of national power. Some in the United States argue the defense budget must be included with other federal programs in any cuts to spending designed to reduce annual deficits and the gross national debt. Such a position is nonsensical. A decade of sustained military activity at a very high tempo puts tremendous strain on military personnel and the equipment they use in defense of the United States and its citizens. Cuts to the defense budget result in a loss of capability that cannot be risked in an international security environment as dangerous as that in which the United States is currently engaged. This is not an area where the nation can afford to cut corners, nor should it seek to do so. China and Russia are investing significant portions of their national budgets in the modernization and qualitative improvement of their forces, making it critical that the U.S. defense budget be largely exempt from cuts that could reduce the United States' deterrent capability. There is waste in the Department of Defense, to be sure. Inefficiencies and unneeded programs and weapons platforms are legitimate targets for trimming if the savings can then be used to bolster areas of the defense budget that are short on resources. Efforts to rein in government spending must not target America's armed forces just because they receive hundreds of billions of dollars from U.S. taxpayers each year. Protecting American citizens and American interests around the world from potential conventional threats and Muslim extremists acting in the name of Islam will require a strong and balanced military force, and that force will not be had without a sizable price tag.

The Economic Element

The United States is by far the world's leading economic powerhouse, a status that gives America's elected leaders the ability to exert significant economic leverage against other nations and nonstate actors, making the economic element of national power a critical component of the overall U.S. strategy for combating the Islamic extremist threat. Instruments of the economic element of power can be employed either to promote the continuation of a given behavior through incentive or reward, or to encourage or compel a change in state or nonstate actor behavior through the imposition of punitive economic measures. The provision of economic development aid to struggling states can be accompanied by conditions requiring the aid be used to improve governance capability and the quality of life for the recipient nation's people. Programs that support an impartial law enforcement and judicial system, free and fair elections, open media, transparent government, and officials accountable to the people reduce the likelihood that terrorists will find conditions conducive to the establishment of safe havens in struggling nations.

Open and equitable trade relations between the United States and developing countries facilitate commerce that expands markets, increases interdependence, improves quality of life, and undermines the terrorist argument that the United States and other Western nations are benefiting from the exploitation of non-Western countries.

Sanctions, the most commonly thought of punitive economic measures employed in the international system, can be imposed to cut off terrorist funding from states providing both direct and indirect support for terrorist operations and to deny the ability of nonstate groups to participate in the global marketplace. Economic sanctions can include freezing the assets of state sponsors and supporters of terrorism or groups known to funnel money to terrorist organizations, adopting embargoes or boycotts, imposing quotas, tariffs, or export controls, suspending foreign aid, restricting travel, and limiting trade. Although popular in the international system as a means for addressing global security concerns, sanctions often fail to have the full effect desired by the state or states imposing them. In a globalized world that features high levels of interdependence and trade among nation-states, many countries are reluctant to impose economic sanctions that could have a financial impact not only on the targeted state but on themselves as well. Sanctions work best when they are multilateral, but true multilateralism is difficult to achieve for sanctions severe enough to have the potential to change behavior that is undesirable. With the exception of the apartheid government in South Africa, sanctions have a historically poor record of getting states to change behaviors deemed objectionable by other nations. For evidence of the relative futility of sanctions regimes in the contemporary international environment, one only has to look at the case of Iran's suspected nuclear weapons program and the international community's failure to act in a timely and decisive manner. Sanctions can be used effectively for issues deemed nonvital to the national interest of the targeted state and for restricting the ability of terrorist organizations to secure adequate funding. For issues considered nonnegotiable or vital to the national interests of a targeted nation, sanctions generally accomplish little more than allowing imposing states the ability to appear as though they are taking meaningful action without actually doing anything substantive to correct irresponsible behavior in the international system.

Finally, the economic health of the United States is critically important in determining just how much leverage American officials will be able to exercise with the economic element of national power. It is extremely difficult for the nation's elected leadership to justify economic development aid or favorable trade conditions to other countries while American citizens are struggling with a weak economy and high rates of job loss.

Elevated rates of unemployment and a heavy debt burden weaken U.S. economic influence abroad and limit the funds available for economic development aid programs, offsetting the effect of sanctions, and for the operation and maintenance of the United States military while it is engaged in multiple theaters of conflict around the world where Islamic extremists threaten U.S., allied, and partner interests. With the size and scope of U.S. military operations across the international system set to decrease in the years ahead, the economic element of power will grow in importance as the United States seeks to reduce or eliminate funding streams that allow Islamic radicals to execute their acts of terror against American citizens and the publics of allied and partner nations. A weak or unhealthy U.S. economy shifts the focus of the American public and American political leaders away from everything but domestic economic concerns, ultimately restricting the ability of the United States to effectively employ the economic element of national power.

The Intelligence and Law Enforcement Elements

Intelligence information about the goals, plans, actions, movements, or any other data on Islamic terrorists and extremist organizations that might be of value to the United States is critical to disrupting terrorist operations and preventing attacks on the American homeland and on U.S. interests abroad. For intelligence information to be useful, it must be timely, accurate, and actionable. Timely intelligence is collected information that is current enough to be relevant to policymakers and top governmental decision authorities. Finding out the goals, plans, actions, or movements of Muslim extremists after an attack, or after it is too late to prevent an attack, is not much better than not getting the intelligence information at all. Accurate intelligence information is critical to the ability of the United States to take necessary action in response to threats to the nation, a lesson learned by the United States in its invasion of Iraq in 2003. That invasion was based, in part, on the belief that Saddam Hussein possessed chemical weapons of mass destruction, weapons that have never been located in the years since Saddam's Ba'athist government was deposed by American military forces. Intelligence information that is actionable is information that allows the United States to undertake measures to thwart extremists' plans before they can be executed. The United States cannot protect all potential targets at home and in countries far from America's shores. There are simply too many options available to the radical Islamists that threaten the United States, its people, and its national interests.

Quality intelligence that contains enough detail to facilitate preventive action is essential if the United States is to be successful in defending itself against Muslim extremists. Quality intelligence information also enables the United States to bolster its efforts against radical groups through the employment of the other elements of national power. Limited U.S. resources preclude aggressive offensive action in every place Muslim extremists live, train, and operate, making it vital for the United States to focus its efforts where success is most likely to be achieved. Prioritized operations that provide for the defense of American citizens and interests and that facilitate targeted offensive operations that take radical Islamists out of the fight are impossible without intelligence information that is timely, accurate, and actionable. The United States can give itself the best possible chance to secure current and relevant intelligence information by seriously investing in the various types of intelligence-gathering assets, especially the human ones. Human intelligence, or HUMINT, is arguably the most critical intelligence capability the United States can possess in its arsenal of intelligence resources, particularly when it exists at the grassroots level in the communities where Islamic terrorists seek the cover and support of the local populace. Intelligence gathering is an inexact science, and the United States will never know everything it needs to know to be completely effective in stopping terrorist strikes. Investing in the proper intelligence assets to facilitate the collection of timely, accurate, and actionable information and the subsequent sharing of critical intelligence across the government and with allies and partners working with the United States to combat Islamic extremists will increase the likelihood of success in the employment of the intelligence element of national power.

Law enforcement personnel will continue to play a vital role in U.S. efforts to reduce the threat posed by transnational Islamic extremists. It is important that the law enforcement effort not be separated from or elevated above the other elements of national power, as some in the United States and abroad have argued. As with each of the other elements of power, law enforcement is just one component of a comprehensive grand strategy for managing the violence that is a product of radical Islamist ideology. While some Muslim terrorists will rightly be classified as dangerous criminals subject to civilian detention and judicial proceedings, others will require classification, detention, and treatment as unlawful enemy combatants if they are to be neutralized as threats to the United States. Suspected terrorists detained within the United States may, if they are U.S. citizens, be entitled to the legal protections provided for in the Constitution. Foreign nationals detained within the United States or on battlefields abroad, however, should not be granted the same rights and privileges as those who hold American citizenship. Granting such rights does not enhance the safety or security of American citizens but instead increases the likelihood that dangerous actors will be set free to continue to their conflict with the United States and the West. Evidence collection methods and chains of custody that result from normal law enforcement operations are not practical in battlefield situations, where soldiers are engaged in active combat operations with hostile forces. Furthermore, the prosecution of key terrorist leaders and operatives in normal criminal courts could potentially compromise covert intelligence sources and methods, putting intelligence personnel and their contacts in danger of capture or death.

Two sets of rules are needed for the detention and prosecution of suspected Islamic terrorists: one for those instances, most likely involving homegrown extremists who are American citizens, where civilian criminal proceedings might be appropriate, and one for those instances when key terrorist leaders and foreign fighters are detained by the United States military during combat operations, where some sort of tribunal for cases resulting from armed conflict are appropriate. It is understandable that some in the United States would want to treat Islamic terrorists as ordinary criminals best dealt with in U.S. civilian courts of law instead of under military jurisdiction, especially given the problems the United States has encountered with its military tribunals. Their argument is bolstered by the fact that the U.S. Department of Justice has successfully prosecuted more than four hundred individuals in terrorism-related cases since the 9/11 attacks.[9] Elevating law enforcement efforts to such a position, though, is neither the most efficient nor the most effective way to confront the threat from Muslim radicals. Instead, it must be understood that the law enforcement element has to work in concert with the other elements of national power, including the military element, if the United States is going to be successful in reducing the Islamist threat to a level that is manageable and acceptable to the American people.

Finally, the security of the United States' land, sea, and air borders must be addressed as an immediate U.S. national security concern. The first physical line of defense against Islamic radicals seeking to enter the United States to conduct attacks has to be at the point of entry. Stopping terrorists from entering the American homeland is not an easy task by any measure. The U.S. Border Patrol is underresourced, and funding for technological assets along the border with Mexico continues to be problematic in Congress. Even if it could, the United States should not want to stop all immigrants from entering its territory. The American economy is dependent upon labor provided by individuals taking advantage of legal immigration policies and procedures, and the United States cannot afford to cut off completely those immigrants who are simply seeking a better life for themselves and their families. Sealing the border is not a realistic or desirable option. The ultimate goal, and it is a tricky one, must be to secure the nation by air, land, and sea as much as possible, stopping those attempting to enter the country illegally without impeding normal commerce or critically needed legal immigration. To provide the best measure of protection for American citizens at home, the Department of Homeland Security must continue to refine the methods it uses to provide timely and accurate threat information to first responders and to support those local and state governments with the responsibility for taking immediate action in the aftermath of a terrorist attack on U.S. soil. Coordination at the international, national, regional, and local levels is critical. Bureaucracies as large as the United States government are typically inefficient and slow to respond to unfolding events. Some progress has been made since the 9/11 terrorist attacks, but much remains to be done if Americans are going to be protected to the greatest degree possible from the Islamic terrorist threat.

U.S. Leadership in the Fight against Islamic Terrorism

The United States is by far the most powerful nation in the international system, not only in terms of its military and economic strength, but also in the amount of influence it wields with the other nations in the international community. No other country in the world even comes close, and no other nation is likely to approach the level of power enjoyed by the United States for many decades to come, if ever. American technologic, military, and economic superiority provide the United States with an unprecedented degree of global reach that has led the international effort for global security for the better part of a century. That degree of power does not come without a price. America's status as the world's strongest nation means other countries look to the United States for leadership and guidance in an uncertain, complex, and dangerous international security environment. Those who believe the United States is in a state of declining power because of strategic overreach in Afghanistan and Iraq are premature in their assessment that America is destined to lose its status as the world's only superpower. Succumbing to the isolationist sentiments expressed by many in the United States is not a realistic option. Commitments to allied and partner nations and the interdependence inherent in an increasingly globalized world make isolation from those that threaten the American homeland virtually impossible.

Yearnings for isolation also ignore America's history. Since the late 1800s, the United States has seen its armed forces involved in some capacity in conflicts in Cuba, the Philippines, China, Nicaragua, Mexico, Haiti, the Dominican Republic, Europe, Korea, Lebanon, Vietnam, Grenada, Panama, Iraq, Somalia, Bosnia, Kosovo, Yemen, and Afghanistan. Some of these countries have seen U.S. boots on the ground more than once. Almost half of the United States' history since its emergence as a global power has been in armed conflict across the international system, and incidents of American armed intervention have increased steadily since the end of the Cold War. There is no going back to the world that existed prior to the 9/11 attacks. Even if Americans wanted to return to that world, the enemy gets a vote on how future events are going to play out. The United States is the only nation in the international system capable of globally projecting the power and influence necessary to reduce the threat from Islamic terrorism to a level that is both controllable and acceptable. America's allies and partners expect U.S. power to be exercised responsibly and in consultation with the international community. It is an expectation that, if heeded, has the potential to hinder U.S. action against Islamic extremists who have the United States squarely in their crosshairs. Ultimately, the right to act unilaterally must always be maintained.

Muslim radicals seeking to block Western influence and subjugate Muslims and non-Muslims alike under their extremist interpretation of Islam also understand the greatness of American power and view the United States as their primary non-Muslim target in the global security environment. The American approach to the threat posed by Islamic radicalism must be a careful one because the other nations of the world, friend and foe alike, are watching closely every move made by America's political leaders in Washington. If the United States is going to lead the global fight against Muslim extremists, it will need to adhere to the values and beliefs that have made it a beacon of hope for much of the rest of the world. America is not just another country in the broader international system. It is not perfect, to be sure, but it is without doubt a special country that other nations and their peoples look to as a force for good and, in many cases, aspire to be like. It is, simply put, an exceptional nation. If the United States loses the moral high ground in the battle against the radicals, it will be virtually impossible to enlist the help of other nations in places where their vital national interests might not be at stake, but where the United States could nonetheless use the help and support of the international community.

America and its allies and partner countries have made great progress against the threat posed by Muslim extremists, especially the core al Qaeda of Osama bin Laden and its multiple franchises and affiliates around the world. But there is no end in sight, and Americans need to understand that this conflict, in its present form with active combat theaters and aggressive offensive

U.S. action in multiple hot spots around the world, is at a minimum a generational struggle in which various Islamic terrorist groups will come and go and U.S. goals and objectives will frequently change over time in response to new opportunities and new threats. Shifts in the international security environment will require periodic adjustments by the United States that see America engaged in new places and against groups and individuals that have thus far not been of concern, or, in some cases, that have not yet even formed into viable terrorist threats. Given the wide range of tools available to the United States under the elements of American national power, actions will in many cases take place in countries or failed and failing states where America is not actively involved in military operations. Some of these actions will necessarily be unknown to the general public, while others will be widely publicized. Ultimately, it is the national interests of the United States that will determine the measures undertaken by the federal government in defense of its homeland and its people, even if that means snubbing a few allies on occasion. Pulitzer Prize–winning columnist Charles Krauthammer once said,

> In October 1962, during the Cuban Missile Crisis, we came to the edge of the abyss. Then, accompanied by our equally shaken adversary, we both deliberately drew back. On September 11, 2001, we saw the face of Armageddon again, but this time with an enemy that does not draw back. This time the enemy knows no reason. Were that the only difference between now and then, our situation would be hopeless. But there is a second difference between now and then: the uniqueness of our power, unrivaled, not just today but ever. That evens the odds. The rationality of the enemy is something beyond our control. But the use of our power is within our control. And if that power is used wisely, constrained not by illusions and fictions but only by the limits of our mission—which is to bring a modicum of freedom as an antidote to nihilism—we can prevail.[10]

The United States will never return to the way it was on September 10, 2001, and the sooner Americans understand this simple reality, the sooner their government will be able to take all the actions necessary to achieve the only logical objective or end state: a reduction of the threat from Islamist radicals to a level that minimally disrupts Americans' daily lives. The way to reach this objective is through the coordinated and integrated employment of all the elements of national power under one comprehensive grand strategy that is focused on a long-term time line. The means or instruments utilized by the United States will necessarily be dependent upon each unique terrorism-related challenge America is forced to confront. Patience and a determination to do what it takes to ensure the security of the United States will be critical. The terrorist attacks of September 11, 2001, ushered in an era of persistent conflict in which the United States will continue to find itself under unrelenting attack from Islamic radicals for decades to come, if not indefinitely. Some attacks will be stopped before they can do harm to citizens or infrastructure, and some will not. The core challenge is to stop as many plots and attacks as possible while minimizing the damage done from those that cannot be prevented. When Islamic terrorism becomes nothing more than a nuisance requiring minimal containment action and occasional military strikes, the United States will finally be able to say it has prevailed.

Notes

Chapter 1

1. Samuel P. Huntington, "The Lonely Superpower," in *American Foreign Policy*, 8th ed., ed. Glenn P. Hastedt (Guilford: McGraw-Hill/Dushkin, 2002), 33.

2. FBI, "First Strike: Global Terror in America," Federal Bureau of Investigation, http://www.fbi.gov/news/stories/2008/february/tradebom_022608 (accessed January 3, 2010).

3. Thomas H. Kean et al., *9/11 Commission Report*, National Commission on Terrorist Attacks Upon the United States, July 22, 2004, 71–73, http://www.9-11commission.gov/report/911report.pdf (accessed July 10, 2008).

4. NATO, "The North Atlantic Treaty," North Atlantic Treaty Organization, http://www.nato.int/cps/en/natolive/official_texts_17120.htm (accessed August 23, 2010).

5. Thomas P. M. Barnett, *The Pentagon's New Map: War and Peace in the Twenty-First Century* (New York: Putnam, 2004), 34.

6. Thomas Friedman, "National Strategies and Capabilities for a Changing World: Globalization and National Security" (luncheon address presented at the Fletcher Conference for the Institute for Foreign Policy Analysis, Arlington, VA, November 15–16, 2000), http://www.ifpafletcherconference.com/oldtranscripts/2000/friedman.htm (accessed September 28, 2009).

7. Donald Snow, *National Security for a New Era* (New York: Pearson Longman, 2004), 5.

Chapter 2

1. George W. Bush, "Presidential Address to the Nation, October 7, 2001," Johnston's Archive, http://www.johnstonarchive.net/terrorism/bush911d.html (accessed January 3, 2011).

2. Donald H. Rumsfeld, *National Defense Strategy of the United States of America* (Washington, D.C.: U.S. Department of Defense, 2005), 2.

3. "Human Security Report 2009/2010: The Causes of Peace and the Shrinking Costs of War, Part 1: Causes of Peace," Human Security Report Project of the Simon Fraser University, http://www.hsrgroup.org/docs/publications/hsr20092010/2009201 0humansecurityreport-part1-causesofpeace.pdf (accessed February 15, 2011).

4. John T. Bennett, "Commission: China Bolsters Fighters, Missiles, 'Supports' Cyberattacks," *Defense News*, November 17, 2010, http://www.defensenews.com/story.php?i=5064294 (accessed November 17, 2010).

5. Jeremy Page, "China's New Drones Raise Eyebrows," *Wall Street Journal*, November 18, 2010, http://online.wsj.com/article/sb10001424052748703374304575622350604500556.html (accessed November 18, 2010).

6. Katherine Hille, "China Reveals Aircraft Carrier Plans," *Financial Times*, December 17, 2010, http://www.ft.com/cms/s/0/fa7f5e6a-09cc-11e0-8b29-00144fe-abdc0.html#axzz1eomyykck (accessed December 18, 2010).

7. Jeremy Page, "Test Flight Signals Jet Has Reached New Stage," *Wall Street Journal*, January 12, 2011, http://online.wsj.com/article/SB10001424052748704515904576 075852091744070.html (accessed January 12, 2011).

8. Nabi Abdullaev, "Russia Announces Sharp Hike in Defense Spending," *Defense News*, November 9, 2010, http://www.defensenews.com/story.php?i=5016720 (accessed November 9, 2010).

9. Alexei Anishchuk, "Russia Plans New Naval Bases Abroad," *Guardian (UK)*, November 25, 2010, http://www.guardian.co.uk/world/2010/nov/25/russia-new-naval-bases-abroad (accessed November 25, 2010).

10. "Putin Pledges $646 Billion to Modernize Russia's Army," Radio Free Europe Radio Liberty, December 13, 2010, http://www.rferl.org/content/putin_pledges_646_billion_to_modernize_russian_army/2247315.html (accessed December 13, 2010).

11. Al Neuharth, "Why It's OK for Iran to Join 'Nuclear Age,'" *USAToday*, December 10, 2010, http://www.usatoday.com/news/opinion/forum/2010-12-10-column10_ST_N.htm (accessed December 10, 2010).

12. Karen DeYoung, "Pakistan Doubles Its Nuclear Arsenal," *Washington Post*, January 31, 2011, http://www.washingtonpost.com/wp-dyn/content/article/2011/01/30/AR2011013004682.html (accessed January 31, 2011).

13. Ibid.

14. Martin Harrow, "Inside a Wave of Terrorism: The Dynamic Relation between Terrorism and the Factors Leading to Terrorism," *Journal of Global Change and Governance*, 1 (2008): 2, Human Security Report Project: Human Security Gateway, http://www.humansecuritygateway.info/documents/HARROW_InsideWaveOfTerrorism.pdf (accessed June 28, 2009).

15. David C. Rapoport, *The Four Waves of Modern Terrorism* (Los Angeles: UCLA International Institute, 2006), 47, http://www.international.ucla.edu/cms/files/Rapoport-Four-Waves-of-Modern-Terrorism.pdf (accessed May 21, 2010).

16. Todd Sandler et al., "Terrorism" (paper presented to the Copenhagen Consensus 2008 Challenge, February 2008), 5.

17. "Title 22, United States Code, Section 2656f," Cornell University Law School, http://www.law.cornell.edu/uscode/22/usc_sec_22_00002656---f000-.html (accessed March 29, 2009).

18. John Baylis, *Strategy in the Contemporary World: An Introduction to Strategic Studies* (New York: Oxford University Press, 2003), 211.

19. Paul R. Pillar, *Terrorism and U.S. Foreign Policy* (Washington, D.C.: Brookings Institution Press, 2001), 13–14.

20. Ibid, 130–31.

21. "Getting Inside the Terrorist Mind," Rand Corporation, 2007, http://www.rand.org/content/dam/rand/pubs/research_briefs/2007/RAND_RB9258.pdf (accessed July 2, 2008).

22. Chairman of the Joint Chiefs of Staff, *National Military Strategic Plan for the War on Terrorism* (Washington, D.C.: U.S. Department of Defense, 2006), 4.

23. Rick Nelson et al., *A Threat Transformed: Al Qaeda and Associated Movements in 2011* (Washington, D.C.: Center for Strategic and International Studies, 2011), 2.

24. Daniel L. Byman, "Al Qaeda's M & A Strategy," *Foreign Policy*, December 7, 2010, http://www.foreignpolicy.com/articles/2010/12/07/al_qaedas_m_and_a_strategy (accessed December 7, 2010).

25. Dale C. Eikmeier, "Qutbism: An Ideology of Islamic-Fascism," *Parameters* 37, no. 1 (2007): 90–91.

26. Christopher M. Blanchard, *Al Qaeda: Statements and Evolving Ideology*, Congressional Research Service (Washington, D.C.: 2007), 5.

27. Bruce Hoffman, "Al-Qaeda Has a New Strategy. Obama Needs One, Too," *Washington Post*, January 10, 2010, http://www.washingtonpost.com/wp-dyn/content/article/2010/01/08/AR2010010803555.html (accessed January 10, 2010).

28. Daveed Gartenstein-Ross, "Threat Matrix: Reflections on Osama bin Laden, and His Continuing Relevance," *Long War Journal*, November 4, 2010, http://www.longwarjournal.org/threat-matrix/archives/2010/11/reflections_on_osama_bin_laden_1.php (accessed November 4, 2010).

29. Donald Snow, *National Security for a New Era* (New York: Pearson Longman, 2004), 288.

30. Christine Bartolf and Bernard I. Finel, *Are We Winning? Measuring Progress in the Struggle against al Qaeda and Associated Movements*, American Security Project, 2009, 19.

31. "Title 50, United States Code, Section 2405," Cornell University Law School, http://www.law.cornell.edu/uscode/html/uscode50a/usc_sec_50a_00002405----000-.html (accessed March 29, 2009).

32. *Unclassified Report on Military Power of Iran*, United States Department of Defense, April, 2010, 8, http://www.foxnews.com/projects/pdf/IranReportUnclassified.pdf (accessed May 1, 2010).

33. Robert M. Gates, *Report on Progress toward Security and Stability in Afghanistan*, Report to Congress in accordance with Section 1230 of the National Defense Authorization Act for Fiscal Year 2008 (Washington, D.C.: U.S. Department of Defense, 2010), 43.

34. Ibid., 2–3.

35. "Country Reports on Terrorism, 2009," United States Department of State, August 5, 2010, chapter 3, http://www.state.gov/s/ct/rls/crt/2009/140889.htm (accessed December 21, 2010).

36. "Country Reports on Terrorism, 2007," United States Department of State, April 30, 2008, chapter 3, http://www.state.gov/s/ct/rls/crt/2007/103711.htm (accessed August 12, 2008).

37. Pillar, *Terrorism and U.S. Foreign Policy*, 170.

38. "Foreign Terrorist Organization Designation," United States Department of State, September 1, 2010, http://www.state.gov/r/pa/prs/ps/2010/09/146554.htm (accessed November 12, 2010).

39. "2008 Report on Terrorism," National Counterterrorism Center, April 30, 2009, 10, http://www.fas.org/irp/threat/nctc2008.pdf (accessed August 3, 2009).

40. "Press Release for Country Reports on Terrorism, 2009," United States Department of State, August 5, 2010, http://www.state.gov/r/pa/prs/ps/2010/08/145737.htm (accessed August 31, 2010).

41. George W. Bush, *National Strategy for Combating Terrorism* (Washington, D.C.: The White House, 2006), 3, http://georgewbush-whitehouse.archives.gov/nsc/nsct/2006/ (accessed July 7, 2007).

42. George W. Bush, *National Strategy for Homeland Security* (Washington, D.C.: Homeland Security Council, 2007), 3, http://www.dhs.gov/xlibrary/assets/nat_strat_homelandsecurity_2007.pdf (accessed April 23, 2008).

43. *Merriam-Webster Online Dictionary*, s.v. "war," http://www.merriam-webster.com/dictionary/war (accessed October 4, 2007).

44. Caleb Carr, *The Lessons of Terror* (New York: Random House, 2002), 11.

45. United States Army, *U.S. Army Field Manual 5-0: The Operations Process* (Washington, D.C.: Department of the Army, 2010), 3–4.

46. Ibid.

Chapter 3

1. John D. Johnson, "Root Causes of Islamist Extremism: Nine Years Later," *Small Wars Journal*, January 10, 2011, http://smallwarsjournal.com/blog/2011/01/root-causes-of-islamist-extrem/ (accessed January 11, 2011).

2. David Kilcullen, *The Accidental Guerrilla: Fighting Small Wars in the Midst of a Big One* (New York: Oxford University Press, 2009), 7–27.

3. *The Royal College of Defence Studies Strategy Handbook*, 2nd ed., The Royal College of Defence Studies, Defence Academy of the United Kingdom, February 15, 2010, 9, http://www.mod.uk/NR/rdonlyres/9E28927E-733F-49E1-A0AB-7BA46AF3F8F6/0/rcdsstrategyhandbook.pdf (accessed March 31, 2010).

4. Seth Cropsey, "Anchors Away: American Sea Power in Dry Dock," *World Affairs Journal,* January/February 2011, http://www.worldaffairsjournal.org/articles/2011-JanFeb/full-Cropsey-JF-2011.html (accessed February 23, 2011).

5. Andrew F. Krepinevich, *7 Deadly Scenarios: A Military Futurist Explores War in the 21st Century* (New York: Bantam, 2009), 291–94.

6. Colin S. Gray, *Modern Strategy* (New York: Oxford University Press, 1999), 361.

7. Richard H. Yarger, "Towards a Theory of Strategy: Art Lykke and the Army War College Strategy Model," https://dde.carlisle.army.mil/authors/stratpap.htm (accessed November 15, 2007).

8. Ibid.

9. J. Boone Bartholomees, ed., *U.S. Army War College Guide to National Security Issues, Volume II: National Security Policy and Strategy,* 3rd ed., (Carlisle, Pa.: U.S. Army War College, 2008), 276.

10. Barack H. Obama, *National Security Strategy* (Washington, D.C.: The White House, 2010), 7.

11. Richard H. Yarger, "Towards a Theory of Strategy: Art Lykke and the Army War College Strategy Model," https://dde.carlisle.army.mil/authors/stratpap.htm (accessed November 15, 2007).

12. Chairman of the Joint Chiefs of Staff, *National Military Strategic Plan for the War on Terrorism* (Washington, D.C.: U.S. Department of Defense, 2006), 5.

13. David Jablonsky, "National Power," in *U.S. Army War College Guide to National Security Issues, Volume I: Theory of War and Strategy,* 3rd ed., ed. J. Boone Bartholomees (Carlisle, Pa.: U.S. Army War College, 2008), 148.

14. Donald Snow, *National Security for a New Era* (New York: Pearson Longman, 2004), 174–75.

15. Chairman of the Joint Chiefs of Staff, *Joint Publication 3-16: Multi-national Operations* (Washington, D.C.: U.S. Department of Defense, 2007), I-1.

16. NATO, "The North Atlantic Treaty," North Atlantic Treaty Organization, http://www.nato.int/cps/en/natolive/official_texts_17120.htm (accessed August 23, 2010).

17. Rafael L. Bardaji, "NATO at 60," *Weekly Standard,* March 24, 2009, http://www.weeklystandard.com/Content/Public/Articles/000/000/016/322ndlep.asp (accessed March 24, 2009).

18. Ahto Lobjakas, "NATO Looks to Evolve without Shedding DNA," *International Relations and Security Network,* April 23, 2010, http://www.isn.ethz.ch/isn/Current-Affairs/Security-Watch/Detail/?ots591=4888caa0-b3db-1461-98b9-e20e7b9c13d4&lng=en&id=115320 (accessed April 23, 2010).

19. "Active Engagement, Modern Defence: Strategic Concept for the Defence and the Security of the Members of the North Atlantic Treaty Organization," North Atlantic Treaty Organization, November 19, 2010, http://www.nato.int/cps/en/natolive/official_texts_68580.htm (accessed November 20, 2010).

20. Judy Dempsey, "The Peril That NATO Can't Ignore," *New York Times,* November 10, 2010, http://www.nytimes.com/2010/11/11/world/europe/11iht-letter.html (accessed November 10, 2010).

21. "Defence Data 2009," European Defence Agency (2010), 2–3.

22. Henry Chu, "As Europe Cuts Military Budgets, Some Worry about Its Clout," *Los Angeles Times*, December 5, 2010, http://articles.latimes.com/2010/dec/05/world/la-fg-europe-military-20101205 (accessed December 5, 2010).

23. Andrew R. Hoehn and Sarah Harting, *Risking NATO: Testing the Limits of the Alliance in Afghanistan*, Rand Corporation, 2010, 71, http://www.rand.org/pubs/monographs/2010/RAND_MG974.pdf (accessed December 3, 2010).

Chapter 4

1. Reed J. Fendrick, "Diplomacy as an Instrument of National Power," in *U.S. Army War College Guide to National Security Issues, Volume I: Theory of War and Strategy*, 3rd ed., ed. J. Boone Bartholomees (Carlisle, Pa.: U.S. Army War College, 2008), 190.

2. *The Royal College of Defence Studies Strategy Handbook*, 2nd ed., The Royal College of Defence Studies, Defence Academy of the United Kingdom, February 15, 2010, 9, http://www.mod.uk/NR/rdonlyres/9E28927E-733F-49E1-A0AB-7BA46AF3F8F6/0/rcdsstrategyhandbook.pdf (accessed March 31, 2010).

3. Kristin M. Lord and Richard Fontaine, *Managing 21st Century Diplomacy: Lessons from Global Corporations*, (Washington, D.C.: Center for a New American Security, 2010), 8.

4. United Nations, "Charter of the United Nations," http://www.un.org/en/documents/charter/chapter1.shtml (accessed September 21, 2008).

5. *USAID Strategic Plan, FYs 2004–2009*, Publication Number 11084, (Washington, D.C.: U.S. Department of State, 2003), 4.

6. Brett D. Schaefer and Anthony B. Kim, *U.S. Aid Does Not Build Support at the U.N.*, Heritage Foundation, 2007, 3, http://www.heritage.org/research/reports/2007/03/us-aid-does-not-build-support-at-the-un (accessed May 15, 2008).

7. *Issues 2010: The Candidate's Briefing Book*, Heritage Foundation, 2009, 150, http://www.issues2010.com/ (accessed December 13, 2010).

8. Ibid., 151.

9. "U.S. Dues and Contributions to the United Nations," Better World Campaign, http://www.betterworldcampaign.org/issues/funding/us-dues-and-contributions.html (accessed January 2, 2011).

10. John R. Bolton, *The Key to Changing the United Nations System*, American Enterprise Institute for Public Policy Research, October 10, 2010, http://www.aei.org/outlook/101000 (accessed November 1, 2010).

11. Daniel Trachsler, *UN Security Council Reform: A Gordian Knot?* CSS Analysis in Security Policy Number 72, International Relations and Security Network (Zurich: April 2010), 2.

12. Kara C. McDonald and Stewart M. Patrick, *UN Security Council Enlargement and U.S. Interests* (Washington, D.C.: Council on Foreign Relations, 2010), 21–22.

13. United Nations, "Charter of the United Nations," http://www.un.org/en/documents/charter/chapter1.shtml (accessed September 21, 2008).

14. Amos A. Jordan et al., *American National Security*, 5th ed. (Baltimore: Johns Hopkins University Press, 1999), 483–84.

15. "Foreign Terrorist Organization Designation," United States Department of State, September 1, 2010, http://www.state.gov/r/pa/prs/ps/2010/09/146554.htm (accessed November 12, 2010).

16. Angel Rabasa et al., *Deradicalizing Islamist Extremists* (Washington, D.C.: Rand Corporation, 2010), 1.

Chapter 5

1. Antulio J. Echevarria II, "Wars of Ideas and the War of Ideas," Strategic Studies Institute, United States Army War College, June, 2008, 3, http://www.carlisle.army.mil/DIME/documents/Echevarria.pdf (accessed August 21, 2008).

2. Chairman of the Joint Chiefs of Staff, *National Military Strategic Plan for the War on Terrorism* (Washington, D.C.: U.S. Department of Defense, 2006), 12.

3. Martin Harrow, "Inside a Wave of Terrorism: The Dynamic Relation between Terrorism and the Factors Leading to Terrorism," *Journal of Global Change and Governance* 1, no. 3 (2008): 4, Human Security Report Project: Human Security Gateway, http://www.humansecuritygateway.info/documents/HARROW_InsideWaveOfTerrorism.pdf (accessed June 28, 2009).

4. Hassan Mneimneh, "Islamism," American Enterprise Institute's Critical Threats Project, October 1, 2009, http://www.criticalthreats.org/basics/islamism (accessed December 10, 2009).

5. Gregory M. Davis, "Islam 101," Jihad Watch, http://www.jihadwatch.org/islam-101.html (accessed October 10, 2010).

6. "Understanding the Muslim Brotherhood," *The Week*, February 11, 2011, http://theweek.com/article/index/211951/understanding-the-muslim-brotherhood (accessed February 11, 2011).

7. "Controversial Gathering of Islamic Scholars Refutes Al-Qaeda's Ideological Cornerstone," *Terrorism Monitor* 8, no. 14 (2010), Jamestown Foundation, http://www.jamestown.org/single/?no_cache=1&tx_ttnews%5Btt_news%5D=36248&tx_ttnews%5BbackPid%5D=381&cHash=ea30c780ba (accessed May 1, 2010).

8. Ibid.

9. Brian M. Jenkins, "Building an Army of Believers: Jihadist Radicalization and Recruitment," Rand Corporation, April 5, 2007, 3, http://www.rand.org/content/dam/rand/pubs/testimonies/2007/RAND_CT278-1.pdf (accessed May 1, 2008).

10. Shibley Telhami, *2008 Annual Arab Public Opinion Poll*, Survey of the Anwar Sadat Chair for Peace and Development at the University of Maryland (with Zogby International), March 2008, http://www.brookings.edu/~/media/Files/events/2008/0414_middle_east/0414_middle_east_telhami.pdf (accessed June 5, 2009).

11. Shibley Telhami, *2010 Annual Arab Public Opinion Poll*, Survey of the Anwar Sadat Chair for Peace and Development at the University of Maryland (with Zogby International), July 2010, http://www.brookings.edu/~/media/Files/rc/reports/

2010/08_arab_opinion_poll_telhami/08_arab_opinion_poll_telhami.pdf (accessed August 10, 2010).

12. Donna Abu-Nasr and Lee Keath, "200 Web Sites Spread Al-Qaida's Message in English," Associated Press, November 20, 2009, http://www.huffingtonpost.com/2009/11/19/increasing-number-of-web_n_364635.html (accessed November 20, 2009).

13. "The Jihadist Social Network Underworld," Investigative Project on Terrorism, December 10, 2010, http://www.investigativeproject.org/2398/the-jihadist-social-network-underworld (accessed December 10, 2010).

14. Katherine Zimmerman, "Expanding the Campaign of Violence: Al Qaeda in the Arabian Peninsula's English-Language Magazine," American Enterprise Institute's Critical Threats Project, July 13, 2010, http://www.criticalthreats.org/yemen/expanding-campaign-violence-al-qaeda-arabian-peninsulas-english-language-magazine-july-13-2010 (accessed July 14, 2010).

15. Bob Drogin, "The 'Vanity Fair' of Al Qaeda," *Los Angeles Times*, November 27, 2010, http://articles.latimes.com/2010/nov/26/nation/la-na-terror-magazine-20101126 (accessed November 27, 2010).

16. Alexander Meleagron-Hitchens, "New English-Language Al-Qaeda Explosives Manual Released Online," International Centre for the Study of Radicalisation and Political Violence, December 31, 2010, http://www.icsr.info/news/icsr-insight-new-english-language-al-qaeda-explosives-manual-released-online (accessed December 31, 2010).

17. Mohammed Ali Musawi, *Cheering for Osama: How Jihadists Use Internet Discussion Forums*, Quilliam Foundation, September 27, 2010, 12.

18. Daniel Kimmage, *The Al-Qaeda Media Nexus: The Virtual Network behind the Global Message*, Radio Free Europe/Radio Liberty, March 2008, 18, http://docs.rferl.org/en-US/AQ_Media_Nexus.pdf (accessed June 1, 2008).

19. Antulio J. Echevarria II, "Wars of Ideas and the War of Ideas," Strategic Studies Institute, United States Army War College, June, 2008, 28, http://www.carlisle.army.mil/DIME/documents/Echevarria.pdf (accessed August 21, 2008).

20. Kristin M. Lord and Marc Lynch, *America's Extended Hand: Assessing the Obama Administration's Global Engagement Strategy* (Washington, D.C.: Center for a New American Security, 2010), 11.

21. Scott Helfstein et al., *Deadly Vanguards: A Study of Al-Qa'ida's Violence against Muslims* (West Point, N.Y.: United States Military Academy, Combating Terrorism Center, 2009), 2.

22. Jarret M. Brachman and William F. McCaints, *Stealing Al-Qa'ida's Playbook* (West Point, N.Y.: United States Military Academy, Combating Terrorism Center, 2006), 12.

23. "Prominent Egyptian Preacher Dissects Al-Qaeda Strategy," *Terrorism Monitor* 8, no. 30 (2010), Jamestown Foundation, http://www.jamestown.org/uploads/media/TM_008_72.pdf (accessed August 1, 2010).

24. UN Counter-Terrorism Implementation Task Force, *First Report of the Working Group on Radicalisation and Extremism That Lead to Terrorism* (September 2008), 5, in *Deradicalizing Islamist Extremists*, ed. Angel Rabasa et al. (Rand Corporation: 2010).

25. "Rand Proposes Blueprint for Building Moderate Muslim Networks," Rand Corporation, 2007, http://www.rand.org/pubs/research_briefs/2007/RAND_RB9251.pdf (accessed February 22, 2008).

26. Paul R. Pillar, *Terrorism and U.S. Foreign Policy* (Washington, D.C.: Brookings Institution Press, 2001), 197.

Chapter 6

1. William S. Lind et al., "The Changing Face of War: Into the Fourth Generation," Global Guerrillas, http://globalguerrillas.typepad.com/lind/the-changing-face-of-war-into-the-fourth-generation.html (accessed May 16, 2010).

2. Amos A. Jordan et al., *American National Security*, 5th ed. (Baltimore: Johns Hopkins University Press, 1999), 30–31.

3. Ibid., 43–44.

4. Ibid., 272.

5. Paul R. Pillar, *Terrorism and U.S. Foreign Policy* (Washington, D.C.: Brookings Institution Press, 2001), 102.

6. Chairman of the Joint Chiefs of Staff, *Joint Publication 1-02, Department of Defense Dictionary of Military and Associated Terms* (Washington, D.C.: U.S. Department of Defense, 2001), 415.

7. Ibid., 333.

8. Richard N. Haass, *Intervention* (Washington, D.C.: The Brookings Institution Press, 1999), 50.

9. Joshua Partlow, *Milestone in Training Afghan Forces*, Washington Post, November 9, 2010, http://www.washingtonpost.com/wp-dyn/content/article/2010/11/08/AR2010110806052.html (accessed November 9, 2010).

10. Ibid.

11. Introduction to *Afghan Army Growing, but Additional Trainers Needed*, report to congressional addressees (Washington, D.C.: Government Accountability Office, 2011).

12. Spencer Ackerman, "Yearly Price Tag for Afghan Forces: $6 Billion, Indefinitely," *Danger Room*, December 16, 2010, http://www.wired.com/danger-room/2010/12/yearly-price-tab-for-afghan-forces-6-billion-indefinitely/ (accessed December 16, 2010).

13. Walter Pincus, "Gauging the Price Tag for Afghanistan's Security," *Washington Post*, December 21, 2010, http://www.washingtonpost.com/wp-dyn/content/article/2010/12/20/AR2010122004829.html (accessed December 21, 2010).

14. Bijan R. Kian and Wayne Porter, "A New Deal: A Plan for Sustainable Afghan Security," New America Foundation, December 6, 2010, http://www.newamerica.net/publications/policy/a_new_deal_a_plan_for_sustainable_afghan_stability (accessed December 10, 2010).

15. Chairman of the Joint Chiefs of Staff, *Joint Publication 3-16, Multinational Operations* (Washington, D.C.: U.S. Department of Defense, 2007), I-4.

16. Vice Chairman of the Joint Chiefs of Staff, *An Evolving Joint Perspective: U.S. Joint Warfare and Crisis Resolution in the 21st Century*, Joint Staff, J7 Division (Washington, D.C.: U.S. Department of Defense, 2003), 61.

17. A. E. Stahl and William F. Owen, "Targeted Killings Work," *Infinity Journal* no. 1 (2010): 10, http://www.infinityjournal.com/article/3/Targeted_Killings_Work (accessed January 2, 2011).

Chapter 7

1. *Issues 2010: The Candidate's Briefing Book*, Heritage Foundation, 2009, 143, http://www.issues2010.com/ (accessed December 13, 2010).

2. William Antholis and Strobe Talbott, "Tackling Trade and Climate Change," in *Opportunity '08: Independent Ideas for America's Next President*, ed. Michael E. O'Hanlon (Washington, D.C.: Brookings Institution Press, 2007), 64.

3. Paul Miller, "What Is Foreign Aid For?" *Foreign Policy*, January 27, 2011, http://shadow.foreignpolicy.com/posts/2011/01/27/what_is_foreign_aid_for (accessed January 27, 2011).

4. Raphael Perl, *Terrorism, the Future, and U.S. Foreign Policy*, issue brief for Congress (Washington, D.C.: Congressional Research Service, 2003), 9–10.

5. David C. Gompert and John Gordon IV, *War by Other Means: Building Complete and Balanced Capabilities for Counterinsurgency* (Washington, D.C.: Rand Corporation, 2008), 34.

6. "Foreign Aid and Economic Development," in *Cato Handbook for Policymakers*, 7th ed. (Washington, D.C.: Cato Institute, 2009), 656.

7. Perl, *Terrorism, the Future, and U.S. Foreign Policy*, 9.

8. Paul R. Pillar, *Terrorism and U.S. Foreign Policy* (Washington, D.C.: Brookings Institution Press, 2001), 167–69.

9. "Country Reports on Terrorism, 2009," United States Department of State, August 5, 2010, 213, http://www.state.gov/s/ct/rls/crt/2009/140889.htm (accessed December 21, 2010).

10. Eric Lichtblau and Eric Schmitt, "Cash Flow to Terrorists Evades U.S. Efforts," *New York Times*, December 5, 2010, http://www.nytimes.com/2010/12/06/world/middleeast/06wikileaks-financing.html (accessed December 6, 2010).

11. Frank G. Hoffman, "Striking a Balance: Posturing the Future Force for COIN and Conventional Warfare," *Armed Forces Journal*, July 2009, http://www.armedforcesjournal.com/2009/07/4099782/ (accessed September 1, 2009).

12. "Federal Spending Chart 10," *2010 Budget Chart Book*, Heritage Foundation, 2010, http://www.heritage.org/budgetchartbook/obama-budget-defense-spending (accessed January 10, 2011).

13. David Barboza, "China Passes Japan as Second-Largest Economy," *New York Times*, August 15, 2010, http://www.nytimes.com/2010/08/16/business/global/16yuan.html (accessed August 16, 2010).

14. *Issues 2010: The Candidate's Briefing Book*, Heritage Foundation, 2009, 41, http://www.issues2010.com/ (accessed December 13, 2010).

15. Peter A. Buxbaum, "Balancing the Budget on DoD's Back," *International Relations and Security Network*, January 31, 2011, http://www.isn.ethz.ch/isn/Current-Affairs/ISN-Insights/Detail?lng=en&id=126477&contextid734=126477&contextid735=126476&tabid=126476126477 (accessed February 2, 2011).

16. "Table 7.1, Federal Debt at the End of the Year: 1940–2015," Government Printing Office, http://www.gpoaccess.gov/usbudget/fy11/sheets/hist07z1.xls (accessed January 21, 2011).

17. Buxbaum, "Balancing the Budget on DoD's Back."

Chapter 8

1. Paisley Dodds, "Spy Agencies Use Ex-Captives to Infiltrate Al Qaeda," *Miami Herald*, November 5, 2010, http://www.miamiherald.com/2010/11/05/1910118/spy-agencies-infiltrate-al-qaida.html (accessed November 6, 2010).

2. David Kris, remarks to Law Enforcement as a Counterterrorism Tool Panel, Brookings Institution, June 10, 2010, http://www.brookings.edu/events/2010/0611_law_enforcement.aspx (accessed November 24, 2010).

3. Charles Krauthammer, "Travesty in New York," *Washington Post*, November 20, 2009, http://www.washingtonpost.com/wp-dyn/content/article/2009/11/19/AR2009111903434.html (accessed November 21, 2009).

4. George Friedman, "Deciphering the Mohammed Trial," Strategic Forecasting, November 16, 2009, http://www.stratfor.com/weekly/20091116_postsept_11_legal_dilemma (accessed November 16, 2009).

5. James Clapper, *Summary of the Reengagement of Detainees Formerly Held at Guantanamo Bay, Cuba* (Washington, D.C.: Office of the Director of National Intelligence, 2010), http://www.dni.gov/electronic_reading_room/120710_Summary_of_the_Reengagement_of_Detainees_Formerly_Held_at_Guantanamo_Bay_Cuba.pdf (accessed January 2, 2011).

6. Peter Finn and Anne E. Kornblut, "Indefinite Detention Possible for Suspects at Guantanamo Bay," *Washington Post*, December 22, 2010, http://www.washingtonpost.com/wp-dyn/content/article/2010/12/21/AR2010122105523.html (accessed December 23, 2010).

7. Thomas P. M. Barnett, *Great Powers: America and the World After Bush* (New York: G. P. Putnam's Sons, 2009), 56–58.

8. Richard M. Stana, introduction to *Border Security: Preliminary Observations on Border Control Measures for the Southwestern Border*, testimony before the Subcommittee on Border and Maritime Security, Committee on Homeland Security, U.S. House of Representatives (Washington, D.C.: Government Accountability Office, 2011).

9. "Immigration," in *Cato Handbook for Policymakers*, 7th ed. (Washington, D.C.: Cato Institute, 2009), 625.

10. Jeffrey S. Passel and D'Vera Cohn, *Unauthorized Immigrant Population: National and State Trends, 2010* (Washington, D.C.: Pew Hispanic Center, 2011), 1.

11. Ken Ellingwood, "More Than 12,000 Killed in Mexican Drug War This Year, Officials Say," *Los Angeles Times*, December 16, 2010, http://articles.latimes.com/2010/dec/16/world/la-fg-mexico-death-toll-20101217 (accessed December 16, 2010).

12. *Issues 2010: The Candidate's Briefing Book*, Heritage Foundation, 2009, 9, http://www.issues2010.com/ (accessed December 13, 2010).

13. Douglas V. Johnson II, *Borders: Technology and Security—Strategic Responses to New Challenges*, United States Army War College and New Mexico State University Colloquium Brief, Strategic Studies Institute, April, 2008, 2.

14. Janet Napolitano, *Quadrennial Homeland Security Review Report: A Strategic Framework for a Secure Homeland* (Washington, D.C.: U.S. Department of Homeland Security, 2010), 19.

15. "Domestic Security," in *Cato Handbook for Policymakers*, 7th ed. (Washington, D.C.: Cato Institute, 2009), 499.

Chapter 9

1. Harry R. Yarger, *Strategic Theory for the 21st Century: The Little Book on Big Strategy*, Strategic Studies Institute (Carlisle, Pa.: 2006), 18.

2. "Operation Enduring Freedom," Global Security, http://www.globalsecurity. org/military/ops/enduring-freedom-intro.htm (accessed January 23, 2007).

3. Thomas H. Kean et al., *9/11 Commission Report*, National Commission on Terrorist Attacks upon the United States, July 22, 2004, 337–78, http://www.9-11com-mission.gov/report/911report.pdf (accessed July 10, 2008).

4. Jeffrey A. Dressler, *The Haqqani Network: From Pakistan to Afghanistan* (Washington, D.C.: Institute for the Study of War, 2010), 4.

5. Haider Ali Hussein Mullick, *Al Qa'eda and Pakistan: Current Role and Future Considerations*, Institute for Social Policy and Understanding, October, 2010, 7, http://ispu.org/files/PDFs/Al_Qaeda_and_Pakistan_Report_-_Haider_Mullick.pdf (accessed November 1, 2010).

6. David Wood, "White House Mulls Grim Picture of 'Deteriorating Stalemate' in Afghanistan," *Politics Daily*, December 3, 2010, http://www.politicsdaily. com/2010/12/03/white-house-mulls-grim-picture-of-deteriorating-stalemate-in-a/ (accessed December 4, 2010).

7. "KGS Nightwatch," Kforce Government Solutions, December 2, 2010, http://www.kforcegov.com/Services/IS/NightWatch/NightWatch_10000300.aspx (accessed December 2, 2010).

8. *Afghanistan: Exit versus Engagement*, Asia Briefing No. 115, International Crisis Group, November 28, 2010, 2.

9. Jim Garamone, "2014 Is 'Aspirational Goal' for Security Turnover to Afghans," *American Forces Press Service*, November 18, 2010, http://www.defense.gov/news/ newsarticle.aspx?id=61753 (accessed November 18, 2010).

10. Robert M. Gates, "Report on Progress toward Security and Stability in Afghanistan," report to Congress in accordance with Section 1230 of the National Defense Authorization Act for Fiscal Year 2008 (Washington, D.C.: U.S. Department of Defense, 2010), 11.

11. Bob Woodward, *Obama's Wars* (New York: Simon & Schuster, 2010), 290.

12. "Afghan Taliban Issue Guidelines for Establishment of Islamic Emirate," *Terrorism Monitor* 9, no. 5 (2011), Jamestown Foundation, http://www.jamestown.org/ programs/gta/single/?tx_ttnews%5Btt_news%5D=37454&cHash=e60326b681 (accessed February 4, 2011).

13. Woodward, *Obama's Wars*, 15.

14. Shuja Nawaz, *FATA—A Most Dangerous Place* (Washington, D.C.: Center for Strategic and International Studies, 2009), 7.

15. Daniel Markey, *Securing Pakistan's Tribal Belt* (Washington, D.C.: Council on Foreign Relations, 2008), 3.

16. Faryal Leghari, "Dealing with FATA: Strategic Shortfalls and Recommendations," *Perspectives on Terrorism* 2, no. 10 (2010), http://www.terrorismanalysts.com/pt/index.php?option=com_rokzine&view=article&id=61 (accessed December 21, 2010).

17. Peter Bergen and Katherine Tiedemann, "Jihadistan," *Foreign Policy*, http://www.foreignpolicy.com/articles/2009/07/03/jihadistan (accessed January 10, 2011).

18. "Karachi Target Killings, Highest in 15 Years," *Times of Pakistan*, http://thetimesofpakistan.com/2010/10/30/karachi-target-killings-highest-in-15-years/ (accessed November 3, 2010).

19. Jayshree Bajoria, "Foreign Policy and the 2010 Midterms: War in Afghanistan," Council on Foreign Relations, October 28, 2010, http://www.cfr.org/afghanistan/foreign-policy-2010-midterms-war-afghanistan/p23259 (accessed November 1, 2010).

20. Douglas J. Feith, "Why We Went to War in Iraq," *Wall Street Journal*, July 3, 2008, http://online.wsj.com/article/SB121504452359324921.html (accessed July 4, 2008).

21. Kevin Woods and James Lacey, *Saddam and Terrorism: Emerging Insights from Captured Iraqi Documents*, vol. 1 (redacted) (Alexandria: Iraqi Perspectives Project, 2007), 42.

22. Joseph Felter and Brian Fishman, *Al-Qa'ida's Foreign Fighters in Iraq: A First Look at the Sinjar Records* Carlisle, Pa.: United States Military Academy at West Point, Combating Terrorism Center, 2007), 4.

23. Jim Michaels, "Bloodshed Ebbed in Iraq Last Year," *USA Today*, January 11, 2011, http://www.usatoday.com/printedition/news/20110111/iraqviolence11_st.art.htm (accessed January 12, 2011).

24. *Loose Ends: Iraq's Security Forces between U.S. Drawdown and Withdrawal*, Middle East Report No. 99, International Crisis Group, October 26, 2010, 1.

25. Anne Gearan, "Gates: US Open to Request from Iraq to Stay," *Washington Times*, November 9, 2010, http://www.washingtontimes.com/news/2010/nov/9/gates-says-us-open-request-iraq-stay/ (accessed November 10, 2010).

26. Walter Pincus, "Report Details Inadequacies of Iraqi Defense Ministry," *Washington Post*, November 22, 2010, http://www.washingtonpost.com/wp-dyn/content/article/2010/11/22/AR2010112206420.html (accessed November 22, 2010).

27. Alan G. Stolberg, "The International System in the 21st Century," in *U.S. Army War College Guide to National Security Issues, Volume II: National Security Policy and Strategy*, 3rd ed., ed. J. Boone Bartholomees (Carlisle, Pa.: U.S. Army War College, 2008), 124.

28. David Kilcullen, *The Accidental Guerrilla: Fighting Small Wars in the Midst of a Big One* (New York: Oxford University Press, 2009), 35–38.

29. Michael Lund, *Engaging Fragile States: An International Policy Primer*, Woodrow Wilson International Center for Scholars, 2010, 3, http://wilsoncenter.org/topics/pubs/Colloquium%20Report-Engaging%20Fragile%20States.pdf (accessed December 30, 2010).

30. "U.S. Policy toward Sub-Saharan Africa," in *Cato Handbook for Policymakers*, 7th ed. (Washington, D.C.: Cato Institute, 2009), 647.

31. Jeff Azarva, "Theater of Jihad," American Enterprise Institute's Critical Threats Project, October 1, 2009, http://www.criticalthreats.org/theater-jihad-africa (accessed October 1, 2009).

32. Mawassi Lahcen, "Kidnapping, Drug Trafficking Dominate AQIM Activities," *Magharebia*, August 12, 2010, http://www.magharebia.com/cocoon/awi/xhtml1/en_GB/features/awi/features/2010/12/08/feature-01 (accessed August 12, 2010).

33. "Operation Enduring Freedom Trans Sahara," United States Africa Command, http://www.africom.mil/oef-ts.asp (accessed August 12, 2010).

34. Richard Spencer, "Terrorists Posing as Refugees in Yemen," *Telegraph* (United Kingdom), November 29, 2010, http://www.telegraph.co.uk/news/worldnews/middleeast/yemen/8149993/Terrorists-posing-as-refugees-in-Yemen.html (accessed November 30, 2010).

35. "Somalia: Jihadist Propaganda Aimed at Recruiting Children," ADNKronos International, April 16, 2010, http://www.adnkronos.com/AKI/English/Security/?id=3.1.261331670 (accessed April 17, 2010).

36. Christopher Harnisch, *The Terror Threat from Somalia: The Internationalization of Al Shabaab*, American Enterprise Institute's Critical Threats Project, February 12, 2010, 3.

37. Katherine Zimmerman, "Looking Ahead in Mogadishu: Tough Decisions," American Enterprise Institute's Critical Threats Project, November 1, 2010, http://www.criticalthreats.org/somalia/looking-ahead-mogadishu-tough-decisions-november-1-2010 (accessed November 1, 2010); Muhyadin Ahmed Roble, "Somali Forces Sell Weapons to Islamists," Africa News, October 29, 2010, http://www.africanews.com/site/Somali_forces_sell_weapons_to_Islamists/list_messages/35708 (accessed October 29, 2010).

38. "Combined Joint Task Force–Horn of Africa," United States Africa Command, http://www.hoa.africom.mil/AboutCJTF-HOA.asp (accessed March 2, 2010).

39. "2010 Command Brief," United States Africa Command, http://www.scribd.com/doc/28163958/2010-US-Africa-Command-Command-Brief-USAFRICOM (accessed October 16, 2010).

40. Craig Whitlock, "Pentagon Hunting for Home for Africom," *Washington Post*, November 27, 2010, http://www.washingtonpost.com/wp-dyn/content/article/2010/11/26/AR2010112604889.html (accessed November 27, 2010).

41. "Hamas Backgrounder," Council on Foreign Relations, http://www.cfr.org/israel/hamas/p8968 (accessed January 31, 2009).

42. Greg Bruno, "Iran's Nuclear Program," Council on Foreign Relations, http://www.cfr.org/iran/irans-nuclear-program/p16811 (accessed March 10, 2010).

43. Shibley Telhami, *2008 Annual Arab Public Opinion Poll*, Survey of the Anwar Sadat Chair for Peace and Development at the University of Maryland (with Zogby International), March, 2008, http://www.brookings.edu/~/media/Files/events/2008/0414_middle_east/0414_middle_east_telhami.pdf (accessed June 5, 2009).

44. Varun Vira et al., "Sanctions on Iran: Reactions and Impact," American Enterprise Institute's Iran Tracker, http://www.irantracker.org/us-policy/sanctions-iran-reactions-and-impact (accessed November 5, 2010).

45. "Comprehensive Iran Sanctions, Accountability, and Divestment Act," Council on Foreign Relations, July 1, 2010, http://www.cfr.org/iran/comprehensive-iran-sanctions-accountability-divestment-act-hr-2194/p22484 (accessed July 1, 2010).

46. Borzou Daragahi, "U.S. Announces New Sanctions against Iran," *Los Angeles Times*, November 30, http://articles.latimes.com/2010/nov/30/world/la-fg-iran-nu-clear-20101201 (accessed December 2, 2010).

47. Peter Brookes, "The Post-Iran Proliferation Cascade," *Journal of International Security Affairs* 19 (2010): 9.

48. Frederick Kagan and Christopher Harnisch, *Yemen: Fighting al Qaeda in a Failing State, The Security and Economic Situation and Considerations for the Way Forward*, American Enterprise Institute's Critical Threats Project, January 12, 2010, 19.

49. Andrew M. Exum and Richard Fontaine, *On the Knife's Edge: Yemen's Instability and the Threat to American Interests* (Washington, D.C.: Center for a New American Security, 2009), 1.

50. Craig Whitlock, "Al-Qaeda's Yemen Branch Spreads Its Reach for Recruits, Targets," *Washington Post*, November 30, 2010, http://www.washingtonpost.com/wp-dyn/content/article/2010/11/29/AR2010112905615.html (accessed November 30, 2010).

51. Katherine Zimmerman, "Militant Islam's Global Preacher: The Radicalizing Effect of Sheikh Anwar Al Awlaki," American Enterprise Institute's Critical Threats Project, March 12, 2010, http://www.criticalthreats.org/yemen/militant-islams-global-preacher-radicalizing-effect-sheikh-anwar-al-awlaki (accessed March 12, 2010).

52. Jarret Brachman, "Agent Provocateurs: Al-Qaida's New Strategy in Yemen," *International Relations and Security Network*, December 9, 2010, http://www.isn.ethz.ch/isn/Current-Affairs/ISN-Insights/Detail?lng=en&id=125023&contextid734=125023&contextid735=125022&tabid=125022 (accessed December 10, 2010).

53. Sara Schoenhardt, "Religious Tensions Rise in Indonesia," *Voice of America News*, December 15, 2010, http://www.voanews.com/english/news/Religious-Tension-Increases-in-Indonesia-111910634.html (accessed December 15, 2010).

54. Mark A. Groombridge, "In Search of a North Korea Policy: Time to Pursue 'Aggressive Isolation,'" *National Security Policy Proceedings* 3 (2010): 59–60.

55. Shibley Telhami, *2008 Annual Arab Public Opinion Poll*, Survey of the Anwar Sadat Chair for Peace and Development at the University of Maryland (with Zogby International), March, 2008, http://www.brookings.edu/~/media/Files/events/2008/0414_middle_east/0414_middle_east_telhami.pdf (accessed June 5, 2009).

Chapter 10

1. David Bukay, "Peace or Jihad? Abrogation in Islam," *Middle East Quarterly* 14, no. 4 (Fall 2007): 3–11.

2. Seth G. Jones, *Defeating Terrorist Groups*, Rand Corporation, 2008, 1, http://www.rand.org/pubs/testimonies/CT314.html (accessed April 1, 2010).

3. George W. Bush, Introduction to *The National Security Strategy of the United States of America* (Washington, D.C.: The White House, 2002).

4. Hillary Clinton, *Leading through Civilian Power: The First Quadrennial Diplomacy and Development Review* (Washington, D.C.: U.S. Department of State, 2010), iv.

5. Eric Schmitt, "Governments Go Online in Fight against Terrorism," *New York Times*, January 31, 2011, http://www.nytimes.com/2011/01/31/world/middleeast/31terror.html (accessed January 30, 2011).

6. Micah Zenko, "Between Threats and War: U.S. Discrete Military Operations in the Post–Cold War World," excerpt from the Council on Foreign Relations, December 2010, http://www.cfr.org/united-states/between-threats-war/p22621?excerpt=1 (accessed January 22, 2011).

7. Mackenzie Eaglen and Julia Pollack, *How to Save Money, Reform Processes, and Increase Efficiency in the Defense Department*, Heritage Foundation, January 10, 2011, http://www.heritage.org/research/reports/2011/01/how-to-save-money-reform-processes-and-increase-efficiency-in-the-defense-department (accessed January 11, 2011).

8. *Issues 2010: The Candidate's Briefing Book*, Heritage Foundation, 2009, 105, http://www.issues2010.com/ (accessed December 13, 2010).

9. David Kris, remarks to Law Enforcement as a Counterterrorism Tool Panel, Brookings Institution, June 10, 2010, http://www.brookings.edu/events/2010/0611_law_enforcement.aspx (accessed November 24, 2010).

10. Charles Krauthammer, "Democratic Realism: An American Foreign Policy for a Unipolar World" (Irving Kristol lecture at the American Enterprise Institute, Washington, D.C., February, 2004), http://www.aei.org/book/755 (accessed February 22, 2007).

Bibliography

Abdullaev, Nabi. "Russia Announces Sharp Hike in Defense Spending." *Defense News,* November 9, 2010. http://www.defensenews.com/story.php?i=5016720 (accessed November 9, 2010).

Abu-Nasr, Donna, and Lee Keath. "200 Web Sites Spread Al-Qaida's Message in English." *Associated Press,* November 20, 2009. http://www.huffingtonpost.com/2009/11/19/increasing-number-of-web_n_364635.html (accessed November 20, 2009).

Ackerman, Spencer. "Yearly Price Tag for Afghan Forces: $6 Billion, Indefinitely." *Danger Room,* December 16, 2010. http://www.wired.com/dangerroom/2010/12/yearly-price-tab-for-afghan-forces-6-billion-indefinitely/ (accessed December 16, 2010).

ADNKronos International. "Somalia: Jihadist Propaganda Aimed at Recruiting Children." http://www.adnkronos.com/AKI/English/Security/?id=3.1.261331670 (accessed April 17, 2010).

Anishchuk, Alexei. "Russia Plans New Naval Bases Abroad." *Guardian* (United Kingdom), November 25, 2010. http://www.guardian.co.uk/world/2010/nov/25/russia-new-naval-bases-abroad (accessed November 25, 2010).

Antholis, William, and Strobe Talbott. "Tackling Trade and Climate Change." In *Opportunity '08: Independent Ideas for America's Next President,* edited by Michael E. O'Hanlon. Washington, D.C.: Brookings Institution Press, 2007.

Azarva, Jeff. "Theater of Jihad." American Enterprise Institute's Critical Threats Project, 2009. http://www.criticalthreats.org/theater-jihad-africa (accessed October 1, 2009).

Bajoria, Jayshree. "Foreign Policy and the 2010 Midterms: War in Afghanistan." Council on Foreign Relations, 2010. http://www.cfr.org/afghanistan/foreign-policy-2010-midterms-war-afghanistan/p23259 (accessed November 1, 2010).

Barboza, David. "China Passes Japan as Second-Largest Economy." *New York Times*, August 15, 2010. http://www.nytimes.com/2010/08/16/business/global/16yuan. html (accessed August 16, 2010).

Bardaji, Rafael L. "NATO at 60." *Weekly Standard*, March 24, 2009. http://www. weeklystandard.com/Content/Public/Articles/000/000/016/322ndlep.asp (accessed March 24, 2009).

Barnett, Thomas P. M. *Great Powers: America and the World After Bush*. New York: G. P. Putnam's Sons, 2009.

———. *The Pentagon's New Map: War and Peace in the Twenty-First Century*. New York: G. P. Putnam's Sons, 2004.

Bartholomees, J. Boone, ed. *U.S. Army War College Guide to National Security Issues, Volume II: National Security Policy and Strategy*. 3rd ed. Carlisle, Pa.: United States Army War College, 2008.

Bartolf, Christine, and Bernard I. Finel. *Are We Winning? Measuring Progress in the Struggle against al Qaeda and Associated Movements*. Washington, D.C.: American Security Project, 2009.

Baylis, John. *Strategy in the Contemporary World: An Introduction to Strategic Studies*. New York: Oxford University Press, 2003.

Bennett, John T. "Commission: China Bolsters Fighters, Missiles, 'Supports' Cyber-attacks." *Defense News*, November 17, 2010. http://www.defensenews.com/story. php?i=5064294 (accessed November 17, 2010).

Bergen, Peter, and Katherine Tiedemann. "Jihadistan." *Foreign Policy*. http://www. foreignpolicy.com/articles/2009/07/03/jihadistan (accessed January 10, 2011).

Better World Campaign. "U.S. Dues and Contributions to the United Nations." http://www.betterworldcampaign.org/issues/funding/us-dues-and-contributions. html (accessed January 2, 2011).

Blanchard, Christopher M. *Al Qaeda: Statements and Evolving Ideology*. CRS Report for Congress. Washington, D.C.: Congressional Research Service, 2007.

Bolton, John R. *The Key to Changing the United Nations System*. American Enterprise Institute for Public Policy Research, October 10, 2010. http://www.aei.org/out-look/101000 (accessed November 1, 2010).

Brachman, Jarret. "Agent Provocateurs: Al-Qaida's New Strategy in Yemen." *International Relations and Security Network*, December 9, 2010. http://www.isn.ethz.ch/ isn/Current-Affairs/ISN-Insights/Detail?lng=en&id=125023&contextid734=12502 3&contextid735=125022&tabid=125022 (accessed December 10, 2010).

Brachman, Jarret M., and William F. McCaints. *Stealing Al-Qa'ida's Playbook*. West Point, N.Y.: Combating Terrorism Center, 2006.

Brookes, Peter. "The Post-Iran Proliferation Cascade." *Journal of International Security Affairs* 19 (2010): 7–13.

Bruno, Greg. "Iran's Nuclear Program." Council on Foreign Relations. http://www. cfr.org/iran/irans-nuclear-program/p16811 (accessed March 10, 2010).

Bukay, David. "Peace or Jihad? Abrogation in Islam." *Middle East Quarterly* 14, no. 4 (Fall 2007): 3–11.

Bush, George W. Introduction to *The National Security Strategy of the United States of America*. Washington, D.C.: The White House, 2002.

————. *National Strategy for Combating Terrorism.* Washington, D.C.: The White House, 2006. http://georgewbush-whitehouse.archives.gov/nsc/nsct/2006/ (accessed July 7, 2007).

————. *National Strategy for Homeland Security.* Washington, D.C.: Homeland Security Council, 2007. http://www.dhs.gov/xlibrary/assets/nat_strat_homelandsecurity_2007.pdf (accessed April 23, 2008).

————. "Presidential Address to the Nation, October 7, 2001." Johnston's Archive. http://www.johnstonsarchive.net/terrorism/bush911d.html (accessed January 3, 2011).

Buxbaum, Peter A. "Balancing the Budget on DoD's Back." *International Relations and Security Network,* January 31, 2011. http://www.isn.ethz.ch/isn/Current-Affairs/ISN-Insights/Detail?lng=en&id=126477&contextid734=126477&contextid735=126476&tabid=126476126477 (accessed February 2, 2011).

Byman, Daniel M. "Al Qaeda's M & A Strategy." *Foreign Policy,* December 7, 2010. http://www.foreignpolicy.com/articles/2010/12/07/al_qaedas_m_and_a_strategy (accessed December 7, 2010).

Carr, Caleb. *The Lessons of Terror.* New York: Random House, 2002.

Cato Institute. "Domestic Security." In *Cato Handbook for Policymakers.* 7th ed. Washington, D.C.: Cato Institute, 2009, 497–505.

————. "Foreign Aid and Economic Development." In *Cato Handbook for Policymakers.* 7th ed. Washington, D.C.: Cato Institute, 2009, 655–70.

————. "Immigration." In *Cato Handbook for Policymakers, 7th Edition,* 625–35. Washington: The Cato Institute, 2009.

————. "U.S. Policy toward Sub-Saharan Africa." In *Cato Handbook for Policymakers.* 7th ed. Washington, D.C.: Cato Institute, 2009, 645–53.

Chairman of the Joint Chiefs of Staff. *Joint Publication 1-02, Department of Defense Dictionary of Military and Associated Terms.* Washington, D.C.: U.S. Department of Defense, 2001.

————. *Joint Publication 3-16: Multi-national Operations.* Washington, D.C.: U.S. Department of Defense, 2007.

————. *National Military Strategic Plan for the War on Terrorism.* Washington, D.C.: U.S. Department of Defense, 2006.

Chu, Henry. "As Europe Cuts Military Budgets, Some Worry about Its Clout." *Los Angeles Times,* December 5, 2010. http://articles.latimes.com/2010/dec/05/world/la-fg-europe-military-20101205 (accessed December 5, 2010).

Clapper, James. *Summary of the Reengagement of Detainees Formerly Held at Guantanamo Bay, Cuba.* Washington, D.C.: Office of the Director of National Intelligence, 2010. http://www.dni.gov/electronic_reading_room/120710_Summary_of_the_Reengagement_of_Detainees_Formerly_Held_at_Guantanamo_Bay_Cuba.pdf (accessed January 2, 2011).

Clinton, Hillary. *Leading through Civilian Power: The First Quadrennial Diplomacy and Development Review.* Washington, D.C.: U.S. Department of State, 2010.

Cornell University Law School. "Title 22, United States Code, Section 2656f." http://www.law.cornell.edu/uscode/22/usc_sec_22_00002656---f000-.html (accessed March 29, 2009).

———. "Title 50, United States Code, Section 2405." http://www.law.cornell.edu/uscode/html/uscode50a/usc_sec_50a_00002405----000-.html (accessed March 29, 2009).

Council on Foreign Relations. "Comprehensive Iran Sanctions, Accountability, and Divestment Act." http://www.cfr.org/iran/comprehensive-iran-sanctions-accountability-divestment-act-hr-2194/p22484 (accessed July 1, 2010).

———. "Hamas Backgrounder." http://www.cfr.org/israel/hamas/p8968 (accessed January 31, 2009).

Cropsey, Seth. "Anchors Away: American Sea Power in Dry Dock." *World Affairs Journal*, January/February 2011. http://www.worldaffairsjournal.org/articles/2011-JanFeb/full-Cropsey-JF-2011.html (accessed February 23, 2011).

Daragahi, Borzou. "U.S. Announces New Sanctions against Iran." *Los Angeles Times*, November 30, 2010. http://articles.latimes.com/2010/nov/30/world/la-fg-iran-nuclear-20101201 (accessed December 2, 2010).

Davis, Gregory M. "Islam 101." Jihad Watch. http://www.jihadwatch.org/islam-101.html (accessed October 10, 2010).

Dempsey, Judy. "The Peril That NATO Can't Ignore." *New York Times*, November 10, 2010. http://www.nytimes.com/2010/11/11/world/europe/11iht-letter.html (accessed November 10, 2010).

DeYoung, Karen. "Pakistan Doubles Its Nuclear Arsenal." *Washington Post*, January 31, 2011. http://www.washingtonpost.com/wp-dyn/content/article/2011/01/30/AR2011013004682.html (accessed January 31, 2011).

Dodds, Paisley. "Spy Agencies Use Ex-Captives to Infiltrate Al Qaeda." *Miami Herald*, November 5, 2010. http://www.miamiherald.com/2010/11/05/1910118/spy-agencies-infiltrate-al-qaida.html (accessed November 6, 2010).

Dressler, Jeffrey A. *The Haqqani Network: From Pakistan to Afghanistan*. Washington, D.C.: Institute for the Study of War, 2010.

Drogin, Bob. "The 'Vanity Fair' of Al Qaeda." *Los Angeles Times*, November 27, 2010. http://articles.latimes.com/2010/nov/26/nation/la-na-terror-magazine-20101126 (accessed November 27, 2010).

Eaglen, Mackenzie, and Julia Pollack. *How to Save Money, Reform Processes, and Increase Efficiency in the Defense Department*. Heritage Foundation, January 10, 2011. http://www.heritage.org/research/reports/2011/01/how-to-save-money-reform-processes-and-increase-efficiency-in-the-defense-department (accessed January 11, 2011).

Echevarria, Antulio J. II. "Wars of Ideas and the War of Ideas." Strategic Studies Institute, U.S. Army War College, 2008. http://www.carlisle.army.mil/DIME/documents/Echevarria.pdf (accessed August 21, 2008).

Eikmeier, Dale C. "Qutbism: An Ideology of Islamic-Fascism." *Parameters* 37, no. 1 (Spring 2007): 85–97.

Ellingwood, Ken. "More Than 12,000 Killed in Mexican Drug War This Year, Officials Say." *Los Angeles Times*, December 16, 2010. http://articles.latimes.com/2010/dec/16/world/la-fg-mexico-death-toll-20101217 (accessed December 16, 2010).

European Defence Agency. "Defence Data 2009."

Exum, Andrew M., and Richard Fontaine. *On the Knife's Edge: Yemen's Instability and the Threat to American Interests*. Washington, D.C.: Center for a New American Security, 2009.

Federal Bureau of Investigation. "First Strike: Global Terror in America." http://www.fbi.gov/news/stories/2008/february/tradebom_022608 (accessed January 3, 2010).

Feith, Douglas J. "Why We Went to War in Iraq." *Wall Street Journal,* July 3, 2008. http://online.wsj.com/article/SB121504452359324921.html (accessed July 4, 2008).

Felter, Joseph, and Brian Fishman. *Al-Qa'ida's Foreign Fighters in Iraq: A First Look at the Sinjar Records.* West Point, N.Y.: Combating Terrorism Center, 2007.

Fendrick, Reed J. "Diplomacy as an Instrument of National Power." In *U.S. Army War College Guide to National Security Issues, Volume I: Theory of War and Strategy,* edited by J. Boone Bartholomees. 3rd ed., 189–194. Carlisle, Pa.: U.S. Army War College, 2008.

Finn, Peter, and Anne E. Kornblut. "Indefinite Detention Possible for Suspects at Guantanamo Bay." *Washington Post,* December 22, 2010. http://www.washingtonpost.com/wp-dyn/content/article/2010/12/21/AR2010122105523.html (accessed December 23, 2010).

Friedman, George. "Deciphering the Mohammed Trial." Strategic Forecasting, November 16, 2009. http://www.stratfor.com/weekly/20091116_postsept_11_legal_dilemma (accessed November 16, 2009).

Friedman, Thomas. "National Strategies and Capabilities for a Changing World: Globalization and National Security." Luncheon address presented at the Fletcher Conference for the Institute for Foreign Policy Analysis, Arlington, Va., November 15–16, 2000. http://www.ifpafletcherconference.com/oldtranscripts/2000/friedman.htm (accessed September 28, 2009).

Garamone, Jim. "2014 is 'Aspirational Goal' for Security Turnover to Afghans." *American Forces Press Service,* November 18, 2010. http://www.defense.gov/news/newsarticle.aspx?id=61753 (accessed November 18, 2010).

Gartenstein-Ross, Daveed. "Threat Matrix: Reflections on Osama bin Laden, and His Continuing Relevance." *Long War Journal,* November 4, 2010. http://www.longwarjournal.org/threat-matrix/archives/2010/11/reflections_on_osama_bin_laden_1.php (accessed November 4, 2010).

Gates, Robert M. "Report on Progress toward Security and Stability in Afghanistan." Report to Congress in accordance with Section 1230 of the National Defense Authorization Act for Fiscal Year 2008. Washington, D.C.: U.S. Department of Defense, 2010.

Gearan, Anne. "Gates: US Open to Request from Iraq to Stay." *Washington Times,* November 9, 2010. http://www.washingtontimes.com/news/2010/nov/9/gates-says-us-open-request-iraq-stay/ (accessed November 10, 2010).

Global Security. "Operation Enduring Freedom." http://www.globalsecurity.org/military/ops/enduring-freedom-intro.htm (accessed January 23, 2007).

Gompert, David C., and John Gordon IV. *War by Other Means: Building Complete and Balanced Capabilities for Counterinsurgency.* Washington, D.C.: Rand Corporation, 2008.

Government Accountability Office. *Afghan Army Growing, but Additional Trainers Needed.* Report to Congressional Addressees. Washington, D.C.: Government Accountability Office, 2011.

Government Printing Office. "Table 7.1, Federal Debt at the End of the Year: 1940–2015." http://www.gpoaccess.gov/usbudget/fy11/sheets/hist07z1.xls (accessed January 21, 2011).

Gray, Colin S. *Modern Strategy*. New York: Oxford University Press, 1999.

Groombridge, Mark A. "In Search of a North Korea Policy: Time to Pursue 'Aggressive Isolation.'" *National Security Policy Proceedings* 3 (2010): 53–62.

Haass, Richard N. *Intervention*. Washington, D.C.: Brookings Institution Press, 1999.

Harnisch, Christopher. *The Terror Threat from Somalia: The Internationalization of Al Shabaab*. American Enterprise Institute's Critical Threats Project, 2010.

Harrow, Martin. "Inside a Wave of Terrorism: The Dynamic Relation between Terrorism and the Factors Leading to Terrorism." *Journal of Global Change and Governance* 1, no. 3 (2008): 1–18. Human Security Report Project, Human Security Gateway. http://www.humansecuritygateway.info/documents/HARROW_Inside-WaveOfTerrorism.pdf (accessed June 28, 2009).

Helfstein, Scott, Nassir Abdullah, and Muhammad al-Obaidi. *Deadly Vanguards: A Study of Al-Qa'ida's Violence against Muslims*. West Point, N.Y.: Combating Terrorism Center, 2009.

Heritage Foundation. "Federal Spending Chart 10." *2010 Budget Chart Book*. http://www.heritage.org/budgetchartbook/obama-budget-defense-spending (accessed January 10, 2011).

———. *Issues 2010: The Candidate's Briefing Book*. http://www.issues2010.com/ (accessed December 13, 2010).

Hille, Katherine. "China Reveals Aircraft Carrier Plans." *Financial Times*, December 17, 2010. http://www.ft.com/cms/s/0/fa7f5e6a-09cc-11e0-8b29-00144feabdc0.html#axzz1eomyykck (accessed December 18, 2010).

Hoeh, Andrew R., and Sarah Harting. *Risking NATO: Testing the Limits of the Alliance in Afghanistan*. Rand Corporation, 2010. http://www.rand.org/pubs/monographs/2010/RAND_MG974.pdf (accessed December 3, 2010).

Hoffman, Bruce. "Al-Qaeda Has a New Strategy. Obama Needs One, Too." *Washington Post*, January 10, 2010. http://www.washingtonpost.com/wp-dyn/content/article/2010/01/08/AR2010010803555.html (accessed January 10, 2010).

Hoffman, Frank G. "Striking a Balance: Posturing the Future Force for COIN and Conventional Warfare." *Armed Forces Journal* (2009). http://www.armedforcesjournal.com/2009/07/4099782/ (accessed September 1, 2009).

Human Security Report Project of the Simon Fraser University. "Human Security Report 2009/2010: The Causes of Peace and the Shrinking Costs of War, Part 1: Causes of Peace." http://www.hsrgroup.org/docs/publications/hsr20092010/20092010humansecurityreport-part1-causesofpeace.pdf (accessed February 15, 2011).

Huntington, Samuel P. "The Lonely Superpower." In *American Foreign Policy*, edited by Glenn P. Hastedt. 8th ed., 33–37. Guilford: McGraw-Hill/Dushkin, 2002.

International Crisis Group. *Loose Ends: Iraq's Security Forces between U.S. Drawdown and Withdrawal*. Middle East Report No. 99, 2010.

———. *Afghanistan: Exit versus Engagement*. Asia Briefing Number 115, 2010.

Investigative Project on Terrorism. "The Jihadist Social Network Underworld." http://www.investigativeproject.org/2398/the-jihadist-social-network-underworld (accessed December 10, 2010).

Jablonsky, David. "National Power." In *U.S. Army War College Guide to National Security Issues, Volume I: Theory of War and Strategy*, edited by J. Boone Bartholomees. 3rd ed., 145–161. Carlisle, Pa.: U.S. Army War College, 2008.

Jamestown Foundation. "Afghan Taliban Issue Guidelines for Establishment of Islamic Emirate." *Terrorism Monitor* 9, no. 5 (2011). http://www.jamestown.org/programs/gta/single/?tx_ttnews%5Btt_news%5D=37454&cHash=e60326b681 (accessed February 4, 2011).

———. "Controversial Gathering of Islamic Scholars Refutes Al-Qaeda's Ideological Cornerstone." *Terrorism Monitor* 8, no. 14 (2010). http://www.jamestown.org/single/?no_cache=1&tx_ttnews%5Btt_news%5D=36248&tx_ttnews%5BbackPid%5D=381&cHash=ea30c780ba (accessed May 1, 2010).

———. "Prominent Egyptian Preacher Dissects Al-Qaeda Strategy." *Terrorism Monitor* 8, no. 30 (2010). http://www.jamestown.org/uploads/media/TM_008_72.pdf (accessed August 1, 2010).

Jenkins, Brian. "Building an Army of Believers: Jihadist Radicalization and Recruitment." Rand Corporation, 2007. http://www.rand.org/content/dam/rand/pubs/testimonies/2007/RAND_CT278-1.pdf (accessed May 1, 2008).

Johnson, Douglas V. II. *Borders: Technology and Security—Strategic Responses to New Challenges*. Strategic Studies Institute. Carlisle, Pa.: U.S. Army War College, 2008.

Johnson, John D. "Root Causes of Islamist Extremism: Nine Years Later." *Small Wars Journal*, January 10, 2011. http://smallwarsjournal.com/blog/2011/01/root-causes-of-islamist-extrem/ (accessed January 11, 2011).

Jones, Seth G. *Defeating Terrorist Groups*. Rand Corporation, 2008. http://www.rand.org/pubs/testimonies/CT314.html (accessed April 1, 2010).

Jordan, Amos A., William J. Taylor Jr., and Michael J. Mazarr. *American National Security*. 5th ed. Baltimore: Johns Hopkins University Press, 1999.

Kagan, Frederick, and Christopher Harnisch. *Yemen: Fighting al Qaeda in a Failing State, The Security and Economic Situation and Considerations for the Way Forward*. American Enterprise Institute's Critical Threats Project, 2010.

Kean, Thomas H., Lee H. Hamilton, Richard Ben-Veniste, Bob Kerrey, Fred F. Fielding, John F. Lehman, Jamie S. Gorelick, Timothy J. Roemer, Slade Gorton, and James R. Thompson. *9/11 Commission Report*. National Commission on Terrorist Attacks upon the United States, July 22, 2004. http://www.9-11commission.gov/report/911report.pdf (accessed July 10, 2008).

Kforce Government Solutions. "KGS Nightwatch." http://www.kforcegov.com/Services/IS/NightWatch/NightWatch_10000300.aspx (accessed December 2, 2010).

Kian, Bijan R., and Wayne Porter. "A New Deal: A Plan for Sustainable Afghan Security." New America Foundation, 2010. http://www.newamerica.net/publications/policy/a_new_deal_a_plan_for_sustainable_afghan_stability (accessed December 10, 2010).

Kilcullen, David. *The Accidental Guerrilla: Fighting Small Wars in the Midst of a Big One*. New York: Oxford University Press, 2009.

Kimmage, Daniel. *The Al-Qaeda Media Nexus: The Virtual Network Behind the Global Message.* Radio Free Europe/Radio Liberty, March 2008. http://docs.rferl.org/en-US/AQ_Media_Nexus.pdf (accessed June 1, 2008).

Krauthammer, Charles. "Democratic Realism: An American Foreign Policy for a Unipolar World." Irving Kristol lecture at the American Enterprise Institute, Washington, D.C., February, 2004. http://www.aei.org/book/755 (accessed February 22, 2007).

Krauthammer, Charles. "Travesty in New York." *Washington Post,* November 20, 2009. http://www.washingtonpost.com/wp-dyn/content/article/2009/11/19/AR2009111903434.html (accessed November 21, 2009).

Krepinevich, Andrew F. *7 Deadly Scenarios: A Military Futurist Explores War in the 21st Century.* New York: Bantam, 2009.

Kris, David. Remarks to Law Enforcement as a Counterterrorism Tool Panel, Brookings Institution, June 10, 2010. http://www.brookings.edu/events/2010/0611_law_enforcement.aspx (accessed November 24, 2010).

Lahcen, Mawassi. "Kidnapping, Drug Trafficking Dominate AQIM Activities." *Magharebia,* August 12, 2010. http://www.magharebia.com/cocoon/awi/xhtml1/en_GB/features/awi/features/2010/12/08/feature-01 (accessed August 12, 2010).

Leghari, Faryal. "Dealing with FATA: Strategic Shortfalls and Recommendations." *Perspectives on Terrorism* 2, no. 10 (2010). http://www.terrorismanalysts.com/pt/index.php?option=com_rokzine&view=article&id=61 (accessed December 21, 2010).

Lichtblau, Eric, and Eric Schmitt. "Cash Flow to Terrorists Evades U.S. Efforts." *New York Times,* December 5, 2010. http://www.nytimes.com/2010/12/06/world/middleeast/06wikileaks-financing.html (accessed December 6, 2010).

Lind, William S., Colonel Keith Nightengale, Captain John F. Schmitt, Colonel Joseph W. Sutton, and Lieutenant Colonel Gary I. Wilson. "The Changing Face of War: Into the Fourth Generation." Global Guerrillas. http://globalguerrillas.typepad.com/lind/the-changing-face-of-war-into-the-fourth-generation.html (accessed May 16, 2010).

Lobjakas, Ahto. "NATO Looks to Evolve without Shedding DNA." *International Relations and Security Network,* April 23, 2010. http://www.isn.ethz.ch/isn/Current-Affairs/Security-Watch/Detail/?ots591=4888caa0-b3db-1461-98b9-e20e7b9c13d4&lng=en&id=115320 (accessed April 23, 2010).

Lord, Kristin M., and Richard Fontaine. *Managing 21st Century Diplomacy: Lessons from Global Corporations.* Washington, D.C.: Center for a New American Security, 2010.

Lord, Kristin M., and Marc Lynch. *America's Extended Hand: Assessing the Obama Administration's Global Engagement Strategy.* Washington, D.C.: Center for a New American Security, 2010.

Lund, Michael. *Engaging Fragile States: An International Policy Primer.* Woodrow Wilson International Center for Scholars, 2010. http://wilsoncenter.org/topics/pubs/Colloquium%20Report-Engaging%20Fragile%20States.pdf (accessed December 30, 2010).

Markey, Daniel. *Securing Pakistan's Tribal Belt.* Washington, D.C.: Council on Foreign Relations, 2008.

McDonald, Kara C., and Stewart M. Patrick. *UN Security Council Enlargement and U.S. Interests.* Washington, D.C.: Council on Foreign Relations, 2010.

Meleagron-Hitchens, Alexander. "New English-Language Al-Qaeda Explosives Manual Released Online." International Centre for the Study of Radicalisation and Political Violence, December 31, 2010. http://www.icsr.info/news/icsr-insight-new-english-language-al-qaeda-explosives-manual-released-online (accessed December 31, 2010).

Merriam-Webster Online Dictionary. "War." http://www.merriam-webster.com/dictionary/war (accessed October 4, 2007).

Michaels, Jim. "Bloodshed Ebbed in Iraq Last Year." *USA Today*, January 11, 2011. http://www.usatoday.com/printedition/news/20110111/iraqviolence11_st.art.htm (accessed January 12, 2011).

Miller, Paul. "What Is Foreign Aid For?" *Foreign Policy*, January 27, 2011. http://shadow.foreignpolicy.com/posts/2011/01/27/what_is_foreign_aid_for (accessed January 27, 2011).

Mneimneh, Hassan. "Islamism." American Enterprise Institute's Critical Threats Project, 2009. http://www.criticalthreats.org/basics/islamism (accessed December 10, 2009).

Mullick, Haider Ali Hussein Mullick. *Al Qa'eda and Pakistan: Current Role and Future Considerations.* Institute for Social Policy and Understanding, 2010. http://ispu.org/files/PDFs/Al_Qaeda_and_Pakistan_Report_-_Haider_Mullick.pdf (accessed November 1, 2010).

Musawi, Mohammed Ali. *Cheering for Osama: How Jihadists Use Internet Discussion Forums.* Quilliam Foundation, September 27, 2010.

Napolitano, Janet. *Quadrennial Homeland Security Review Report: A Strategic Framework for a Secure Homeland.* Washington, D.C.: U.S. Department of Homeland Security, 2010.

National Counterterrorism Center. "2008 Report on Terrorism." http://www.fas.org/irp/threat/nctc2008.pdf (accessed August 3, 2009).

Nawaz, Shuja. *FATA—A Most Dangerous Place.* Washington, D.C.: Center for Strategic and International Studies, 2009.

North Atlantic Treaty Organization. "Active Engagement, Modern Defence: Strategic Concept for the Defence and the Security of the Members of the North Atlantic Treaty Organization." http://www.nato.int/cps/en/natolive/official_texts_68580.htm (accessed November 20, 2010).

———. "Charter of the North Atlantic Treaty Organization." http://www.nato.int.cps/en/natolive/official_texts_17120.htm (accessed August 23, 2010).

Nelson, Rick, Thomas M. Sanderson, Amrit Bagia, Ben Bodurian, and David A. Gordon. *A Threat Transformed: Al Qaeda and Associated Movements in 2011.* Center for Strategic and International Studies, 2011.

Neuharth, Al. "Why It's OK for Iran to Join 'Nuclear Age.'" *USA Today*, December 10, 2010. http://www.usatoday.com/news/opinion/forum/2010-12-10-column10_ST_N.htm (accessed December 10, 2010).

Obama, Barack H. *National Security Strategy.* Washington, D.C.: The White House, 2010.

Page, Jeremy. "China's New Drones Raise Eyebrows." *Wall Street Journal*, November 18, 2010. http://online.wsj.com/article/sb10001424052748703374304575622350604500556.html (accessed November 18, 2010).

———. "Test Flight Signals Jet Has Reached New Stage." *Wall Street Journal*, January 12, 2011. http://online.wsj.com/article/SB100014240527487045159045760758520917744070.html (accessed January 12, 2011).

Partlow, Joshua. "Milestone in Training Afghan Forces." *Washington Post*, November 9, 2010. http://www.washingtonpost.com/wp-dyn/content/article/2010/11/08/AR2010110806052.html (accessed November 9, 2010).

Passel, Jeffrey S., and D'Vera Cohn. *Unauthorized Immigrant Population: National and State Trends, 2010*. Washington, D.C.: Pew Hispanic Center, 2011.

Perl, Raphael. *Terrorism, the Future, and U.S. Foreign Policy*. Washington, D.C.: Congressional Research Service, 2003.

Pillar, Paul R. *Terrorism and U.S. Foreign Policy*. Washington, D.C.: Brookings Institution Press, 2001.

Pincus, Walter. "Gauging the Price Tag for Afghanistan's Security." *Washington Post*, December 21, 2010. http://www.washingtonpost.com/wp-dyn/content/article/2010/12/20/AR2010122004829.html (accessed December 21, 2010).

Pincus, Walter. "Report Details Inadequacies of Iraqi Defense Ministry." *Washington Post*, November 22, 2010. http://www.washingtonpost.com/wp-dyn/content/article/2010/11/22/AR2010112206420.html (accessed November 22, 2010).

Rabasa, Angel, Stacie L. Pettyjohn, Jeremy J. Ghez, and Christopher Boucek. *Deradicalizing Islamist Extremists*. Washington, D.C.: Rand Corporation, 2010.

Radio Free Europe/Radio Liberty. "Putin Pledges $646 Billion to Modernize Russia's Army." http://www.rferl.org/content/putin_pledges_646_billion_to_modernize_russian_army/2247315.html (accessed December 13, 2010).

Rand Corporation. "Getting Inside the Terrorist Mind." Rand Research Brief, 2007. http://www.rand.org/content/dam/rand/pubs/research_briefs/2007/RAND_RB9258.pdf (accessed July 2, 2008).

———. "Rand Proposes Blueprint for Building Moderate Muslim Networks." Rand Center for Middle East Public Policy, 2007. http://www.rand.org/pubs/research_briefs/2007/RAND_RB9251.pdf (accessed February 22, 2008).

Rapaport, David C. *The Four Waves of Modern Terrorism*. Los Angeles: UCLA International Institute, 2006. http://www.international.ucla.edu/cms/files/Rapoport-Four-Waves-of-Modern-Terrorism.pdf (accessed May 21, 2010).

Roble, Muhyadin Ahmed. "Somali Forces Sell Weapons to Islamists." *Africa News*, October 29, 2010. http://www.africanews.com/site/Somali_forces_sell_weapons_to_Islamists/list_messages/35708 (accessed October 29, 2010).

Royal College of Defence Studies. *The Royal College of Defence Studies Strategy Handbook*. 2nd ed. Defence Academy of the United Kingdom, February 15, 2010. http://www.mod.uk/NR/rdonlyres/9E28927E-733F-49E1-A0AB-7BA46AF3F8F6/0/rcdsstrategyhandbook.pdf (accessed March 31, 2010).

Rumsfeld, Donald H. *National Defense Strategy of the United States of America*. Washington, D.C.: U.S. Department of Defense, 2005.

Sandler, Todd, Daniel G. Arce, and Walter Enders. "Terrorism." Paper presented to the Copenhagen Consensus 2008 Challenge, February 2008.

Schaefer, Brett D., and Anthony B. Kim. *U.S. Aid Does Not Build Support at the U.N.* Heritage Foundation, 2007. http://www.heritage.org/research/reports/2007/03/us-aid-does-not-build-support-at-the-un (accessed May 15, 2008).

Schmitt, Eric. "Governments Go Online in Fight against Terrorism." *New York Times*, January 31, 2011. http://www.nytimes.com/2011/01/31/world/middleeast/31terror.html (accessed January 30, 2011).

Schoenhardt, Sara. "Religious Tensions Rise in Indonesia." *Voice of America News*, December 15, 2010. http://www.voanews.com/english/news/Religious-Tension-Increases-in-Indonesia-111910634.html (accessed December 15, 2010).

Snow, Donald. *National Security for a New Era.* New York: Pearson Longman, 2004.

Spencer, Richard. "Terrorists Posing as Refugees in Yemen." *Telegraph* (United Kingdom), November 29, 2010. http://www.telegraph.co.uk/news/worldnews/middleeast/yemen/8149993/Terrorists-posing-as-refugees-in-Yemen.html (accessed November 30, 2010).

Stahl, A. E., and William F. Owen. "Targeted Killings Work." *Infinity Journal* no. 1 (2010): 10–13. http://www.infinityjournal.com/article/3/Targeted_Killings_Work (accessed January 2, 2011).

Stana, Richard M. Introduction to *Border Security: Preliminary Observations on Border Control Measures for the Southwestern Border.* Government Accountability Office Testimony before the Subcommittee on Border and Maritime Security, Committee on Homeland Security, U.S. House of Representatives. Washington, D.C.: Government Accountability Office, 2011.

Stolberg, Alan G. "The International System in the 21st Century." In *U.S. Army War College Guide to National Security Issues, Volume II: National Security Policy and Strategy,* edited by J. Boone Bartholomees. 3rd ed., 121–34. Carlisle, Pa.: U.S. Army War College, 2008.

Telhami, Shibley. *2008 Annual Arab Public Opinion Poll.* Survey of the Anwar Sadat Chair for Peace and Development at the University of Maryland (with Zogby International), March 2008. http://www.brookings.edu/~/media/Files/events/2008/0414_middle_east/0414_middle_east_telhami.pdf (accessed June 5, 2009).

———. *2010 Annual Arab Public Opinion Poll.* Survey of the Anwar Sadat Chair for Peace and Development at the University of Maryland (with Zogby International), July 2010. http://www.brookings.edu/~/media/Files/rc/reports/2010/08_arab_opinion_poll_telhami/08_arab_opinion_poll_telhami.pdf (accessed August 10, 2010).

Times of Pakistan. "Karachi Target Killings, Highest in 15 Years." http://thetimesofpakistan.com/2010/10/30/karachi-target-killings-highest-in-15-years/ (accessed November 3, 2010).

Trachsler, Daniel. *UN Security Council Reform: A Gordian Knot?* International Relations and Security Network, 2010.

"Understanding the Muslim Brotherhood." *Week*, February 11, 2011. http://theweek.com/article/index/211951/understanding-the-muslim-brotherhood (accessed February 11, 2011).

United Nations. "Charter of the United Nations." http://www.un.org/en/documents/charter/chapter1.shtml (accessed September 21, 2008).

———. *First Report of the Working Group on Radicalisation and Extremism That Lead to Terrorism.* UN Counter-Terrorism Implementation Task Force, 2008. In Rabasa,

Angel, et al. *Deradicalizing Islamist Extremists.* Washington, D.C.: Rand Corporation, 2010.

United States Africa Command. "Combined Joint Task Force–Horn of Africa." http://www.hoa.africom.mil/AboutCJTF-HOA.asp (accessed March 2, 2010).

———. "2010 Command Brief." http://www.scribd.com/doc/28163958/2010-US-Africa-Command-Command-Brief-USAFRICOM (accessed October 16, 2010).

———. "Operation Enduring Freedom Trans Sahara." http://www.africom.mil/oef-ts.asp (accessed August 12, 2010).

United States Army. *U.S. Army Field Manual 5-0: The Operations Process.* Washington, D.C.: Department of the Army, 2010.

United States Department of Defense. *Unclassified Report on Military Power of Iran.* http://www.foxnews.com/projects/pdf/IranReportUnclassified.pdf (accessed May 1, 2010).

United States Department of State. "Country Reports on Terrorism, 2007." http://www.state.gov/s/ct/rls/crt/2007/103711.htm (accessed August 12, 2008).

———. "Country Reports on Terrorism, 2009." http://www.state.gov/s/ct/rls/crt/2009/140889.htm (accessed December 21, 2010).

———. "Foreign Terrorist Organization Designation." http://www.state.gov/r/pa/prs/ps/2010/09/146554.htm (accessed November 12, 2010).

———. "Press Release for Country Reports on Terrorism, 2009." http://www.state.gov/r/pa/prs/ps/2010/08/145737.htm (accessed August 31, 2010).

———. *USAID Strategic Plan, FYs 2004–2009.* Publication Number 11084. Washington, D.C.: U.S. Department of State, 2003.

Vice Chairman of the Joint Chiefs of Staff. *An Evolving Joint Perspective: U.S. Joint Warfare and Crisis Resolution in the 21st Century.* Joint Staff, J7 Division. Washington, D.C.: U.S. Department of Defense, 2003.

Vira, Varun, John Karian, David Pupkin, Stephen Szrom, Maseh Zarif, Daniel Katz, Eiman Behzadi, and Kerry Harris. "Sanctions on Iran: Reactions and Impact." American Enterprise Institute's Iran Tracker. http://www.irantracker.org/us-policy/sanctions-iran-reactions-and-impact (accessed November 5, 2010).

Whitlock, Craig. "Al-Qaeda's Yemen Branch Spreads Its Reach for Recruits, Targets." *Washington Post,* November 30, 2010. http://www.washingtonpost.com/wp-dyn/content/article/2010/11/29/AR2010112905615.html (accessed November 30, 2010).

———. "Pentagon Hunting for Home for Africom." *Washington Post,* November 27, 2010. http://www.washingtonpost.com/wp-dyn/content/article/2010/11/26/AR2010112604889.html (accessed November 27, 2010).

Wood, David. "White House Mulls Grim Picture of 'Deteriorating Stalemate' in Afghanistan." *Politics Daily,* December 3, 2010. http://www.politicsdaily.com/2010/12/03/white-house-mulls-grim-picture-of-deteriorating-stalemate-in-a/ (accessed December 4, 2010).

Woods, Kevin, and James Lacey. *Saddam and Terrorism: Emerging Insights from Captured Iraqi Documents,* vol. 1 (redacted). Alexandria, Va.: Iraqi Perspectives Project, 2007.

Woodward, Bob. *Obama's Wars.* New York: Simon & Schuster, 2010.

Yarger, Harry R. *Strategic Theory for the 21st Century: The Little Book on Big Strategy.* Strategic Studies Institute. Carlisle, Pa.: U.S. Army War College, 2006.

Yarger, Richard H. "Towards a Theory of Strategy: Art Lykke and the Army War College Strategy Model." https://dde.carlisle.army.mil/authors/stratpap.htm (accessed November 15, 2007).

Zenko, Micah. "Between Threats and War: U.S. Discrete Military Operations in the Post–Cold War World". Excerpt from the Council on Foreign Relations, December, 2010. http://www.cfr.org/united-states/between-threats-war/p22621?excerpt=1 (accessed January 22, 2011).

Zimmerman, Katherine. "Expanding the Campaign of Violence: Al Qaeda in the Arabian Peninsula's English-Language Magazine." American Enterprise Institute's Critical Threats Project, July 13, 2010. http://www.criticalthreats.org/yemen/expanding-campaign-violence-al-qaeda-arabian-peninsulas-english-language-magazine-july-13-2010 (accessed July 14, 2010).

———. "Looking Ahead in Mogadishu: Tough Decisions." American Enterprise Institute's Critical Threats Project, November 1, 2010. http://www.criticalthreats.org/somalia/looking-ahead-mogadishu-tough-decisions-november-1-2010 (accessed November 1, 2010).

———. "Militant Islam's Global Preacher: The Radicalizing Effect of Sheikh Anwar Al Awlaki." American Enterprise Institute's Critical Threats Project, March 12, 2010. http://www.criticalthreats.org/yemen/militant-islams-global-preacher-radicalizing-effect-sheikh-anwar-al-awlaki (accessed March 12, 2010).

Index

About the Author

Greg Reeson is a United States Army strategist who has worked on strategic-level plans and policies for more than four years. He holds a graduate degree in international relations (national security studies) and undergraduate degrees in Russian area studies and history, and is a graduate of the United States Army War College's Basic Strategic Arts Program and Defense Strategy Course. Mr. Reeson has written dozens of articles on foreign policy and defense-related issues for online and print publications.